Gifts of Many Cultures

Gifts of Many Cultures

Worship Resources for the Global Community

Maren C. Tirabassi and Kathy Wonson Eddy

United Church Press   Cleveland, Ohio

United Church Press, Cleveland, Ohio 44115
© 1995 by Maren C. Tirabassi and Kathy Wonson Eddy

Printed in the United States of America on acid-free paper

00 99 98 97 96 95   5 4 3 2 1

Library of Congress Cataloging-in-Publication Data

Tirabassi, Maren C.
      Gifts of many cultures : worship resources for the global community / Maren C. Tirabassi and Kathy Wonson Eddy.
          p.   cm.
      Includes bibliographical references and indexes.
      ISBN 0-8298-1029-3 (alk. paper)
        1. Liturgical adaptation.   2. Worship programs.   3. Church year.   I. Eddy, Kathy Wonson, 1951–   .   II. Title.
      BV178.T57   1995
      264—dc20   94-39951
                                                                              CIP

Contents

Foreword

Sharing gifts . . . sharing resources . . . sharing all life, the great gifts of God!

Liturgy, a willing service of those who serve the Holy One, is a community feast of life. When we think of celebration, we think of communion: shared home, table, food . . . common faith, dreams, and desires . . .

Nobody celebrates alone! It's not enough. Still many people today prefer to be alone, far from crying and suffering, or noisy and crazy people . . .

Nowadays, liturgical renewal is a multifaced task that involves a lot of people, groups, communities throughout the world—our big home. Our gracious God has blessed the human community with so many charismas, abilities, and possibilities for expression.

Gifts of Many Cultures, a four-hands production, received inspiration from many members of the human family. Much anguish, many fights, and discoveries are expressed in these words, sounds, colors, pictures . . . and it reflects the faith of daily life and manifestations of the Holy Spirit that cry through God's people for a new creation . . . new heavens and new earth . . . free and abundant life for *all* . . . humankind, creatures, universe!

Here you can find resources for worship, daily meditations, Bible studies, and small groups . . . to enrich the global faith community and to share what we have kindly received from the Giver.

May God inspire and strengthen you and others through these pages full of life to spread these messages and experiences.

ERNESTO BARROS CARDOSO
Deputy Executive Secretary of the Institute for Studies on Religion, Rio de Janeiro, Brazil, and General Coordinator of the Latin American Council of Churches Liturgy Network

Words from the Authors

This book is a handful of prayer
held open to offer
the words of the world
in the patient silence of our
hope.

God is tortilla, cassava, coffee,
cinnamon, wheat,
rice.
God is broken
for all of us.

Between invocation and benediction
is the possibility
of speaking
justice.
Like a bleeding woman
God's people have suffered long.
Between invocation and benediction
our fingers reach out for
the shawl-fringes of
peace.

And for such speech-reaching and
eucharist
did we write this book.

     MAREN C. TIRABASSI

Have you ever had the experience of waking in the night, startled by the luminous beauty of the moon in your room? Have you
seen it spreading a gossamer cloth of light over your bed, creating
shimmering pools on the floor?

I had the experience of being stunned by Light in working on
this book. It happened about five months after Maren and I had
sent our first thousand letters seeking worship resources from
around the world. The first responses seemed meager to me, not
very expressive of the unique cultures from which they came, and
certainly not very plentiful. Maren and I each had driven an hour
and a half in frigid temperatures (it was -38°F in Vermont!) to meet
for reading and sorting these early responses. It was easy at that

point in the process to be discouraged. We closed our meeting with prayer for this book. During the prayer I saw an image in my mind's eye of our little pile of papers glowing with light—luminous, shining! It is an image that sustained us over and over, and it has proven true: God's light shines bountifully on these gifts of many cultures to grace our worship. It is our prayer that these radiant liturgical resources and graphics will be bringers of light and warmth in your community of faith.

Many times we have been stunned by the beauty and depth of these gifts from around the world. We were filled with awe the first time we opened a packet of He Qi's delicate papercuts of biblical stories from China, so deeply grateful to have had the opportunity to discover his work and the creative explosion of Christian art in Asia.

The brilliant writing of Bill Wallace of Aotearoa/New Zealand, the vibrancy of liturgical renewal in Central and South America, especially through the leadership of Ernesto Barros Cardoso, the poetry of Kate Compston of England and Julia Esquivel of Guatemala, the woodcuts of Rini Templeton, and the prayers from high school students in Zimbabwe are all gifts that are woven with God's grace.

We were inspired by the worship at the United Theological College in Bangalore, India, and the Protestant Church of Bali with its beautiful emphasis on breathing and stillness, on symbols and dance.

We were moved by the courage and pain of all Earth's peoples in struggles for freedom and equality, especially the witness of the people in the parish of Zacamil, El Salvador, which has 623 martyrs. The poem of Amaya Lopez about the loss of her five-year-old son's jaw in a Contra attack moved our typist to tears as she worked on the manuscript. Here is a tapestry of grief and faith, despair and love, suffering and bravery, many-colored and textured.

May these liturgical materials help you realize the beauty and worth of each person on this planet, the gifts that each has to offer us all. In the tender words of the father to the bride in a Popoloca (Mexico) wedding, may the message be woven into each heart, "you are noble, you are precious." As you use these gifts of many cultures may you discover, as we have, God's light shining abundantly.

KATHY WONSON EDDY

Words of Gratitude

The word "acknowledgment" has a technical sound, and it is, in fact, more appropriately applied to the gracious permissions for the reprinting of liturgical material that is found at the end of this book. These are words of gratitude for those who have assisted, supported, and encouraged us in the sometimes uneven journey we have undertaken in this project. We are not including here the wonderful individual contributors whom we list with their material throughout the book.

We were enticed by Paul Clayton and Andrew White into the original workshop at the New England Global Mission Seminar I, from which this book was developed. Liaisons to the seven denominations who shared names and addresses with us were: Scott Libbey, United Church of Christ; Marilee Blanchard, Presbyterian Church (U.S.A.); Joyce M. Bowers, Evangelical Lutheran Church in America; Lillian Moir, Christian Church (Disciples of Christ); Joseph A. Perez, United Methodist Church; Dorothy Gist, Episcopal Church; and Corene Garrison, American Baptist Church.

Others in denominational offices who have given us particular help on the way are Armin Schmidt, the Council on American Indian Ministries of the United Church of Christ; Diane Allen, General Board of Global Ministries, United Methodist Church; Susan Dickerman, Massachusetts Conference office, United Church of Christ; Christopher Miller, Presbyterian Church; Angela Kinkead, United Methodist National Youth Ministry Organization; Samuel Arends, United Congregational Church of Southern Africa; Dale Rominger, the United Reformed Church, United Kingdom; and Joanne Goodwin, the Colegio Episcopal da Igreja Metodista.

Particular assistance from ecumenical organizations was offered by Isabel Best, the Conference of European Churches; Souha Khoury, the Middle East Council of Churches; Heather Stunt, World Council of Churches; Eugene Braun, Latin American Council of Churches; Chan Beng Seng and Harold Williams, Christian Conference of Asia; Graham Maule, Iona Community; and Jean-Francois Delteil, World Student Christian Federation.

Administrative staff and professors from several theological seminaries in the United States were helpful to us by asking international students for their contributions. They include David Greenhaw of Lancaster Theological Seminary, M. Douglas Meeks of Wesley Theological Seminary, Michael Kinnamon of Lexington Theological Seminary, and Kathy Black of the School of Theology, Claremont, California. We are also grateful to these international seminaries—United Theological College of Bangalore, India; Nanjing Theological Seminary, Nanjing, China; and Doshisha University, Kyoto, Japan.

Among many publishers and editors, Cathie Hillenbrand of Real Comet Press, Don Parker-Bugard of Friendship Press, and Scott Wright of EPICA were particularly gracious. Michael Rozene of Equal Exchange, a coffee distributor, took particular care in helping us locate graphic art.

Several United Church of Christ missionaries sent us the writings of others and so are not mentioned in the text—June Fleshman from Nepal, James Wilson from Lesotho, Jeffrey Phillips from Zimbabwe, Geraldine Abbott from Zimbabwe, John Moss from Japan, Olgha Sandman from Turkey, and Bruce Van Voorhis from Hong Kong. We are also indebted to Judith Newton from Japan, a United Methodist, for her help with Japanese artists.

Our congregations have certainly become a part of *Gifts of Many Cultures*—from trying out prayers and listening to stories to often waiting patiently for their pastors to return from "a meeting on the book." Kathy's parish is Bethany United Church of Christ in Randolph, Vermont. Maren, who made the transition from settled pastor to intentional interim minister during this time, has been encouraged by three United Church of Christ congregations—First Congregational Church, Somerville, Massachusetts; First Congregational Church, Essex, Massachusetts; and Dane Street Congregational Church, Beverly, Massachusetts.

Halfway between Randolph, Vermont, and Portsmouth, New Hampshire, where Maren lives, is Hopkinton, New Hampshire. For a year and a half the First Congregational Church of Hopkinton has offered us work space, coffee, and friendship, thanks to the hospitality of pastor Ed Horstman and secretary Margaret Serzans.

Our families have loved us through this all (and copied, stapled, sorted, and laughed at us). Many thanks to Bob Eddy and Don Tirabassi and our children, Nathan and Isaac Eddy and Matthew and Maria Tirabassi.

Typists and friends MaryAnne Douglas and Diane Karr have given of their technical and editorial skills and have, as they each said at different times, "prayed their way through the book."

We are deeply grateful that Ernesto Barros Cardoso, coordinator of the Latin American Council of Churches Liturgy Network and the "Gesture, Colors, Sounds: Liturgical and Spiritual Renewal Project" of the Institute of Studies in Religion (ISER) has written the foreword for us. His fresh use of language has been an inspiration to us.

Finally, our fond appreciation and thanks go to Kim Sadler, our editor at United Church Press, who has been both skillful and caring in her support of this project and her warm relationship with us.

Introduction

The purpose of *Gifts of Many Cultures: Worship Resources for the Global Community* is to enrich worship, encourage cross-cultural appreciation, facilitate church mission programming, and deepen spiritual understanding across the global community. To facilitate this, we offer some simple guidelines.

Use of Material

Permission to copy these worship resources is freely given for church bulletins, newsletters, and congregational and educational use with appropriate acknowledgment.

Reprinting these resources in other forms (such as a book or a workshop for which a fee is charged) requires the additional permission of the copyright holders listed in the source notes or the United Church Press.

A Special Word about Inclusive Language

It is our belief that the words and images used in the worship of God should be welcoming of all people and that expressions—both visual and verbal—that cause pain, however unintentional the motivation of the originator, should be avoided in faith communities with a shared understanding of meanings involved.

Issues of gender-inclusive language in particular have been a concern throughout the preparation of this book. The issues are not clear-cut or simple. We have discovered that there is a need to balance the justice concerns of inclusive language with those of cultural integrity. As editors, we have worked with many contributors to adapt their words and images. Translation from many different languages occasionally has complicated this process. Many resources already contain both masculine and feminine names for God. In other cases, we have used placement to create an artistic contrast between pieces that employ masculine and feminine imagery.

However, we have received letters from some contributors who found our suggested changes to go against the grain of their culture and, indeed, to be imperialistic. We have, therefore, included many works that may not be fully usable in all the congregations reading this book. We feel strongly that, as people of faith, we cannot receive only those gifts from other cultures that conform to "our" current linguistic scrutiny. And so we have shared throughout this book many liturgical resources of profound integrity and widely differing imagery and expression.

Suggestions for Use

- Clergy and lay preparation for Sunday morning worship throughout the year.
- Special worship services with an international aspect, such as Pentecost, World-Wide Communion Sunday, One Great Hour of Sharing, Thanksgiving, Integrity of Creation, Peace and Justice Sunday.
- Seasons of the church year from a global perspective (Part III).
- Event resourcing, such as outreach fairs and mission suppers.
- Devotional and workshop materials for church committee meetings.
- Programs for affinity groups such as women's guilds, men's breakfast gatherings, youth groups.
- Worship services for retreats, camps, university or seminary chapels, as well as educational forums discussing such worship.
- Ecumenical, interfaith, multicultural, and communitywide services.

Gifts of Many Cultures

Robert Eddy, U.S.A.

PART I

Resources to Lift Up Our Voices

The first part of our book shares liturgical resources for congregational worship and follows a general outline of a Sunday morning service. Chapter 1, "Gathering Words and Invocations," includes a variety of beginning moments sent to us by contributors throughout our global community. Chapter 2, "Prayers of Confession" includes prayers, statements, poems, and litanies of penitence and reconciliation. Four of the next five chapters, "Prayers of Praise and Thanksgiving," "Prayers of Petition and Intercession," "Offering Resources," and "Benedictions," are straightforward in their content. However, "Resources Relating to Scripture" involved more subjective decisions on our part. In addition to prayers, we include a custom and a procession, stories, and litanies. The scripture reference precedes each particular resource. This section concludes with seven different reprayings of the Prayer of our Savior, which Jesus taught his disciples and which still unites us today.

We invite you to use the prayers and liturgical resources we have gathered here. The citations we have placed after each distinct piece are intended to be helpful in identifying the context from which the resource emerged. The citations are not absolutely uniform because of the diversity of the material, and they do not replace the complete acknowledgments at the end of the book.

We hope that you will be engaged by these prayers and liturgical resources, that you will travel with them, that you will come to care for the people whose words these are, and that you will receive their "gift"—which is to experience them in your own services of worship.

Rini Templeton, U.S.A./Mexico

God of Life
prepare our hands for a touch
a new and different touch
prepare our hands for a touch
a touch of encounter
a touch of awakening
a touch of hope
a touch of feeling
Many are the worn-out gestures
many are the movements frozen in time
Many are the useless excuses just to repeat attitudes. . . .
Give us daring
to create new titles of community
new links of affection
breaking away from old ways of relating,
encouraging true, meaningful ways to move into closeness.

Ernesto Barros Cardoso, Brazil

(Sun Dance Song, which is sung just as the day-sun peeps over the horizon.)

The light of the Great Spirit is upon my people;
It is making the whole earth bright.
My people are now happy!
All beings that move are rejoicing!

Dakota Tribe, U.S.A.

*Lord, oil the hinges
of our hearts' doors
that they may swing gently
and easily to welcome
your coming.*

New Guinea

Like the sun that is far away and yet close at hand to warm us,
so God's Spirit is ever present and around us.
Come Creator into our lives.
We live and move and have our very being in you.
Open now the windows of our souls. Amen.

United Methodist Clergywomen, U.S.A.

Leader: In the beginning, when it was very dark God said, "Let there be light"

Congregation: And there was light.

(A lighted candle is placed on the altar)

Leader: In the beginning, when it was very quiet, the Word was with God

Congregation: And what God was, the Word was.

(An open Bible is placed on the altar)

Leader: When the time was right God sent his Son.

Congregation: He came among us, he was one of us.

(A cross is placed on the altar)

Conference of European Churches, 10th Assembly, 1992, Prague

Leader: Blessed is our God always, now and ever, and unto ages of ages. Amen.

Leader: O Heavenly One, the Comforter, the Spirit of Truth, who art everywhere and fillest all things, Treasury of Blessings, and giver of life: come and abide in us, and cleanse us from every impurity, and save our souls, O Good One. In peace let us pray to the Lord.

Congregation: Lord have mercy.

Leader: For the peace that is from above, and for the salvation of our souls. . . .

Congregation: Lord have mercy.

Leader: For the peace of the whole world; for the welfare of God's holy churches, and for the union of all. . . .

Congregation: Lord have mercy.

Middle East Council of Churches

Middle East Council of Churches

Preparation and Approach to God

Call to Worship   (*The people standing*)

Leader: Thanks be to you O God, that we have risen this day,

All: To the rising of this life itself.

Leader: Be the purpose of God between us and each purpose,

All: The hand of God between us and each hand.

Leader: The pain of Christ between us and each pain,

All: The love of Christ between us and each love.

Leader: Beloved of the waifs, beloved of the naked,

All: Draw us to the shelter house of the Saviour of the poor.

> John L. Bell, Iona, Scotland

Liturgy of Agape Feast

Call to Worship

Leader: Rejoice, people of God!

Celebrate the life within you, and Christ's presence in your midst.

Congregation: Our eyes shall be opened!

The present will have new meaning and the future will be bright with hope.

Leader: Rejoice, people of God!

Bow your heads before the One who is our wisdom and our strength.

Congregation: We place ourselves before our God that we may be touched and cleaned by the power of God's Spirit.

Lighting of Candles   (*For three readers*)

Reader 1: I will light a light in the name of God who lit the world and breathed the breath of life into me.

Reader 2: I will light a light in the name of the Son who saved the world and stretched out His hand to me.

Reader 3: I will light a light in the name of the Spirit who encompasses the world and blesses my soul with yearning.

All: We will light three lights for the Trinity of love:

God above us, God beside us, God beneath us; the beginning, the end, the everlasting one.

> I. Wayan Mastra, Bali

Opening Responses

Leader: We gather today to learn what it is to be a pilgrim community.

Congregation: We gather, bringing our hopes and our fears, our memories and our visions.

Leader: We gather, longing for the guidance of God's Spirit to give us renewal and courage for the days ahead.

Congregation: Come, Christ Jesus, be in our midst. Bless us as we remember those who have shown us your way forward. Help us to find a clear vision for the future, as we learn to be your disciples day by day.

Scottish Students, World Student Christian Federation

Lord Jesus, Holy Spirit, come into this church and lead us in our worship during these two hours. Those who are still coming, bring them safely. Bless those who cannot come because of illness or work duty. Those who are sick in bed, give them healing and peace. Please heal those who are hurting and staying away from Church. God, be with the churches in Nepal, India, and Tibet.

Lord, thank you for your guidance and leading during the past week. Thank you for healing us and our children. We thank you with a large voice.

Thank you for Jesus' sacrifice for us. We want all Nepal to put you highest, higher than the King, make you the highest—most important of all.

We ask you to bless this offering like you blessed the five fish and two loaves near Lake Galilee.

We pray that you will be with today's speaker. We are starting to plan for the Christmas drama. We ask you that the people of Tansen shall know that Jesus was born for all the Nepalese people. We pray for our local CDO (Chief District Officer), who is Hindu, that he will permit the drama to be held in the city auditorium and will see it.

The young people in the villages who are new believers do not know how to pray. They are using their own ideas. We pray that you will give them your wisdom. There are so many small village fellowships without baptized members. We pray that you will help them all.

May God's love, Jesus Christ's grace, and fellowship of the Holy Spirit be with us until the second coming of Jesus. Amen.

Birkha Khadka, Nepal

Leader: Everything as it moves, now and then, here and there, makes pauses.

Congregation: The bird, as it flies, stops on one place to make its nest, and in another to rest in its flight.

Leader: In the same way, God has paused as well.

Congregation: The sun, which is so bright and beautiful, is one place where God has paused.

Leader: The moon, the stars, the winds; God has been with them, too.

Congregation: The trees, the animals, are all places where God has stopped, leaving the touch of the Holy in all these things.

Leader: We, too, have had God pause in us. We, too, have the Holy touch in our beings.

Congregation: Let us now pause ourselves, and listen for the voice of God on our hearts.

Lakota teachings, U.S.A.

Leader: Father, Son, and Holy Spirit. One God, in perfect Community, look now on us, who look to you. . . .

Congregation: And hear our prayer for our community:

Leader: Where there is falseness. . . .

Congregation: Smother it by your truth;

Leader: Where there is any coldness. . . .

Congregation: Kindle the flame of your love;

Leader: Where there is joy and hope. . . .

Congregation: Free us to share it together;

Leader: Where there is something we should do for others. . . .

Congregation: Make us discontent until it is done.

Leader: And make us one. . . .

Congregation: As you are one.

Leader: Before God and you who are near me, I release anything I hold against you. I regret all I have done to harm you. I stand beside the wrong in my life and ask God's forgiveness.

Congregation: Before God and the people gathered here, we release anything we hold against you. We regret all we have done to harm you. We stand beside the wrong in our lives and ask God's forgiveness.

(Silence)

Leader: The Lord Jesus Christ says to us, each one: "Go and sin no more, come and follow me." Now, Lord Jesus, bind our hands with honesty, as we offer them to each other and as we offer our prayers to you.

Conference of European Churches, 10th Assembly, 1992, Prague

Longing for the God of Peace

(The flute plays in plaintive longing, expressing the age-old Indian desire for the God of peace, for the realisation of that transcendent Source and Ground of deep peace. In the opening chant, we combine the Indian 'OM' [itself usually linked with a prayer for peace or shanti] with the Hebrew "Shalom," the latter expressing the wholeness of creation's life for which we hope. The Silence, for meditation on our "Origin" and our "End," should aim to be itself peace-creating. The song following can be sung to any suitably meditative tune, or may be changed. The Christ-Child, and children generally, are taken in this prayer-song as true signs of the peace we long for.)

Leader: Om Shalom, Om Shalom, Om Shalom

(*Silence. We reflect on the Origin of our being and on the End to which we move. Then the following is sung meditatively, all repeating the "Om Shalom."*)

Leader: Om Shalom, Om Shalom, Om Shalom

As the hunted deer for the river longs,

For the God of Peace alone we sing,

Like a dry parched land athirst for rain,

For the God of Peace we deeply yearn.

Congregation: Come, O come Lord God of Peace,

Om Shalom, Om Shalom, Om Shalom

Leader: Where can we find the peace we've sought?

Too long, we've planned, discussed, and fought;

Blessed our children, beyond our feuds,

They point in play to that world of peace.

Congregation: Come, O come Lord God of Peace,

Om Shalom, Om Shalom, Om Shalom

Leader: Given us now a clear peace-sign,

Yet wrapped in peasant rags this Child;

Here Peace breaks in, in love compels;

O show us now your light of peace.

Congregation: Come, O come Lord God of Peace,

Om Shalom, Om Shalom, Om Shalom

Samson Prabhakar, India

Leader: A people marked by life, clubbed with sticks and struck with cannons. A people doomed to exile by cursed oppression.

Congregation: A mixed people: white, black, Indian Americans, with a fore-ordained life, but unhappy and with empty hands.

Leader: Come, Lord, to us. Restore our charm. We want to walk in the force of this song.

Congregation: The blood that runs in our veins makes of our song a cry, joining jungles and deserts, streets, forests and fields.

All: The strength of the wind and the sun shines in the eyes of this people, where the sweet taste of honey gives pleasure to this life.

> World Student Christian Federation

Call to Worship

Come my brothers and sisters.
Let us celebrate!
Let us sing the old missionary songs that burn in our distant memories.
Let us remember our Christian brothers and sisters who weathered severe persecutions on the Korean Peninsula during World War II and the Korean War.
Let us shout joyous proclamations about the rapid fire of the gospel burning across South Korea.
Let us remember how Koreans are building churches across the U.S. with nothing but fervent prayer and love of God in their hearts.
Let us celebrate this worship because we have witnessed God's glory on the face of our brothers and sisters.
Come my brothers and sisters, let us worship.

> Keith Hwang, U.S.A/Korea

Opening Prayer

Open my eyes, that I may see those who have been beaten, robbed and left for dead in Guatemala and other parts of God's world. Open my ears, that I may hear cries of injustice, anger, and pain as people pour out stories of torture and death. Open my mouth, that I may spread the truth without fear, to others who refuse to believe the complicity we all share. Open my heart, illumine me, Spirit Divine.

> Janet Ross-Heiner, U.S.A./Nicaragua

Come to be our hope, O Jesus, come to set our people free.
From oppression come, release us, let us turn to life in Thee.
Come release from every prison those who suffer in our land.
In your love we find the reason still to live and understand.

Come to build your new creation through the road to servanthood;
Give new life to every nation, changing evil into good.
Come and open our tomorrow for a realm, now, so near.
Take away all human sorrow, give us hope against our fear.

> Jaci C. Maraschin, Brazil

Invocation

Saranam,* Saranam, Jagadisvara (God of the universe)
Saranam, Saranam, Hridayesvari (Mother God of the heart)
Saranam, Saranam, Ananda-purna (Fullness of Joy)
Saranam, Saranam, Kalyana-kari (Maker of Good)
Saranam, Saranam, Jivesvara (God of life)
Saranam, Saranam, Sarvesvari (Mother God of all beings)
Saranam, Saranam, Pramata-pita (Wise Father)
Saranam, Saranam, Karuna-mata (Compassionate Mother)

Leader: Let us acknowledge the pervasive presence of God that breaks in amidst us, his children, in the togetherness of male and female.

*Refuge.

United Theological Seminary, Bangalore, India

(The following call to worship is not limited to use only at the advent of a service, but may be exchanged at any point during the worship experience. It serves then as a communal affirmation which may be called out as a "uniting statement or rallying cry" at any time in the worship event. I mean worship in Zaire is quite literally an event!)

Leader: Yesu Azali Na Bomoi!! (Jesus has Life!!)
Congregation: (shouting) Hallelujah!! Yesu Azali Na Bomoi!! (Jesus has Life!!)
Leader: Hallelujah!! (thus completing the circle or exchange)

This statement expresses for the Zairean Christian the kernel (or seed, as they might envision) which is at the very core of our confessional faith. The profound double meaning of this Lingala phrase (one of the official languages widely used) is that of:

1. Jesus has Life (Jesus is alive); the equivalent of our Easter proclamation of 'He is Risen!'

2. Jesus has life (to offer). Jesus has in his possession (of your) eternal life.

This is the message of grace in salvation.

Quite literally, this call to worship or affirmation in praise has also taken on an existential reality during these troubled days. As the Israelites in the desert depended on God for daily manna, so too Zaireans see themselves as totally dependent on the church of Jesus Christ for any future life or resurrection of their "underdeveloping" country.

Suzette Goss-Geffrard, Zaire

O God, we thank You for this worship time. We pray that all ways of all peoples come together in understanding. We pray that world leaderships come together to end the needless waste of war spending. We pray that the ways of the Native people live on. We pray that our environment becomes cleaner and less polluted. We pray for our friends who are sick and need help. O God, we pray for this world so that all these nuclear weapons and other bad things that we point at each other will some day soon be all destroyed. We pray that adversaries will communicate and all of the mistrust will be healed. We pray for the renewal of our Mother Earth. We thank You again for this ceremony. Hetchetu aloh. (It is good.) Mitaquye oyasin. (All is related. All the four-legged, the winged, the swimming, the two-legged, even the rock, are all related to one another and all are equal.)

Eagle Man, Lakota, U.S.A.

2   *Prayers of Confession*

Prodigal Son, He Qi, China

Lord, thanks to you the dividing wall of the temple is no longer a problem for us, but the separating walls which we continue to build most certainly are. So Lord, whether we are in Berlin, Soweto, or on the 38th parallel, or a member of an ordinary Christian congregation somewhere, putting up all the barriers common to human communities the world over, show us how we may begin instead to take them down. Amen.

Korea

Grandfather, Grandmother, look at our brokenness. We know that in all creation only the human family has strayed from the Sacred Way. We know that we are divided, and we are the ones who must come back together to walk in the Sacred Way. O God, Sacred One, teach us love, compassion, and honor, that we may heal the earth and heal each other.

Ojibway, Canada

Mercifully hear this prayer which rises to you from the tumult and desperation of a world in which you are forgotten, in which your name is not invoked, your laws are derided and your presence is ignored. Because we do not know you, we have no peace.

Conference of European Churches, 9th Assembly, 1986, Stirling, Scotland

Forgiveness

All-loving God, you do not delight in holding our sins against us, but instead long for us to grow into greater maturity. Help us to forgive ourselves, as you forgive us, so that we may also be able to forgive others.

Affirmation

I am a lovable person created by God. I give myself permission to enjoy being myself, to use my power responsibly and to be a singer and dancer of God's new age.

Bill Wallace, Aotearoa/New Zealand

Prayer of Confession

God of mercy, God of forgiveness.
Forgive us for our insistence that
Korean ways are sometimes more important than the gospel message.

Forgive us for our insistence that
we will take care of our Korean brothers and sisters,
not all brothers and sisters as you commanded.

Forgive us for our insistence that
we will carry on our proud Korean Christian traditions,
not the love of God in our daily lives.

Forgive us for our insistence that
working hard and being successful is more important than being your
    faithful servant.

Forgive us for our insistence that
saving face is more important than
risking our all to proclaim the selfless love of Christ to our neighbors.

God of Hope, God of Love.
Plant your eternal hope and invincible love in our heart
so that we may be bold enough to give up Korean ways
when they become dead weight
rather than a crucible in which
the gospel can burn bright and strong.
Amen.

    Keith Hwang, U.S.A./Korea

(This poem is taken from a sermon that Mr. Simpson, a Jamaican migrant worker, preached at Bethany Church, Randolph, Vermont, 1989.)

In Jamaica, we are poor.
Sometimes I wake up in the morning,
and there is only tea in the house.
I get down on my knees and say,
"Thank you, God, for the tea."
In America, you have so many things.
Yet I am confused:
I see so much around me, in your country,
but I don't see your people saying,
"Thank you, God."

    George Simpson, U.S.A./Jamaica

Eternal God
We confess to you our sinfulness.
You made the world a paradise
but we have turned our lands into
places of tears and unhappiness.
People are fighting with each
    other
race against race.
The holocaust of chauvinism
sweeps through countries
devouring humanity
terrorising us into submission.
Liberating One
free us from all bondage
so that our faith in you
will make us free
to create with courage
a new world—
new societies.

> Sri Lanka

Prayer of Confession

Leader: Shining, surprising, grace-full God, for avoiding the searchlight of your desire for us and running away from your love:

All: Forgive us;

Leader: For preferring the safe, familiar and certain to the risky, unknown and mysterious:

All: Forgive us;

Leader: For failing to believe in the vulnerability of power and the power of vulnerability:

All: Forgive us;

Leader: For taking no delight in variety and insisting on sameness and conformity:

All: Forgive us;

Leader: For fearing those different from ourselves, and projecting onto them what we cannot accept within our own depths:

All: Forgive us;

Leader: For assuming we are superior to the rest of creation, for abusing, despoiling and failing to celebrate our relationship with the earth and the web of life:

All: Forgive us;

Leader: For not noticing your presence in darkness as in light, in body as in spirit, in feeling as in intellect, in pain as in healing, in Good Friday as in Easter Day:

All: Forgive us;

Leader: Set us free, we pray, to be whole human beings and to live our lives graciously and without fear.

(Pause)

Leader: God forgives us:

All: God makes peace within us:

we claim this healing, in faith and hope.

> Kate Compston, England

Earthmaker, our Father, listen to me.
On earth, most pitiable is the life we lead.
Falling and dying, we stumble along the road.
True it is that You told us what to do so that
we might obtain the goods and benefits of life.
That we are aware of.
To achieve the good life as You ordained, this too,
we know and we shall attempt.
We shall indeed attempt to secure light and life.
But You, nevertheless, cause real life to
appear among us.
This is what we ask of You in all humility.

      Winnebago, U.S.A.

Rini Templeton, U.S.A./Mexico

Our Hawaiian sisters and brothers remind us, however, that as important as an apology is, true reconciliation depends on rectification, making right (pono) that which is wrong, so that we can walk, with integrity, toward a common future. That is our task. As we respond in faith to that task, we will be the faithful people that these times demand.

The native Hawaiian people have suffered greatly. Their sovereignty has been taken from them. Their culture has been denigrated. They have been denied their land. Many among them suffer greatly from poverty, and from a lack of educational opportunity and decent health care. Reconciliation demands rectification of these ugly abuses, in the name of justice and mercy. But rectification demands also that the leadership for this journey toward justice and mercy rest in the hands of the native Hawaiian people. And as we of the United Church of Christ respond, as we seek to make right that which is wrong, may God grant that the reconciliation we seek will indeed come to pass.

Acts of repentance and reconciliation remind us that our God is not finished with us yet. In a world of injustice and hostility, we are all tempted to despair. We wonder if the truth will ever be told, if the hungry will be fed, if the excluded will find a home, if justice will be served and mercy received. But even as we wonder, we trust that, since our God is with us, our journey is not in vain. In the midst of the brokenness, God forgives, God renews, God transforms.

This day, far too long delayed, we ask the forgiveness of God and of the native Hawaiian people and we re-commit ourselves to continue the journey toward a world of justice and mercy, for all people, everywhere.

      Paul H. Sherry, U.S.A.

Revelation

The words of the poor
are knives
that bury themselves in our flesh
and cut,
and hurt,
and draw out
infection.

The cry of the poor
is clear water
that rinses off our makeup;
we can let the mask fall.

The eyes of the poor
are two mirrors,
we need not be afraid
to see ourselves there.

The nearness of the poor
reveals Jesus,
excellent Counselor,
God with us,
Prince of Peace,
Fire that burns away
all chaff
and purifies gold!

      Julia Esquivel, Guatemala

Lord, God, we have given more weight to our successes and our happiness than to your will. We have eaten without a thought for the hungry. We have spoken without an effort to understand others. We have kept silence instead of telling the truth.
We have judged others, forgetful that you alone are the Judge.
We have acted rather in accordance with our opinions than according to your commands. Within your Church we have been slow to practice love of our neighbours. And in the world we have not been your faithful servants. Forgive us and help us to live as disciples of Jesus Christ, your Son, our Saviour.

      Conference of European Churches, 9th Assembly, 1986, Stirling, Scotland

Penitence

Leader: Jesus, you came to call the humble and the little ones,
  Christ, you came to call the pure in heart,
  Jesus, you came to call women and men to serve, not to be served,
  Christ, you came to teach us love,

Congregation: We ask your forgiveness for failing to follow what you taught.

Leader: Knowing full well that the situation of the sick today is at its worst, with
  so little medical resources available, that our salary is not enough to eat well
  or maintain our health, and often the sick, especially the victims of AIDS,
  do not have the love and support of their families;
  Knowing full well that the situation of women in all sections of society is
  one of marginalization, of discrimination, of exploitation and domination,

Congregation: We ask pardon for our failings (our societal sins)

Leader: God, forgive our intolerance, our authoritarianism, our self-indulgence,
  self-sufficiency, our lack of community feeling. Forgive our machoism, which
  has caused so much suffering for women.

Congregation: God have mercy upon us.

Leader: God, Father and Mother of women and men who say they love one another but accept a life of unfaithfulness, disrespect, indifference, exploitation
  in a society of oppressed and oppressors; forgive our omissions, our willingness to accept these injustices, and have mercy upon us.

Congregation: Christ have mercy upon us;

Leader: God, who is revealed to us throughout history as a God who hears the
  clamors of the poor and oppressed, of the blind, the sick, who showed yourself in the face of Christ who cured the woman with the hemorrhage of
  blood, who gave sight to the blind, sound to the deaf, remove the mask that
  hides our egoism so that we, reconciled with you and all our brothers and
  sisters, can begin to live a new life, one that reflects your love, and sense of
  justice and equality.

Congregation: God have mercy upon us.

Leader: God, our God, God of all humankind, have compassion for us, your sons
  and daughters, forgive us for our sins. Accept our confession of these sins of
  omission and lack of love, and lead us to eternal life. Hear us, O God who
  created women and men in your image. Amen.

  Barbara de Souza, Brazil

The Liturgy of 1997,* Hong Kong

Leader: We humbly confess our sins:

Congregation: We confess that we have the mentality of refugees, live under refuge willingly, and do not pay any concern to Hong Kong. We labour only for ourselves and our own families, we are apathetic to politics.

Leader: May the Lord forgive us.

Congregation: We confess that we have an intellectual mentality. We shout out for the abstract ideas of "nationalism" while we neglect the real situation. We do not think that the return of Hong Kong to China may be harmful to China. We are the victims of unreal nationalism.

Leader: May the Lord forgive us.

Congregation: We confess that we have a merchant's mentality, always looking for profit. We would do anything in order to earn as much as we can before 1997, including selling our local properties and transferring our capital outside Hong Kong. We are the victims of capitalism.

Leader: May the Lord forgive us.

Congregation: We confess that we do not take up the responsibility of being social leaders. Although we often voice out our concern for the future of Hong Kong, we do not realise that the five million citizens do not have the chance to express their feelings. We know there are negotiations among China, British and the local merchants; but we forget to include the mass of the citizens in the negotiations. We think of ourselves as the representatives of the people, but in fact we are the victims of honour and prestige.

Leader: May the Lord forgive us.

Congregation: We confess that we only pay attention to voicing our own ideas, trying to shape public opinion, so revealing that we are concerned only with individualistic freedom and the welfare of a certain class. We never think of 1997 as the optimum opportunity to reflect on our political and economic order and on the struggle for social justice. We totally forget our role to be the prophetic voice of the people.

Leader: May the Lord forgive us.

Congregation: We confess that we are conservative on social issues. Though we sometimes discuss the future of Hong Kong, we seldom care for the unification of China, and do not seek God's will revealed in human history. We only think from our own situation, and consider the benefits of our own class.

All: May the Lord forgive us.

Hong Kong

*1997 is the expiration date on the lease of the New Territories and their return to the People's Republic of China.

*. . . we ask with humility, our loving and merciful God, that you would have
mercy on us. Cleanse us from sin, cause the gifts of your Holy Spirit to grow
and multiply upon us day by day, that our true repentance may produce the
fruits of conversion which are precious in your sight.*

Dr. Kalman Csiha, Romania

Prayer of Confession

Christ, Jesus, Lord,
I bear your name.
No eyes can see it.
It is not written on my forehead.
No hand can touch it,
it is not tattooed on my skin.
I bear your Name,
Christ, Jesus, Lord,
engraved in the depths
of my heart,
with letters of love.
Who can take it away?
Christ, Jesus, Lord,
I bear your name.
Nothing can take it away.
I shall not shout it from the house-
   tops
but people will be able to tell it
from my eyes and my hands
and my lips,
which, because of you,
bring happiness.
Then people will say:
"It's true! He/She bears his name."
Lord, forgive your Church, for not
   having known
at all times
how to convey you and announce
   you
to the ends of the earth.

Forgive your Church, for having
   lived, often,
among the powerful
and for having been firmly iden-
   tified with them,
instead of with those who perish in
   prison
because they talk too much about
   love.
Forgive your Church, for having
   used your name
as a lie;
for having closed its eyes instead of
   opening them.
Forgive your Church, for having
   been legalistic
instead of promoting liberty.
Forgive your Church, for having
   hidden its poverty
under the appearance of wealth,
and for having hidden its weakness
under the cloak of saintliness.
Forgive your Church,
and give it the strength of renewed
   Hope
so that it may live in your love
and gather all people together
united in this love.
In Jesus' Name. Amen.

Assurance of Pardon

Christ is our peace;
those who are divided
he has made one.
He has broken down the barriers
   of separation
by his death and he has built us up
into one body, with God.
To whomsoever repents and believes
he has promised reconciliation.
So, live as people reconciled.
   Amen.

The United Congregational
Church of Southern Africa

Prayers of Praise and Thanksgiving

Rini Templeton, U.S.A./Mexico

We thank you God for this land of
   Aotearoa*
our place of belonging.
We thank you for the sight of
towering mountain peaks
rolling countryside
checkered plains
multi-hued bush.
We thank you for the sound of
tui and korimako*
rushing mountain streams
gurgling braided rivers
waves pounding the shore
the silence of solitary places.
We thank you for the smell of
rain soaked forests
city gardens' perfumes
fresh frosted air
earth itself.
We thank you for the touch of
soft moist moss
sharp mountain rock
smooth coastal stones
crisp leaf and snow
tender hands of friends and lovers
the heart-beat of all that lives.

*Aotearoa—see note p. 41.
*Bellbird.

   Bill Wallace, Aotearoa/New Zealand

Leader: Thank you, Creator of the universe, for the people gathered around us today. We give thanks for the things of the earth that give us the means of life.

Congregation: Thank you for the plants, animals, and birds that we use as food
   and medicine.

Leader: Thank you for the natural world, in which we find the means to be
   clothed and housed.

Congregation: Thank you, Lord, for the ability to use these gifts of the natural
   world.

Leader: Help us to see our place among these gifts, not to squander them or think
   of them as means for selfish gain.

Congregation: May we respect the life of all you have made. May our spirits be
   strengthened by using only what we need, and may we use our strength to
   help those who need us. Amen.

   Sue Ellen Herne, Mohawk, U.S.A.

(According to my language [Rukiga], at home in Uganda, this is how the prayer should be used. The translation has carefully followed the meaning of the prayer.)

We thank you God for your creation.
You created earth and heaven.
You created man and woman.
You created sun and moon.
You are the only God to be worshipped.

Thank you God for giving us life.
We thank you for the good sunshine.
Thank you for the good rain, that causes the crops to grow.
God be praised for the plenty of good harvest.
We thank you for our food,
for our bananas, sorghum, beans,
Maize and others, O Lord.

God we thank you for our cows, goats,
sheep that give us milk and meat.
Thank you God for giving us children.
You are the source of life, we thank you.
We, your children, are happy enjoying
the fruits of your creation.
Therefore, we thank you.

Divine Intelligence, give us peace in our country.
We want peace in our homes.
Give peace to the world of which you saved
from the power of Satan.
Lord Jesus Christ, we thank you,
and praise you for our Salvation.

Bless us today, Lord.
Bless our children as they play together in school or at home.
Lord, Bless the President and our nation.

    Jack K. Kabahikyeho, Uganda

Shepherd, I bless you for what you give me.
If nothing you give me, I also do bless you.
I follow you laughing, through roses and thorns;
Through brambles and thistles, I joyously follow.
With you when there's plenty, with you when I want
Still always with you.

    Amado Nervo, Central America (Elena M. Huegel, translator, Paraguay)

Ho! Grandfather, Grandmother, You have made everything and are in everything. You sustain everything, guide everything, provide everything, and protect everything because everything belongs to You. We are weak, poor, and lowly, nevertheless help us to care in appreciation and gratitude to You and for everything. We love the stars, the sun, and the moon, and we thank You for our beautiful mother, the earth, whose many beasts nourish the fish, the fowl, and the animals too. May we never deceive mother earth, may we never deceive other people, may we never deceive ourselves, and above all may we never deceive You.

    Bishop Vine deLoria, Lakota, U.S.A.

Leader: For the earth, and all that is part of it:

Congregation: We praise you, Father.

Leader: For rocks, signs of your strength and your steadfast love:

Congregation: We praise you, Father.

Leader: For shells, signs of your variety and your joy in creating this world, which you have given to our care:

Congregation: We praise you, Father.

Leader: For coconuts and taro,* signs of your providence to us:

Congregation: We praise you, Father.

Leader: For the birds, signs of the freedom that is ours when we recognize that we are your children:

Congregation: We praise you, Father.

Leader: For the fish of the sea and animals that walk on the land, a reminder to us that the new earth is to be a place where your people live, work and share in peace:

Congregation: We praise you, Father.

Leader: For insects, their variety, spontaneity and way of growth, signs of the dying and rising to new life that is the central message to us of your son Jesus:

Congregation: We praise you, Father.

Leader: For the similarities of one group of people to another, signs of your desire that there is but one fold, and one shepherd:

Congregation: We praise you, Father.

Leader: For the difference between one group of people and another expressed in these islands through the variety of language, tradition, custom, denomination, signs of the challenge of your word and your message to each person:

Congregation: We praise you, Father.

Leader: For the people present at this celebration, who by their commitment, readiness to learn and listen, and openness of heart and mind are signs of your readiness to forgive the wrongs we commit against you:

Congregation: We praise you, Father.

*Taro are kinds of tropical plants, the roots of which are used for food.

Melanesia

Leader: You found out what we were doing and you interfered: "Come and do it with me," you said.

Congregation: So thank you, Lord, for interfering in our private lives.

Leader: You promised us nothing by way of success, recognition, possessions or reward. "These things will come at the right time when you walk with me," you said.

Congregation: So thank you, Lord, for promising us nothing.

Leader: You gave us no resources apart from ourselves—
hands meant for caring,
lips meant for praising,
hearts meant for loving,
and the Holy Spirit to make us restless until we change.

Congregation: So thank you, Lord, for the essential gifts.

Leader: Then, just when we've got it right as to where we should go and what we should do, just when we're ready to take on the world, you come, like a beggar to our back door, saying "This is the way, I am the Way."

Congregation: So thank you, Lord, for coming again and keeping us right, and showing you care for us and for all people. Amen.

John L. Bell, Iona, Scotland

O Lord, Our God, who fills your children with good things beyond measure and their deserving, give us grace at this time to remember the steadfastness of your love to us and to all people. Especially today, we come before you as Asians and as members of your Church in its many nations.
We thank you for our distinct history, for the vastness and variety of our heritages in art, culture, religion and philosophy. Help us thankfully to learn of the riches of Christ from them and through them.
We thank you for your Church in our midst, and for the work of all your servants in planting it and nurturing it as your promise of life for all our people.
We thank you for the growing sense of oneness among the Churches of Asia, for their drawing together to confess and proclaim the Gospel of your Son, and to be fellow workers in the work of proclaiming release to the captives, recovery of sight to the blind, to set at liberty those who are oppressed, and to preach the good news to the poor.
Above all, we thank you for the gift of yourself in your Son, our Lord, Jesus Christ, and for your gift to us of faith in him. . . .
Lord, you have given us so much. Give us one thing more:
a grateful heart, for Jesus' sake.

Christian Conference of Asia

Blessed Is My God

Blessed is my God
because He made me a woman.
Blessed is *She,*
Even though there are ignorant men
who still say even today
Blessed is *He*
because he didn't make me a woman.

Blessed is my God
because *She* made me a woman,
made in her image.
Blessed is my God
because *She* made me a collaborator in her creation.
Blessed is my God,
because *He* made me a woman
and as a woman I know what it is to be marginalized.
Blessed is my God
because *She* gave me
many sisters who
with me struggle for justice.
Blessed is my God
because He/She comes and makes all things new.

Blessed is my God
because your Reign will come
and men and women will say:
Blessed is my God
because *He* made me a woman,
Blessed is my God
because *She* made me a man!

Barbara de Souza, Brazil

Lord of lords, Creator of all things,
God of all things, God over all gods,
God of sun and rain, you created the earth with a thought
and us with your breath.
Lord, we brought in the harvest.
The rain watered the earth,
the sun drew cassava and corn out of the clay.
Your mercy showered blessing after blessing over our lands.
Creeks grew into rivers; swamps became lakes.
Healthy fat cows graze on the green sea of the savanna.
The rain smoothed out the clay walls:
the mosquitoes perished in the high waters.
Lord, the yam* is fat like meat, the cassava* melts on the tongue, oranges
burst in their peels, dazzling and bright.
Lord, nature gives thanks, your creatures give thanks.
Your praise rises in us like the great river.
Lord of lords, Creator, Provider,
we thank you in the name of Jesus Christ.

*Cassava and yams are edible tubers forming the staple diet in many parts of Africa and the Caribbean.

West Africa

(*Note:* The author of this prayer, Pastor Debusingh, was in jail for his faith and for baptizing people during the time before Nepal's government changed to a constitutional monarchy.)

Let us all stand and worship our Lord, lifting up our hands praising with a loud voice to offer our hearty sacrifices to the living God:
Almighty God, I thank you for the sacrifice of our Lord Jesus Christ, delivering us from the bondage of sin and curse. You made us new people in Christ Jesus, above all you made us your own sons and daughters.

Lord, you led us so far through the dark valley and painful experience of suffering and imprisonment. You proved yourself a faithful God in our time of need.
This Church of yours survived during separation when some of our dear ones were gone away from us. Now we see many young converts who are sitting in your presence to worship and praise you for giving us life and hope. We have all tasted your love and joy of Salvation.
Lord, help us to have the mind of Christ, so that we may be able to teach and preach the life of Christ and serve the poor and needy and homeless. Lord, help us grow in the deeper, deeper life of Christ in our inner being. Give us revelation of your word to understand your mind and live a life well pleasing in your sight.
Lord, deliver this country from the power of darkness, blindness and bondage of sin. Help us to be a faithful peace maker, ambassador, and a humble servant and available to their needs.
We offer this prayer in the precious name of Jesus Christ. Amen.

Debusingh Dahal, Nepal

Almighty and everlasting God, God of the universe, I praise your name and adore you for the opportunity granted me to call and worship you this morning.

Lord, I thank you for your protection and care for my parents, my family, my friends, and all who care for me. Lord, I am before your mercy seat asking for mercy for all the sins I have committed against you and against my neighbours. Forgive me, Lord, and let my cry come unto you.

I am at the beginning of another day asking for your protection, guidance, mercy, health and good relationship with my neighbour; for peace in all homes, work places, schools, colleges, towns, cities, and the world at large.

Lord, look to lands which are full of wars and disunity, misunderstanding and oppression, poverty and homelessness, orphans and refugees, widows and widowers and the aged. My God, be their counsellor and teach them to be like your Son, Jesus Christ, in word and deed; comfort them and grant them eternal peace.

Remember, O God, other world powers who are full of might, progress, hard work, dedication and power in your name. Grant them happiness and peace, and remove from their sight any forms of strife, greed, corruption, evil thought, hatred and pride that may render them unacceptable to you. Teach them to know your mysterious ways and worship you.

My God, be our guide in the days to come and help us to know your ways so that in the end we shall enjoy a world of peace, comfort, and grace through Jesus Christ our Lord. Amen.

Mabel Morny, Ghana

The Directions

(Face east)

Leader: From the East, the direction of the rising sun, we receive peace and light and wisdom and knowledge

Congregation: We are grateful for these gifts, O God.

(Face south)

Leader: From the South comes warmth, guidance, and the beginning and the end of life

Congregation: We are grateful for these gifts, O God.

(Face west)

Leader: From the West comes the rain, purifying waters, to sustain all living things

Congregation: We are grateful for these gifts, O God

(Face north)

Leader: From the North comes the cold and mighty wind, the white snows, giving us strength and endurance

Congregation: We are grateful for these gifts, O God.

(Face upward)

Leader: From the heavens we receive darkness and light, the air of Your breath, and messages from Your winged creatures

Congregation: We are grateful for these gifts, O God.

(Face downward)

Leader: From the earth we come and to the earth we will return.

Congregation: We are grateful for Your creation, Mother Earth, O God.

All: May we walk good paths, O God, living on this earth as brothers and sisters should; rejoicing in one another's blessing, sympathizing in one another's sorrows, and together with You renewing the face of the earth.

Native American, U.S.A.

Leader: Rejoice in the Lord, for he has caused the parched earth to be refreshed, and where there was nothing but brownness, hardness, and death, there is now greenness covering the soft earth. Where there was death there is now newness of life; hope has been restored throughout the land.

Congregation: We rejoice in the Lord.

Reader 2: For the clouds that shelter us from the sun,
for the thunder that shakes the earth,
for the lightning streaking across the sky:

Congregation: We thank you, O Lord.

Reader 1: Rejoice in the rain that falls at night,
sinking immediately into the parched earth,
swelling half cried roots and sealing wide cracks.
Rejoice in the cooler nights and the budding flowers,
the shooting trees and the tender green grass.

Congregation: We thank you, O Lord.

Reader 2: For the rain that falls at night
refreshing the earth where it falls:

Congregation: We thank you, O Lord.

Reader 1: Rejoice in the big drops that fall at noon-day.
Rejoice in the little streams of water
making their way down hills to the valleys below
to swell the rivers and fill the reservoirs
to supply water for cities and for irrigation.

Congregation: We thank you, O Lord.

Reader 2: For the heavy rains
that fill rivers and lakes:

Congregation: We thank you, O Lord.

Reader 1: Rejoice in the activity in the villages
as housewives take hoes and baskets and hurry to the field
to test the responsiveness of the soil
by placing in it seeds of hope and expectation.
Rejoice in those who have already prepared their seedbeds
and now hasten to test the strength of carefully selected seeds.

Congregation: We thank you, O Lord.

Reader 2: For the soil, for rain, for seeds, for tools,
for strength of arms and back,
and for the will to work and a mind to create:

Congregation: We thank you, O Lord.

   Africa

A Thanksgiving Prayer

God of love and kindness, creator of heaven and earth, and everything that exists in this immense universe; of the rocks strewn along the path, which make our walk difficult; the flowers that, with their multitude of color, beautify our world; of small and invisible beings, that we ignore; the vastness of the stars that illuminate the earth; of the animals that live in the jungles and the fields; the people, the crown of your creative work, . . . We thank you.

O Eternal Father, for your grace that knows no limit and the richness of your gifts that do not cease to fall upon us. the food that comes to our table; the fresh water that quenches our thirst; the air that we constantly breathe; the clothes that we wear; the house in which we live; our health that sustains us; and all the many signs that remind us of your care and concern, which is always around us, . . . We thank you.

O Blessed Father, you have made us your partners in creation and in the conservation of this creation, permitting that our intelligence and progress, ever so imperfect as they are, to be useful to the plans for your Kingdom. We give you thanks for that liberating action of your Son, Jesus Christ, that has made us brothers and sisters, keeping us from destroying completely nature and from exploiting human labor in the name of profits and progress. We give you thanks because you invite us to a new life in love and service.

In the name of Jesus Christ, our Lord, who lives and reigns with you, in the unity of the Holy Spirit. Amen.

Jos Carlos de Souza, Brazil

Thanksgiving for the Sun

Leader: From the rising of the sun, unto the going down of the same;

Congregation: The Lord's name is to be praised.

Leader: O magnify the Lord with me;

Congregation: And let us exalt his name together.

Leader: Let us praise God for the sun, which shines so brightly in Hawaii; for the warmth and light which the sun gives, day by day, season by season, year after year;

Congregation: God be praised for the sun.

Leader: Let us praise God for each day's sunrise; for the new hope which each new dawn brings; for the new life and the new chance which come to each and all as the sun comes up on each new day;

Congregation: God be praised for the sunrise.

Leader: Let us praise God for each day's sunset; for the brilliant splash of color on sea and sky as the sun goes down; for the comfort of knowing, as the evening shadows fall, that our day's work is done and we may go now to our rest;

Congregation: God be praised for the sunset.

Edith Wolfe, Hawaii, U.S.A.

4 *Prayers of Petition and Intercession*

Woman at the Well, He Qi, China

O God, that we may receive your blessing,
touch our brows, touch our heads, and do not look upon us in anger.
In a hard year, offer us mercy; in a year of affliction, offer us kindness;
dark spirits banish from us, bright spirits bring close to us;
gray spirits put away from us, good spirits draw near us.
When we are afraid, offer us courage;
when we are ashamed, be our true face;
be over us like a blanket, be under us like a bed of furs. Amen.

> Mongolia

A Prayer for Prisoners

Leader: We pause today to pray for the prisoners of conscience throughout the world. It is altogether fitting that we do this because many before them have died in the cause of freedom:

Congregation: O God, grant that we may not be complacent as long as one person remains in prison for his or her faith or political opinion, lest in our very complacency we dishonour those who have given their lives to the vision that all people everywhere may breathe the breath of freedom.

Our prayer is in the name of our Savior, who wills that all people be free, and that no one undergo torture for any reason—the Savior who wills that the use of torture be forever banned from the human race. Amen.

> Richard Wilcox, Spain

Lord Hear Us

For the presence of children among us and for those gifts which you bestow on us through them, we pray you, O Lord.
For all the poor in Spirit who have accepted joyfully your Word of life, we pray you, O Lord.
For those ministers of the Gospel who, in their poverty, become witnesses allowing your love to shine through, we pray you, O Lord.
For those children who cannot be as children, who lack bread and who are deprived of love, we pray you, O Lord.

> Middle East Council of Churches

O God:
Enlarge my heart, that it may be big enough to receive the greatness of your love.
Stretch my heart, that it may take into it all those who, with me, around the world, believe in Jesus Christ.
Stretch it, that it may take into it all those who do not know him, but who are my responsibility because I know him.
And stretch it, that it may take in all those who are not lovely in my eyes, and whose hands I do not want to touch; through Jesus Christ, my Savior. Amen.

Africa

Lord,
make us realise that our Christianity is like a rice field:
when it is newly planted the paddies are prominent,
but as the plants take root and grow taller,
these divided paddies gradually vanish,
and soon there appears only one vast continuous field.
So give us roots that love,
and help us grow in Christian fellowship and service,
that thy will be done in our lives,
through our Saviour, Jesus Christ.

Philippines

(Based on Anaphora of St. Basil the Great)

Be mindful, O Lord, of us, your people, who are present
together here in this place, and of those who are
absent through age, frailty or sickness.
We commend the children to your care,
the young to your guidance,
the married to your enrichment,
the aged to your support,
the faint-hearted to your strengthening power,
the scattered to your shepherd's love, and
the wandering to your call to repent and be forgiven.
Journey with all travellers; help the bereaved;
release the addicted; heal the sick.
Bring assurance to all who are passing through
trouble, need or anxiety.
Remember for good all those who love us,
those who care nothing for us, and
those who have asked us (unworthy as we are) to pray for them.
There are surely some whom we have forgotten,
but you, Lord, will surely remember them;
for you are the helper of the helpless,
the Saviour of the lost,
the refuge for the wanderer, and
the healer of the sick.
Since you know each one's need, and hear every prayer,
we commend each one to your merciful grace and
your everlasting love.
Grant that together we may praise your great name,
now and forever.

Conference of European Churches, 10th Assembly, 1992, Prague

Lord Hear Us

We pray you, O Lord, for our brothers and sisters who are not ashamed to put their trust in your Word, even in front of their persecutors.

We pray you, O Lord, for those who are still bound by their past and their dreams, and are not yet open to the call of the kingdom which is to come.

We pray you, O Lord, for those who do not dare to hope from you all that you are ready to do for them.

We pray you, O Lord, for all those who, through fear of the necessity of their own transformation, do not dare to hearken to the suffering of their brothers and sisters.

Middle East Council of Churches

Leader: Let us pray for all religious communities and especially for all who teach, preach, instruct and lead; that they may inspire true religion and sincere devotion in the hearts and minds of people.

Congregation: Hear our prayer, O God.

Leader: Let us pray for all artists, poets, dramatists, writers and theologians; that they may serve the cause of justice and peace in the interpretation and application of their faiths.

Congregation: Hear our prayer, O God.

Leader: Let us pray for the places where there is conflict or war in the name of religion. Let us remember places where there is suspicion or prejudice against any religious community; let us pray for places where there is not religious liberty or the freedom to practice one's own faith.

Congregation: Hear our prayer, O God.

Leader: Let us pray for all reformers, for all who seek to correct the wrongs done in the name of religion and its propagation; let us pray for all who work for reconciliation and dialogue, for all who seek to enrich their own faith through their openness to others.

Congregation: Hear our prayer, O God.

Source unknown

Grandfather, Great Spirit,
You have always been, and before
you nothing has been.
There is no one to pray to but you.
The star nations all over the
heaven are yours, and yours are
the grasses of the earth.
You are older than all need, older
than all pain and prayer.
Grandfather, Great Spirit, fill us
with light.
Give us strength to understand
and eyes to see.
Teach us to walk the soft earth as
relatives to all that live.
Help us, for without you we are
nothing. Amen.

Dakota tribe, U.S.A.

You are a Yahweh
God our Messiah,
we are praying to You:
You are a father of day,
father of night

Jesus our Christ,
We are waiting for You
who never present oneself to us;
but we have belief
You are an Abba of liberation,
Abba of peace.

"We are thirsty,
We are hungry,
We are oppressed,
We are not strong."

Why do you keep taciturn?
How long shall we wait for You?
Please tell us
About the way of escape from above.
Are You mute?
Are You deaf?
Are You buried in a rubbish heap?
Are You dead in the dark street?

We believe and hope
You will give us
Peace, justice, righteousness,
equality . . .
and rice.

We don't have jealousy,
but we have the Han.*
You certainly live with Minjung,*
who are the masses of above.
We know,
You are only crying without speaking,
And you exist in the Minjung.
You are Yahweh
who is thought of as having a primordial nature
and a consequent nature.

*Definitions of Han and Minjung appear in Chapter 8, page 65.

Sung-Hwan Park, U.S.A./Korea

Look graciously, O Lord, upon this land.
Where it is in pride, subdue it.
Where it is in need, supply it.
Where it is in error, rectify it.
Where it is in default, restore it.
And where it holds to that which is just and compassionate, support it.
Amen.

Pakistan

God our Creator,
As we join the large spectrum of Christians in different churches who are praying for refugees, we realize that we are, in fact, asking for changes in our own society.
We pray for politicians, that they may be willing to share the prosperity of our country with all people—not only with their own citizens. Send them someone who will give a name and a human face to the refugee problem, and thus show them the inhumanity of the legislation.
We pray for journalists and others who work in the media, and thus influence public opinion. Send into their experience events which will safeguard them from cynicism and invite them to use their capacities to generate a friendlier atmosphere toward refugees.
We pray for the police and immigration officers at our airports, who exercise power over the lives of people—often without a real knowledge of their situation. Send into their lives people who are able to help them understand the reality of the asylum seekers.
We pray for ordinary citizens in our country, that we may not be naive or indifferent, but join those who are working to alleviate the lot of refugees.
God, our Creator, have mercy on us; we, who are acting as if freedom, peace and the well-being of our country were meant for our benefit alone.
God, our Creator, help us to become changed people, and to change our attitudes, as well as our legislation. Amen.

Finland

Lord, most giving and resourceful,
I implore You:
make it Your will that this people enjoy
the goods and riches You naturally give,
that naturally issue from You,
that are pleasing and savory,
that delight and comfort,
though lasting but briefly,
passing away as if in a dream.

Aztec

Leader: Lord, in your mercy, help all the peoples of the vast Pacific Ocean to be good stewards of the sea and its resources; help all people everywhere to acknowledge that you alone have spread out the heavens, and rule over the seas, and that the waters are a gift from you.

Congregation: Lord, in your mercy, hear our prayer.

Leader: Lord, in your mercy, help the scientists and technicians of the world to use their knowledge and skills for the good of all, and not for destructive purposes. May the countries which produce nuclear energy channel such bounty for the good of humankind.

Congregation: Lord, in your mercy, hear our prayer.

Jabez L. Bryce, Polynesia

Prayers of Intercession from Europe

(You may add additional intentions for each sequence of this intercession.)

O God of all the peoples of this earth
we gather in your presence,
aware of the vastness of your world and of the intimacy of your concern.
Your love encompasses our largest dreams and our smallest fears.
In you we trust.
In love you sent your son to bring peace between the nations. Yet the world has such little faith in you that fear drives us to war, and so we remember:
Cyprus, Ireland, the former Yugoslavia, . . .

(Silence)

As a tiny child, your son was a refugee, living in flight, unsure of the future. Yet the world has such little compassion that we exclude strangers from our countries and homes, and so we remember:
all suffering from unjust race and immigrant laws;
refugees in Eastern Europe and the Balkans, . . .

(Silence)

We learn that there is no greater gift than your love, that this is our ideal, our vision. Yet the world turns to ideologies that crumble and states that vanish, and so we remember:
emerging states and nations looking for a voice;
the disillusioned; misguided capitalists, . . .

(Silence)

In the midst of each of these concerns, we pray for the young people and the students, struggling to bring about justice and peace on earth.
Friend, lover, comforter, disturber, we bring these concerns before you in the certainty that you hear—for you hear our largest dreams and our smallest fears. May we never forget. We pray in the name of your Son, Jesus Christ, Amen.

World Student Christian Federation

Let us pray for those who foster violence,
those who do not forgive others.
May the Lord change their hearts,
that they seek peace and love their brothers and sisters.

> Ivory Coast

Prayer for Peace

Let us pray for the world that is immeasurable, a society of millions of
people and newspapers full of news.
Let us pray for the smaller world around us: for the people who belong to
us, for the members of our families, our friends and those who share our
worries, and those who depend on us.
Let us pray for the leaders of governments, and those whose words and actions will influence the situation in the world—that they may not tolerate
injustice, seek refuge in violence, or make rash and ill-considered decisions about the futures of other people.
Let us also pray for all who live in the shadow of world events, for those
who are seldom noticed: the hungry, the poor, the broken, and the
unloved.
We beseech you, O God, send your Holy Spirit to help us give a new face
to this earth that is dear to us. May we help create peace wherever people
live.
Give us the wisdom to see where we can make a difference in the great
nuclear debate that goes on around us, and grant us the courage to form
our conscience in the image of Christ.
Let your Spirit have power over us, and put us on the path that leads to
peace. Amen.

> Pax Christi, U.S.A.

Lord, hear us.
Awaken in us, O Lord, the desire for the unity of all Christians, and convert our hearts.
Purify our faith, removing all merely human interpretations, and make us
open to your Word, entrusted to your Church.
Teach us, O Lord, to discern the ways which you are now opening up for
us to enable your Churches to come together in fellowship.
Make us ready, O Lord, from now on, to do together all the things that
our beliefs do not force us to do apart.

> Middle East Council of Churches

Song and Prayer

Sung: She is crying Lord, Kumba Yah.

Spoken: She is crying Lord, somewhere,
      She is millions, somewhere in many places.
      There are tears of suffering
      There are tears of weakness and disappointment
      There are tears of strength and resistance
      There are tears of the rich, and the tears of the poor.
      She is crying, Lord, redeem the times.

Sung: She is shouting Lord, Kumba Yah.

Spoken: She is shouting out loudly and clearly.
      She has made a choice,
      She stands up against the times
      She is shouting out, offering her life in love and anger
      To fight the death that surrounds us,
      To wrestle with the evils with which we crucify each other.
      She is shouting, Lord, redeem the times.

Sung: She is praying Lord, Kumba Yah.

Spoken: She is praying, Lord.
      We are praying in tears and anger,
      In frustration and weakness, in strength and endurance.
      We are shouting and wrestling to be touched, marked, blessed.
      We are praying, Lord.
      Spur our imagination.
      Sharpen our will.
      She is praying, Lord, redeem the times.

Sung: Kumba Yah, my Lord, Kumba Yah.

Prayer: Through Jesus Christ you have let us know where you want us to be. Help us to be there now. Be with us, touch us, mark us, let us be a blessing. Let your power be present in our weakness. Amen. Amen. Amen.

International Women's Day, World Student Christian Federation

O Great Spirit, Creator of all things;
Human Beings, trees, grass, berries.
Help us, be kind to us.
Let us be happy on earth.
Let us lead our children
To a good life and old age.
These, our people; give them good minds
To love one another.
O Great Spirit,
Be kind to us.
Give these people the favor
To see green trees,
Green grass, flowers, and berries
This next spring.
So we all meet again.
O Great Spirit,
We ask of you.

    Mohawk, U.S.A.

Pray for us, brothers and sisters in Christ, that we may not fail in the oil of comfort, the wine of justice, the involvement of the patient mule, and the generosity which, having given, promises more, until recovery is complete.

    Hong Kong

Grant us prudence in proportion to our power, wisdom in proportion to our science, humaneness in proportion to our wealth and might. And bless our earnest will to help all races and peoples to travel, in friendship with us, along the road to justice, liberty and lasting peace. But grant us above all to see that our ways are not necessarily your ways, that we cannot fully penetrate the mystery of your designs, and that the very storm of power now raging on this earth reveals your hidden will and your inscrutable decision. Grant us to see your face in the lightning of this cosmic storm, O God of holiness, merciful to all. Grant us to seek peace where it is truly found! In your will, O God, is our peace! Amen.

    Conference of European Churches, 9th Assembly, 1986, Stirling, Scotland

Almighty God, we could easily be overwhelmed by despair and hopelessness in view of the uncertainty that most nations on our continent face with impending political change, by the knowledge that essential African traditions and culture are being destroyed as populations are forced to gravitate to urban shanty towns, by the realization of the enormity of the consequences of AIDS to the coming generation, and by the desperation and despondency of our youth facing perpetual unemployment. We pray for your intervention. You are our Hope, our only Hope.

    Dave Grogan, Zambia

The Prayer of Saint Francis of Assisi in Three Languages

(English)

Lord, make me an instrument
   of your peace.
Where there is hatred, let me
   sow love,
Where there is division, unity,
Where there is error, truth,
Where there is injury, pardon,
Where there is doubt, faith,
Where there is despair, hope,
Where there is darkness, light,
Where there is sadness, joy.
O divine master,
Grant that I may not so much
   seek to be consoled as to
   console,
To be understood as to understand,
To be loved as to love.
For it is in giving that we receive,
It is in pardoning that we are
   pardoned,
It is in dying that we are born
   to eternal life.

(French)

Seigneur, fais de nous des instruments de ta paix.
Là où il y a de la haine, que nous
   mettions l'amour,
Là où il y a l'offense, que nous
   mettions le pardon,
Là où il y a la discorde, que nous
   mettions l'union,
Là où il y a l'erreur, que nous
   mettions la vérité,
Là où il y a le doute, que nous
   mettions la foi,
Là où il y a le désespoir, que nous
   mettions l'espérance,
Là où il y a la tristesse, que nous
   mettions la joie.
O Maître, donne-nous de ne pas
   tant chercher à être consolés
   qu'à consoler.
à être compris qu'à comprendre,
à être aimés qu'à aimer.
Car c'est en donnant qu'on reçoit,
c'est en s'oubliant qu'on se trouve,
c'est en pardonnant qu'on est
   pardonné,
c'est en mourant qu'on ressuscite
   à la vie éternelle.

(German)

Herr, mach mich zu einem
   Werkzeug deines Friedens,
dass ich Liebe übe, wo man
   sich hasst,
dass ich Vergebung übe, wo man
   sich beleidigt,
dass ich Glaubewecke, wo man
   zweifelt,
dass ich Hoffnung schaffe, wo
   Verzweiflung herrscht,
dass ich Licht bringe, wo
   Finsternis herrscht,
dass ich Freude bringe, wo
   Traurigkeit herrscht.
Herr unser Gott,
mach, dass ich nicht danach
   strebe,
getröstet zu werden, sondern
   zu trösten,
verstanden zu werden, sondern
   zu verstehen,
geliebt zu werden, sondern
   zu lieben.
Denn indem wir geben, emp-
   fangen wir,
indem wir vergeben, wird uns
   vergeben,
indem wir sterben, werden wir zum
   ewigen Leben geboren.

St. Francis of Assisi (Printed by the
European Conference of Churches)

Isaiah 58:1–12; Matthew 11:30

(As one rides through various parts of Turkey, one can still see oxen plowing. Sometimes they are the long-horned water buffalo one sees in pictures in Pearl Buck's novels. Sometimes they are the oxen we are familiar with. But they are always under a yoke. This prayer comes from Is 58:1–12.)

Dear God:

Isaiah, in Chapter 58, tells us to break every yoke. Help us to see the yokes we put over other people, to use them for our purposes, like we would use oxen. Where we can free others from every restraint without breaking Your law, help us to be de-termined to do so. And help us more and more to hear, and to keep hear-ing, the voice of the Holy spirit of Christ, who said, "My yoke is easy, and my burden light." In Jesus' name, Amen.

Song

Isaý la gi tmeye, kará ar verdim
Isaý la gi tmeye, kará ar verdim
Isaý la gi tmeye, kará ar verdim
Geri donmen, geri donmem.

(English translation)

I have decided to follow Jesus
I have decided to follow Jesus
I have decided to follow Jesus
· No turning back, no turning back.

Doug Wallace, Turkey

Four Kinds of Soil, Kimiyoshi Endo, Japan

Matthew 11:28–30

(If the carrying of enormous loads is a common feature of life in the mountains of Nepal, so also is the provision of burden benches, on which heavy loads may be rested. Used in one church as the design for its Lord's Table, the "chautara" stands as a very local reminder for Christians of the promise of Jesus.)

"Come to me, all who labor and are heavy laden, and I will give you rest." Amen. So be it, Lord.

Nepal

Matthew 18:18–20

(After sharing a scripture, the congregation divided into three groups, with ten persons in each group).

Our heavenly God, we come to You with our thanks and praise. We are grateful to You for the life we have received from You. You made us free from our bondage of sin to serve You. We are Your witnesses to our relatives. Please save our father, mother and other members of our family. I want to be a good neighbor to my friends.

Many Christians are working in hospitals, campuses, schools, and fields. Please give them grace and your presence that they may be good examples of God's children.

At present, many in our country are suffering from landslides and floods that came from heavy rain. Help us to be helpful to all who are going through hard times. We also pray for the underprivileged poor and homeless children. Please provide their needs, as you have done for us. With our thanksgiving, we offer this prayer in the name of Jesus. Amen.

Debusingh Dahal, Nepal

Revelation 3:20

Candleholder: Listen, I stand at the door and knock. If anyone hears my voice and opens the door, I will come into the house. I will eat with those who live there, and they shall eat with me.

Leader: Come, Lord Jesus, be our guest; stay with us, for the day is ending.
Bring to our house your poverty.

All: For then shall we be rich.

Leader: Bring to our house your pain.

All: That, sharing it, we may also share your joy.

Leader: Bring to our house your understanding of us.

All: That we may be freed to learn more of you.

Leader: Bring to our house all those who hurry or hirple* behind you.

All: That we may meet you as the saviour of all.

Leader: With friend, with stranger, With neighbour and the well-known ones,
Be among us this night.

All: For the door of our house we open, and the doors of our hearts we leave ajar.

*Limp.

John L. Bell, Iona, Scotland

Matthew 20:1–16

(Orthodox Liturgy)

May those who love God rejoice;
May the faithful servants enter
    into joy, into their master's joy.
May those who toiled from the
    earliest hour receive their just
    payment this day;
May those who came at the third
    hour rejoice, giving thanks;
May those who came at the sixth
    hour have no hesitation,
for they will lose nothing thereby;
May those who dallied until the
    ninth hour
come forward boldly and without
    fear;
May those who failed to appear
    until the eleventh hour have no
    fear because they came late.
For the Lord is generous.
The Lord receives the last as the
    first;
The Lord grants rest to the worker
    of the eleventh hour
as to the first-comer;
The Lord forgives the latecomer
    and cherishes the first;
The Lord gives to one and grants
    to another;
The Lord accepts the efforts of the
    one and acknowledges the good
    intentions of the other;
The Lord honours work accom-
    plished and praises good resolu-
    tions:
Enter, all of you, into your Master's
joy.

Conference of European Churches,
10th Assembly, 1992, Prague

Genesis 28:17

May this land of Aotearoa*
its peoples
its cultures
their travails
their hopes
be for us all
the very dwelling place of God.

*Aotearoa is the Maori name for the land the
European settlers called "New Zealand."
Aotearoa can be translated "land of the long
white cloud."

Bill Wallace, Aotearoa/New
Zealand

Hebrews 13:1–2

Trim the cruisie's[a] failing light,
The Son of God shall pass tonight;
Shall pass at midnight dreary,
The Son of Mary, weary.
Lift the sneck[b] and the wooden
    bar,
And leave the stranger's door ajar;
Lest Christ may tarry lowly,
The Son of Mary, holy.
Sweep the hearth and pile the
    peat,
And set the board with bread and
    meat[c];
The Son of God may take it,
The Son of Mary break it.
Alleluia.

[a]Cruisie—oil lamp.
[b]Sneck—small wooden piece that drops down
into a door latch from the inside to lock the
house. Therefore, lifting the sneck means keeping the house open for the stranger.
[c]Bread and meat—ancient Celtic Christians often left a door ajar and bread and meat on a
table for a stranger to enjoy during the night,
believing that Christ often comes in the
stranger's guise.

Celtic—Traditional

Psalm 137

Psalm from Ceara

(English)	(Spanish)	(Portuguese)
By the rivers in Fortaleza, we sat down and cried for the cholera victims; in those who lived there we saw sadness and we didn't know what to say. People who lived there did not have songs on their lips. They wanted joy but, with neither water nor health there was no way to be joyful. How could we sing praise to the Lord in the midst of such suffering? If we forget you may we also go thirsty. May our lips be dry if we forget you if we don't bring back water, health and joy. Judge, Lord, our elites, for their neglect and greed have long mistreated us. But remember Fortaleza, your children in Ceara that suffer from thirst and cholera; don't let the earth go dry.	Junto a los ríos de Fortaleza nos sentamos y lloramos por las víctimas del cólera; en aquellos que allí vivían percibíamos tristeza y no sabíamos qué decir. Ahí, los moradores no tenían canciones en los labios. Querían alegría pero, sin agua y sin salud, no había como alegrarse. ¿Cómo podríamos cantar alabanzas al Señor en medio de tanto sufrimiento? Si nos olvidamos de ustedes que también nos venga la sed. Que se sequen nuestros labios si nos olvidamos de ustedes, si no traemos de vuelta agua, salud y alegría. Juzga, Señor, nuestras élites, pues su indiferencia y codicia ya mucho nos maltrató. Pero acuérdate de Fortaleza de los hijos de Ceará que sufren de sed y cólera; no dejes que la tierra se seque.	As margens dos rios de Fortaleza nos sentamos, e choramos pelas vítimas do cólera; naqueles que ali moravam percebíamos tristeza e ño sabíamos o que falar. Lá, os seus moradores, ño tinham nos lábios canções. Queriam alegria mas, sem água e sem saúde ño havia como se alegrar. Como poderíamos cantar louvores ao Senhor em meio a tanto sofrimento? Se nos esquecermos de vocês que também nos venha a sede. Que sequem os nossos lábios se nos esquecermos de vocês, se ño trouxermos de volta água, saúde e alegria. Julga, Senhor, nossas elites, pois sue descaso e cobiça já muito nos maltratou. Mas lembra de Fortaleza, dos filhos do Ceará que sofrem de sede e cólera; ño deixe a terra secar.
Napoleao Marcos Mendes, Brazil	Napoleao Marcos Mendes, Brazil	Napoleao Marcos Mendes, Brazil

Daniel 3

You are the Lord of fire.
Present in a fiery furnace.
Present in the heat of life.
Present in situations of horror and
    despair.
Present in the prisons that incar-
    cerate men and women for their
    beliefs.
Shadrach, Meshach and Abednego
    were lucky ones, Lord.
They came out unscathed.
Not all are so lucky.
Not all withstand the tyrannies of
    life and remain unharmed.
You are with men and women in
    their suffering, in their alone-
    ness and ignominy and death.
Be with them.
Be with them through us who are
    your limbs.
Give even a glimmer of hope in
    hopeless situations:
for where there is no hope, there is
    nothing.

        Rex Chapman

Psalm 107:1–9

Leader: Come, let us do service for God, our Creator!

Congregation: Help us open our eyes wide so that we may see all the glory of Your creation surrounding us.

Leader: We come from all tribes, we come from the plains, deserts, mountains and valleys; we represent many nations and backgrounds and we dwell together in a village that has gathered from a need for survival in this, Your creation.

Congregation: Help us recognize that our survival as a people, as a village, depends first on our willingness to serve You and second on our willingness to serve our brothers and sisters in the ways you have taught us.

Leader: We live in a world of turmoil, O Great Creator. Our people are but a few blades of grass in a great field and our village is but an obscure leaf of a tree.

Congregation: Help us to remember that the blades of grass take root in a soil of moisture and beauty and spread their seeds of life and renewal throughout the land; and that a leaf is what makes the tree beautiful and majestic.

Leader: We feel so inadequate. There is so much to do in our service to You and to our brothers and sisters that oftentimes we are overwhelmed, and we linger in a season of winter when the cold freezes our growth.

Congregation: Help us recognize, Great Spirit, that the brief season of winter adds rich moisture to the soul of the earth; that the growth of all living things is not stunted by the seasons; but is given renewed life, just as you give us the chance to renew our lives in our service for You and all our brothers and sisters.

Leader: We need to drink of Your word daily, O Great Spirit, to regain the strength to grow from Your earth as part of Your circle of life. Give us the wisdom to know that each blade of grass, each leaf, is a little different but yet has a distinct purpose; and to understand that through You and with one another all things are possible.

Congregation: Our lives will adjust to Your stride, Creator God!

        Juanita Helphrey, Hidatsa, U.S.A.

Matthew 13:44

You are a Masotho man who is not educated. You depend on farming. Then you hear that the Boers are opening the mines in the R.S.A. (Republic of South Africa), where they pay the workers (miners) a lot of money.

You leave your place and go to N.R.C. (one of the many mining companies in South Africa). When you get there, they tell you that in order for you to get to the mines, you must pay five cows to N.R.C.. You return home; you get the five cows and take them to the N.R.C. Thus, you are allowed to go to the mines and work and earn a decent living.

Bridget Flazane Makalane, Lesotho

Mark 5:25–34

A Procession for Liberation Done by Women

(Women walking together in a procession saying, or singing)

All: Woman, your faith has saved you; sister, rise up; your faith has saved you.

(The procession comes upon a woman who has blinders on her eyes.)

Leader: For the times we closed our eyes to the reality about us, and did not see our sisters as companions who did not have the means to liberate themselves,

Congregation: Forgive us, God, for the times we were remiss and permitted our sisters to remain blind.

All: My daughter, your faith has saved you; sister, rise up; your faith has saved you.

(The procession goes on and comes to a woman who has her mouth taped shut.)

Leader: For the times we kept our mouths closed and didn't cry out for liberation from male oppression,

Congregation: Forgive us, God, for the times we were neglectful and permitted our sisters to keep their mouths closed.

All: My daughter, your faith has saved you; sister, rise up; your faith has saved you.

(The procession goes on and comes to a woman with her ears taped.)

Leader: For the times we shut our ears (remained deaf) to the cries of so many suffering and oppressed women about us,

Congregation: Forgive us, God, for the times we were neglectful and permitted our sisters to remain deaf.

All: My daughter, your faith has saved you; sister, rise up; your faith has saved you.

(The procession goes on and comes to a woman who is physically challenged.)

Leader: For the times we neglected to recognize the discrimination that our physically challenged women suffered.

Congregation: Forgive us, God, for the times we were remiss and allowed our physically challenged sisters to be discriminated against for being as they are.

All: My daughter, your faith has saved you; sister, rise up; your faith has saved you.

*(The procession goes on and comes to a woman with
her whole head covered with a cloth.)*

Leader: For the times we permitted men, in public media, in mass communication, newspapers, magazines, and society to place us in roles of passivity or submission and we accepted this as "truth."

Congregation: Forgive us for the times we were remiss and permitted our sisters to believe or accept these "truths" as truths.

All: My daughter, your faith has saved you; sister, rise up; your faith has saved you.

(The procession goes on and comes to a woman with her womb tied up in a cloth.)

Leader: For the times that we permitted others to take possession of our bodies, taking away our choices as to whether we should have sons or daughters, or not. For the ignorance concerning the reality of abortions performed in the worst conditions, of mass sterilization, of the use of our bodies as objects, and of the denial of the freedom to exercise our sexuality freely.

Congregation: Forgive us, God, for the times we were neglectful and permitted our sisters to be used and treated as sex objects.

All: My daughter, your faith has saved you; sister, rise up; your faith has saved you.

(The procession goes on and comes to a black woman.)

Leader: For the times we neglected to see the discrimination of color that exists, seeing our black and mulata sisters living on the margin of our society, permitting white ideals to be forced on a country where the majority are Negro.

Congregation: Forgive us, God, for the times we were remiss and permitted our black sisters to suffer, simply because of the color of their skin.

All: My daughter, your faith has saved you; sister, rise up; your faith has saved you.

(The procession goes on and comes to a Native American woman.)

Leader: For the times that we neglected to see the exploitation of our Native American sisters, the abuse of governmental organizations and public services, and other powers which exploit and abuse the native (indigenous) women of Brasil.

Congregation: Forgive us, God, for the times we were remiss and permitted our indigenous sisters (Native American) to suffer, simply for being Native American women.

All: My daughter, your faith has saved you; sister, rise up; your faith has saved you.
    Woman, without a face, without a name, without a voice,

go out on the streets and say what you think,
there are beggars and so many sufferers,
rejected, who have no decent life.

My daughter, your faith has saved you; sister, rise up; your faith has saved you.
And there are so many women hidden,
with no name or fame in their daily life,
their struggles, not recognized,
trying to transmit their desire for liberty.

My daughter, your faith has saved you; sister, rise up; your faith has saved you.
Woman, find your strength, your light,
in the touch of your friend, Jesus, the master;
know that life, true light, life,
emerges in history and the church with Faith.

My daughter, your faith has saved you; sister, rise up; your faith has saved you.
Woman of today, explain yourself,
and denounce all that oppresses you,
You and Jesus, in a commitment of faith,
are involved in bringing in the reign of God.

Barbara de Souza, Brazil

Good Samaritan, He Qi, China

Luke 10:30–37

Aboriginal Traveller

An Aboriginal person was going down the road
from birth to death in Australia.
He fell among good-hearted people who gave him
Grog
Sugar
Tobacco
The Gospel
and they took his land.
They left him by the edge of
the town
the desert
the mining camp
disheartened
dispossessed
and dying.
A church warden came by that way and thought
—"It's only stirrers"
—"It all happened long ago"
—"They share with each other too much"
—"We spend lots of money on them"
—"They should live like me"
and she passed by in the other Australia.
A parish priest came and looked and thought
—"We should pray for them on Sunday"
—"If only they could be like W.A.S.P.A.s*"
—"Sitting with them would be political,
and unacceptable to the congregation"
—"It's all too complex anyway."
and he passed by in his liturgical correctness.
Another Christian came that way.
She got off her stereotype and out of her preconception.
Sitting down she listened and heard the wounds and the treatment.
She poured in the oil of identification and support.

*White Anglo Saxon Protestant Australians.

Fred Wandmaker, Australia

(Prayer after any scripture reading)

*May the God of grace bless this
word, that the word of Christ may
dwell in us richly, and that we may
bear fruit to God's glory.*

Dr. Kalman Csiha, Romania

The Prayer of Our Savior from Many Cultural Traditions

Our Father who art in heaven,
    Great Spirit, whose tepee is in the sky
    and hunting ground is the earth,
Hallowed be Thy name;
    All afraid of You and mighty are You called;
Thy kingdom come,
    Ruler over storms, over people, and birds,
    and beasts, and mountains,
Thy will be done on earth as it is in heaven;
    Have Your way over all,
    over earthways and skyways;
Give us this day our daily bread;
    Find us this day our meat and corn,
    that we may be strong and brave;
And forgive us our trespasses as we forgive
those who trespass against us;
    And put aside from us our wicked ways, as we
    put aside the bad of all who do us wrong;
And lead us not into temptation;
    And let us not have troubles
    that lead into crooked paths;
But deliver us from evil;
    But keep everyone in our camp from all danger;
For Thine is the kingdom, and the power,
and the glory, forever and ever. Amen.
    For Yours is all that is: the earth and sky,
    the streams, the hills, and the valleys, the stars,
    the moon, and the sun; all that live and breathe.
    Wonderful, Shining Mighty Spirit!

        Council of American Indian Ministries

O Great Spirit, You are our Shepherd Chief in the most high place.
Whose home is everywhere, even beyond the stars and moon.
Whatever You want done, let it, also, be done everywhere.
Give us Your gift of bread day by day.
Forgive us our wrongs as we forgive those who wrong us.
Take us away from wrong doings.
Free us from all evil.
For everything belongs to You.
Let Your power and glory shine forever.
Amen.

        Hattie C. Enos, Nez Percé, U.S.A.

Our Father, who are in this our land, may your name be blessed
in our incessant search for justice and peace.
May your kingdom come for those who have for centuries awaited life
with dignity.
May your will be done on earth and in heaven, and in the church of
Central America, a church on the side of the poor.
Give us today our daily bread to build a new society.
Forgive us our trespasses, do not let us fall into the temptation of
believing ourselves already new men and women.
And deliver us from the evil of war, and from the evil of forgetting that
our lives and the life of this country are in your hands.

Nicaragua

Our father who is in heaven,
between gulls and warplanes,
we want you to return before you forget
how to get to this earth,
so you can dance in a ring, not play hide-and-seek.
Our mother, who is in the fields,
help us when we carry water
and we can't go on.
Mother of so many orphans, of beggars for food and shelter,
of us who work when we should be
playing and coming home from school as so many others do.
Our father who watches street children grow
by the thousands in my city,
see how we play on the streetcorners
and ask for money so our parents won't beat us.
Our mother, who is in the cold night,
it seems you hardly ever remember my kids,
hear our prayer mixed with crying.
May your kingdom simply come,
your Kingdom where I dream freely and receive love,
where I have friends and we learn to live,
this Kingdom you said was for the little ones,
the humble and the boys, the girls. . . .

Hugo Venegas, Ecuador

(Adaptation of the Lord's Prayer.)

O Most Compassionate Life-giver,
may we honour and praise you; may
we work with you to establish your
new order of justice, peace and love.
Give us what we need for growth,
and help us, through forgiving others,
to accept forgiveness. Strengthen us
in the time of testing, that we may re-
sist all evil, for all the tenderness,
strength and love are yours, now and
forever. Amen.

Bill Wallace, Aotearoa/New
Zealand

Lord's Prayer in Arabic

Our Father Who Art in Heaven
You are in Istanbul, in our flats and hotels, in Taksim and Beyoglu.
You are within us and with us and in our homes.
You are in Africa, Europe, Asia, Australia and the Americas.
In Yugoslavia and Russia.
You are with the hungry and dying children in Somalia.
Also in Liberia, Bosnia, Ethiopia, Sri Lanka, Kuwait and Iraq.
Hallowed Be Thy Name
Hallowed in the memory of Paul of Tarsus, Martin Luther King, Jr.,
    Bishop Shanahan in Nigeria, Bishop Lumbuin of Uganda, Pastor
    Joseph Ayo Babalola in Nigeria, Dr. Ida Scudder of India, Florence
    Nightingale, David Livingston of Africa, and our parents and grandpar-
    ents who taught us our faith.
And hallowed in the lives of Desmond Tutu of South Africa, Billy
    Graham of the U.S., Benson Idahosa of Nigeria, and Mother Theresa of
    Bombay.
Thy Kingdom Come

A kingdom without police harassment, accidents, soldiers, murder and crime.

A kingdom of freedom and justice.

A kingdom with no borders and only one language.

A kingdom with Christ prevailing and equal rights.

A kingdom with one family, one faith.

A kingdom with harmony between humans and nature.

Thy Will Be Done on Earth as It Is in Heaven

In a creation free from pollution—with clean air, clean water and safe food.

In our homes and in our lives.

With hope and faith in God's will that our world will be free of war, hunger, and poverty.

Give Us This Day Our Daily Bread

The bread of compassion in word and deed.

The bread of protection from evil and injury, and guidance in the way we go.

Give us the bread of goodness and prosperity to share with others to bring them to Christ.

The bread of patience and endurance.

The bread of unity to make us one nation, one people, one destiny.

And Forgive Us Our Trespasses as We Forgive Those Who Trespass against Us

Forgive our selfishness and our greed,

Our unfaithfulness and pride.

That you will treat us as we treat others.

Help us to forgive and give us the grace to forgive and let go.

Help us to fulfill our debts.

And Lead Us Not into Temptation, but Deliver Us from Evil

The temptation of self-righteousness.

Keep us away from the occasions of sin.

Keep us from false use of our tongues and from unnecessarily opening our mouths or inappropriate silence.

Save us from the evils of starvation, war and all injustice.

And help us do good to our neighbor, as we would have God do to us.

For Thine Is the Kingdom and the Power and the Glory Forever and Ever. Amen.

A kingdom of the merciful, where there is love, not hate, peace, not war.

A kingdom without pain, hunger or sorrow.

A kingdom where there is food without money.

A kingdom where no one would be unemployed.

A kingdom where every man and every woman live in equality.

And where all creatures respect each other, living in harmony and life eternal.

A kingdom where God has the power and the control.

Where he has created us with the power to choose good.

Where thine is the Glory, not ours, but thine.

For ever and ever. Amen.

> African refugees meeting with Olgha Sandman,
> African Fellowship of Union Church, Turkey

(This reflection on the Lord's Prayer can be sung to any simple tune. The concluding line in each part, sung by all, is a repetition of the tune of the last line of each verse as sung by the leader.)

Leader: Life's Source and Sustainer, beyond all yet close
    You are Father and Mother—life's sacred to us.
    We seek now to shape this your world as a home.
    to share in the mystery of your holy name.

Congregation: Our Father in heaven, holy be your name.

Leader: We hope and we work for your promised new world.
    Where your dharma of love reigns,
    Where peace-talk is heard,
    Where compassion alone is the weapon we wield,
    Sharing life with all creatures, to their needs we yield.

Congregation: May your kingdom come quickly, your kingdom of love.

Leader: We long for your will to be done on the earth,
    For you've shown us our world has a heavenly worth;
    You call every human your image to bear,
    And in likeness to you for all creatures to care.

Congregation: May your will now be done on the earth as in heaven.

Leader: As we labour on earth, You, who give all life's good,
    Help us share out earth's nurture, earth's life-giving food.
    We can gain nothing good by our violent ways;
    To the gentle come earth's blessings, as by your grace.

Congregation: Give us this day our bread, daily bread for our need.

Leader: We're indebted to you for each gift in our life;
    You have shared so much with us; we ask you, forgive
    Our abusing of all that sustains life around
    Help us mend what is broken, give us all a new mind.

Congregation: Forgive each one's debts, just as we too forgive.

Leader: Do not lead us to testing in which we must fall;
    Save us from earth-destruction, this can't be your will;
    Save from all that is evil, without and within;
    Grant commitment to wholeness, death to all selfish sin.

Congregation: Yours the kingdom, the power and the glory. Amen.

United Theological College, Bangalore, India

6 Offering Resources

Benefactor, Zhang Guijie China

(*Note:* Other Offertory Prayers written by young people are found under "Youth Offerings," pp. 104–13.)

Lord of the far-flung galaxies, we are wide-eyed in contemplation of the possibility that life may exist somewhere else in the universe, but we have blinders on when contemplating the possibilities for life on Planet Earth. We are intrigued by the thought of black holes in the far distant universe, but apathetic toward the "black holes" in which some people have to live here. At this altar and in this sacred moment, grant that we may be concerned about all the black holes everywhere. Amen.

> Richard Wilcox, Spain

All things of Earth are holy,
All things are one in you.
This Earth is filled with your beauty, God,
Charged with your love.

> Bill Wallace, Aotearoa/New Zealand

(*Contributor's note:* "My English translation for response used almost weekly in many Japanese churches.")

We bring these our gifts for Thy service, dear Savior;
Receive them and bless them, for Thy kingdom's sake. Amen.

> John Moss, Japan

O God, to those who have hunger give bread,
and to us who have bread give the hunger for justice.

> Latin America

(May also be used as a table grace.)

For fish and poi,* for bread and meat,
For all Thou givest us to eat;
For hands that help and hearts that share,
Lord, offer we our grateful prayer.

*Hawaiian food made of taro root.

> Edith Wolfe, Hawaii, U.S.A.

Offering

There are offerings of flowers, fruits and plants as signs of the "bounty and beauty" of our earth-life;
There are gifts of money, as we remember the interlinking of our economy and its structures with ecological life;
There is fire or burning camphor, as a sign of energy, human and cosmic; for we remember that true creativity is found in sacrificial giving, and that greedy exploitation of energy-resources is merely destructive of the wholeness of earth's and human life.

United Theological College, Bangalore, India

Offertory

Leader: Let us present with joy our offerings of commitment and support for the work of Christ's church.

Congregation: Let us prepare Christ's table with the offerings of our life and labor.

The United Congregational Church of Southern Africa

We stand before this altar, Lord, like so many cosmic orphans. We are alienated from the life we feel we were destined to live, and estranged even from you, our Maker and Lord. It is as though we have been set down in a strange land where there is little to remind us of our homeland, and even less to call us back to our true vocation as your sons and daughters.

Let, then, this altar be a trysting place in a foreign land, . . . a place in which cosmic orphans can come and feel at home. And may the gifts we place upon this altar lay claim to all the rest of our orphaned selves until that time when all your human family is reunited in its true homeland and orphaned no longer. Our prayer is in the name of the homeless Christ. Amen.

Richard Wilcox, Spain

Sharing, Presbyterian Church, U.S.A.

Special Offerings

The "mujikilezc" for the receiving of offerings is a time of fun and fellowship in the United Congregational churches of Mozambique. Essential ingredients are a blackboard for listing various subgroupings of those present, a table, and several persons to count and record what is received. This is usually done after the benediction for the worship.

Each organized group of the church is called separately, at which time its members leave the church to organize outside, where they line up and choose a Christian chorus with a good beat, which they will sing vigorously as they dance/shuffle in the main door and up the aisle. As they appear at the door, those still in the church will rise to their feet in greeting and respect. They dance past the table, where they deposit money, and back up the aisle—usually to come around again and deposit more money.

Participants will take large bills to the table to get change so they have many small bills. (Paper money in Mozambique has large numbers, but the smallest bill is worth a U.S. penny.) With many pieces of money in hand, they dance past the table many times, enjoying it when their group succeeds in going a long time. If they see someone sitting down and not participating, they will give some of their money to the nonparticipant so that person can get up and join the fun of giving!

The tally is carefully kept of each group's total offering, and even "guests" will be called up as a separate category. If a group is small, persons from other groups will join them to "support" them and not leave them alone in their offering. After the totals are posted, it is frequently the case that a group will be called by its leader to return yet again in order to boost their total, and perhaps be the one to give the most. It is indeed competitive, but it is also truly a time of great fun—indeed, it is better for building community than for raising real money!

The largest of these special offerings is called the "Thanksgiving" offering, and sometimes families, individuals, or groups bring food or other things in kind, as well as money. A cloth for the altar, a hanging for the church wall, a globe, or a bench might be given at such a time. These contribution competitions can last as long as an hour or more after the worship itself, but everybody stays to the very end to hear the report of the total given, congratulate the group that gave most, and sing a hymn joyfully together as they finally all leave.

Ruth Brandon Minter, Mozambique

7 *Benedictions*

Rini Templeton, U.S.A./Mexico

May it be blessed before me,
May it be blessed behind me,
May it be blessed above me,
May it be blessed below me,
May it be blessed all around,
May speech from me be blessed.
May all my surroundings be
blessed.

> Navajo, U.S.A.

May our senses be awakened
to the presence of God
in the beauty of this land.
May our imagination be awakened
to the suffering of God
in the cries of this land.
May our hearts be awakened
to the compassion of God
to the peoples of this land.
May our consciences be awakened
to the commitment of God
in the Treaty* of this land.
May our whole being be awakened
to the Aroha* of God
in the enfolding of this land.

> Bill Wallace, Aotearoa/New
> Zealand

*Treaty—the Treaty of Waitangi, a solemn
covenant between the British Crown and the
indigenous Maori population protecting Maori
sovereignty lands and cultural treasures in the
face of expanding European settlements. The
treaty was, however, subsequently honored by
the European settlers more in the breach than
in the observance.

*Aroha—Maori word for love, affection, compassion.

Go into the world
With a daring and tender love.
The world is waiting.
Go in peace.
And all that you do
Do it for love,
And by the Spirit of Jesus
Who is the Lord.

> Women's Conference, Japan

Closing Responses

Leader: This is the day that God has
made;

All: We will rejoice and be glad in it.

Leader: We will not offer to God

All: Offerings that cost us nothing.

Leader: Go in peace and serve the
Lord;

All: We will seek peace and pursue it.

Leader: Glory to the Creator and to
the Son and to the Holy Spirit

All: As it was in the beginning, is now
and shall be forever.

Amen.

> George MacLeod, Iona, Scotland

Hands that join.
Hands that reach over barriers.
Hands that cause change.
Bodies that organize themselves so
that
other bodies may have life.
Solidarity.

> Brazil

Leader: Sisters and brothers,

Let us claim the treasures Christ holds
out to us,
let us claim the freedom he
gives us
by his own self-giving on
the cross.

All: May he enable us to live and serve
in faith, hope and love.

Leader: Let us, in times of sorrow, as in
times of joy,
celebrate the goodness of God.
Let us go in peace.

All: Thanks be to God. Amen.

Kate Compston, England

May the God of justice and
creativity
empower us
to honour the Treaty,
to share our power
and to create new hope
for all the peoples of this land.

Bill Wallace, Aotearoa/New Zealand

A Blessing

(We have received the blessing of people who love us, now we are going to bless our own
selves. As a sign of incarnation, we will use the ancient gesture of the laying on of hands.)

Touch your eyes with your hands and say: Bless my eyes that I may see clearly.

*Touch your mouth with your hands and say: Bless my mouth which breaks the si-
lence of centuries and speaks now my truth.*

*Touch your ears with your hands and say: Bless my ears that I might hear my
own words, thoughts and feelings and those of every woman near me.*

*Touch your heart with your hands and say: Bless my heart that I might be open to
friendship and love.*

*Touch your womb with your hands and say: Bless my womb so that I might be in
touch with my creative energies and those of the universe.*

*Touch your feet with your hands and say: Bless my feet so that I might travel
each step firmly and with courage during my life's path.*

*Touch your sisters (and brothers) who are about you and say: Bless me and my
sister (and brother)!*

Barbara de Souza, Brazil

O you people, be healed;
Life anew I bring to you.
O you people, be healed;
Life anew I bring to you.
through the Father over all
do I offer healing.
Life anew I bring to you.

Dakota Holy Song, U.S.A.

May the blessing of God who risked everything for our sake, the blessing of the Christ-child who releases in us new visions of hope, and the blessings of the Holy Spirit who guides and directs us into new forms of obedience, be with us all.

Leader: Go forth as preparers and proclaimers.

Congregation: We go to make ready for the birth of God in our midst. We go to announce Christ's coming.

Leader: The Lord go with you.

Congregation: And also with you.

Aotearoa/New Zealand

Go, my Korean brothers and sisters.
You were Koreans before you became Christians.
Now you are Christians before you are Koreans.
Go far and go fast
and make that piercing Light in you
come out of your Korean memories
and let that Light draw new memories
in you and people around you.
Go far and go fast
and let this earthen vessel called Korean traditions
be used by the Holy Spirit
as a cup holding liberating, living water
to all who thirst.
Go far and go fast
and use that Kimchee power
to put the spice of peace and friendship
into the lives of people
who dare to wake up their spirit.
Amen.

Keith Hwang, U.S.A./Korea

Through the days to come, in every time of year or climate, may you know the luminous goodness of God, creator of all things, all people. Amen.

Judy Newton, Japan

Run with the name of the Christ!
Make[a] God's will happen.
Look! The dawn is coming[b] in this difficult life,
So move forward![c]
Christ ignites, enlivens, and raises us up[d.]
Beloved of God, you empower[e] us and lift each other up![d]
Love and trust[f] each other
and share[g] the new light
that is within you. Amen.

[a]Stronger than simply "do God's will," a powerful word in Marshallese.
[b]Literally, "the dawn comes yet."
[c]"Jouru jure jur u jur"—crescendo as you say these words.
[d]Raises the status of all, changing us to "something more."
[e]Clearly a command here.
[f]"Honor" literally.
[g]"Emmelet" means *explode* the new light, not simply share it: a big concept of extravagant energetic giving—not just a "nice" word.

Lauren Buck Medeiros, translator, Hawaii/Micronesia

Blessing and Sending Out in the Closing Worship

Now we are leaving.
Everyone will submerge once again in his or her activities,
some of them important, others, not.
We leave something here: some complications that have arisen, would
    best be left behind because we will run into them in some other place
    too.
We leave very beautiful people, visible and invisible, who have helped us.
We take large suitcases back, full of things: gifts for our children, and gifts
    for ourselves, among them lots of music, angelical voices, children and
    old people dancing samba, gestures and words not found in the dictio-
    nary,
and we take ourselves, not always something easy to do,
and we take Jesus' presence who never leaves us alone,
and we take this beautiful greeting: May God bless you.

    Art and Liturgy Seminar, Rio de Janeiro, Brazil, February 1993

(Spanish)

Bendicion y Envio en el Culto de Clausura

Ahor vamos
cada uno se sumerge otra vez en sus cositas, algunos importantes,
    otros, . . . no tanto.
Dejamos algo aquí: algunas complicaciones que han sucedido, major las
    dejamos porque las encontramos en otro lugar también.
Dejamos personas muy bellas, visibles e invisibles que nos ayudaron.
Llevamos maletas grandes con cosas: regalos para los niños, regalos para
    nosotros, entre ellos, Musica mucha musica, voces angelicales, niños y
    ancianos bailando samba, gestos y palabras que no se encuentran en el
    diccionario.
Llevamos a nosotros mismos, . . . a veces bastante difícil.
Llevamos la presencia de Jesucristo que nunca nos deja sólos.
y a este saludo tan precioso: Que Dios les bendiga.

    Art and Liturgy Seminar, Rio de Janeiro, Brazil, February 1993

We must close the meeting,
my people!

This is merely a resting place,
a place of transit,
where humanity and God pause
before taking to the road again.

Go, my people,
you are ready to set sail,
your country is not here.

You are a wayfaring people,
strangers, never rooted in one place,
pilgrims moving towards an abiding
    city further on.

Go forth, my people,
go and pray further off,
love will be your song
and life your celebration.
Go, you are the house of God,
stones cut according to the measure
    of God's love.

You are awaited, my people,
and I declare to you, Word of God.
I am going with you.

    The United Congregational Church of
    Southern Africa

May the warm winds of heaven
blow softly upon you,
and may the Great Spirit
make Sunrise in your heart.

    Cherokee blessing, U.S.A.

Robert Eddy, U.S.A.

PART II

Resources to Join Hands Together

Brief introductory notes for each chapter elaborate on the materials we have brought together in this part of our book. Unlike the prayers, litanies, and other worship resources found in the first and third parts, which could be "borrowed" into the Sunday service of a North American congregation, these materials—proverbs, descriptions, liturgies, customs, affirmations—call upon us first to understand and appreciate the liturgical experience in its own context and only then to consider how best to share that experience.

8 Words, Proverbs, and Sayings

In the letters we received for this book, often we would find proverbs, sayings, or simply a word with its definition that our correspondent felt was significant in his or her context. We have gathered these brief resources together, not as the result of intense global research but as a sharing of the "little gifts" we were given.

Chile

"Que Dios le Bendiga." (God bless you.) This is the traditional form of greeting among members of the church, before, during and after worship services, as well as in the street, in homes, or when/wherever we encounter one another!

"¡Gloria a Dios!" (Glory to God!) This exclamation is used throughout the worship service, usually in sets of three. It's a form of exaltation, during which all stand and raise their arms above their heads at the invitation of the worship leader: "Glory to God, Glory to God, Glory to God!" The exclamation "¡Aleluya!" is also used in this way.

"Bendito se Su nombre para siempre." (Blessed be God's name forever.) "Alabado sea Su nombre para siempre." (Worshipped be God's name forever.) "¡Amen! ¡Amen!" These, along with the phrases already listed, may be used as interjections by the preacher during a sermon. Congregants also use all of these phrases spontaneously during worship, to affirm what is being said by the worship leader at any given time.

Leader: ¡Cristo vive! (Christ lives!)

All: ¡Si, vive! (Yes, Christ lives!)

Leader: ¿A su nombre? (His name?)

All: ¡Gloria! (Glory!)

Leader: ¿De quien somos? (To whom do we belong?)

All: ¡De Cristo! (To Christ!)

Leader: ¿Con quien vamos? (With whom will we go?)

All: ¡Con Cristo! (With Christ!)

Alison Buttrick, Chile

El Salvador Cross, Sister Helen David Brancato, U.S.A.

India

"Shanti, Shanti, Shanti!" Peace, peace, peace!

Savithri Devanesen, India

*"Shanti" means peace. This word is derived from Sanskrit and so is found in
Hindi, Telugu, Kannada, and many other Indian languages.*
*"Saranam" means refuge. It is also derived from Sanskrit and hence is found in
many Indian languages such as Hindi, Telugu, Kannada, Tamil,
Malayalam, etc.*

Sheila Rubdi, U.S.A./India

"Bhajan"—shared praise—especially prominent at beginning of worship.
*"Bhakti"—paying worshipful homage. The bhakti movements of devotional
ecstasy in Indian religions caught up people of mixed social backgrounds.*

United Theological College, Bangalore, India

A candle-light is a protest at midnight.
It is a non-conformist.
It says to the darkness,
"I beg to differ."

Samuel Rayan, India

Japan

The truth is
Just like a plum blossom.
Dare to bloom
Despite wind and snow.

By Josef H. Neesima, 1843–1890, the founder of Doshisha University; sent by
Masao Takenaka, Japan

Oshieru wa manabu no nakaba nari. (Half of teaching is learning.)

Anonymous

"Hitotsubu no Karashidane"—a grain of mustard seed.
*"Doronuma"—quagmire or swamp—(how easy it is to be bogged down by the
demands of society)*
"The nail that protrudes gets hammered down."

Armin Kroehler, Japan

Brazil

"Axé"—African word meaning "peace" used as a greeting in Brazil.

Barbara de Souza, Brazil

Peace

PAZ SPANISH PORTUGUESE   МИР RUSSIAN

शांति HINDI   AMANI SWAHILI

FRIEDE GERMAN   PAIX FRENCH

平和 CHINESE JAPANESE   שלום HEBREW

EIPHNH GREEK   PACE ITALIAN

Hawaii

"Pono"—to make right.

See the article by Paul Sherry in Chapter 2, page 15.

Benediction: Psalm 19:14

I maikai ka olelo a ko'u waha, a me ka mana'o o ko'u naau, imua o kou alo, e Iehova, e ko'u kaika, a me ko'u Hoola.

(English translation)

Let the words of my mouth, and the meditation of my heart, be acceptable in thy sight, O Lord, my strength and my Redeemer.

Ke nana aku nei makou ia Oe, e ka Haku, no na mea ai i hanai aku, i ko makou kino, ame ka pomaikai, i hooikaika aku i ko makou uhane, ame kou aloha i hoolako ko makou ola. Amene.

(English translation)

We look to Thee, O Lord, for food to nourish our body, and for grace to strengthen our spirit, and for love to enrich our life. Amen.

> Edith Wolfe, Hawaii, U.S.A.

Korea

"Han" is a pent-up anger mixed with depression over situations that cannot be changed: the unfairness and injustice of life; the disappointments and disillusionments of history and politics.

"Minjung theology" is a specific Korean theology, and it is also global. This means that Minjung theology is a constructive theology, and it is one of the famed third world liberation theologies.

"Minjung" has often described its identity as the mass of the poor, economically and politically alienated people in Korean history. Minjung theology proclaims and manifests that the knowledge of today makes a sacrifice of oneself for the practice (praxis) of the future.

> Sung-Hwan Park, U.S.A./Korea

Philippines

(Spoken by a Filipino held in a detention without trial for many years.)

The prison cell is not the deathbed of our dream.

> Anonymous

Native American

Hetchetu aloh (It is good.)

Lakota, U.S.A.

O Great Spirit, help me never to judge other people until I have walked the path for two weeks in their moccasins.

Sioux, U.S.A.

China

If I keep a green bough in my heart, the singing bird will come.

Anonymous

The ultimate goal of farming is not the growing of crops, but the cultivation and perfection of human beings.

Chinese proverb, quoted by Janet Ross-Heiner, U.S.A./Nicaragua

Forgive me O God: I was angry that I had no shoes, then I met someone who had no feet.

Anonymous

"Ping-an"—peace. Every worship service begins with the ping-an, and it is also used as a general greeting among Presbyterians, meaning "hello" and "goodbye."

Virginia Thelin, Taiwan

The Chinese character for peace, "wa," means harmony. It derives from the combination of two words: "rice" and "mouth." When no one is hungry, then truly there is peace.

Anonymous

"Hsing-t'u"—a homeland. It is the Presbyterians' conviction that Taiwanese, and not outsiders, should be masters of Taiwan; it should be theirs and not part of mainland China.

Virginia Thelin, Taiwan

Japan

Spring is approaching on the campus of our church-related high school, Keiwa Garden. The word "Keiwa" comes from two Chinese characters meaning "reverence" and "harmony," corresponding to "love God and love your neighbor."

John Moss, Japan

Lebanon

Salaam alekum (May God's wholeness be with you.)

Lebanon

9 Descriptions of Worship from the Global Community

One of the ways we join hands together is to learn how worship is experienced throughout the world. The following chapter is divided into four sections. In "The Spirit of Worship" we quote from many letters depicting the spontaneity and oral tradition which characterizes worship within many communities. In "Times of Prayer" we offer a rich variety of prayer customs and services. (Be sure to note, for example, the importance of breathing to corporate prayer in Bali and India.) In "Celebrations" we share distinctive worship events for you to appreciate and then perhaps to adapt to your particular situation. In India, where Christians are a minority, the careful incorporation of indigenous cultural symbols enriches Christian liturgy. Two of our sources have written extensively on "Multifaceted Worship in India" and we put those pieces together here as well as including an Indian service in Chapter 10.

Spirit of Worship

In our church in Zimbabwe, much of the worship is spontaneous/ extemporaneous. The prayers are offered by laity and clergy both—but are not written down.

Allen Myrick, Zimbabwe

As I explained to you when I sent you the hymn, there seems to be a paucity of worship materials in the churches in Mexico due to the current emphasis on spontaneous worship, so I am a little hard pressed to come up with something for you, but I will keep you in mind.

John Huegel, Mexico

One of the things that has become very meaningful to many of us is the prayer and praise time in our church services. We usually stand up for it. Each worshipper praises God in his or her own words and own choice of language simultaneously, (but not in unison) for ten to fifteen minutes in the first half of the service. Here you can thank God for answered prayers or nice surprises or praise God by Psalms or by singing. When it is a song we all know, we'll all stop talking to God and join in the song until it's finished.

Phyl Asher, Nepal

Vine and Branches, Kimiyoshi Endo, Japan

The spontaneity of Zairean worship does not lend itself to liturgy as the western mind conceives of it. However, this is not to say that worship in this context is without ritual or tradition. It has simply not been formalized by print. Oral tradition still prevails and the power of the 'spoken' word is very evident. In fact, the worship experience includes lots of verbal interaction between the worship leader, or preacher, and the people.

Suzette Goss-Geffrard, Zaire

. . . then I will return hopefully to a new assignment in Rio de Janeiro with a project called, "Women, Theology and Citizenship: The Health and Sexuality Project." Also, as the situation gets worse and worse here with an inflation of 0.8 to 1 percent per day, women and children are the most affected and cholera is here, I have found it difficult to think about what worship for the first world has to do with the suffering in the third. But I will try to give you some things, not in Portuguese but in translation. Most of what I have to offer will reflect the situation I have portrayed, but this is what our worship consists of!

Barbara de Souza, Brazil

It is the rare occasion that we, of the U.S. Protestant church community, pull out all of the stops and really let loose in celebration of the living Christ in our midst, shouting and dancing and clashing cymbals. Here in Chile, however, in the congregations of the Pentecostal Church of Chile (IPC), I witness this celebration daily, in the church, on the streets, and in the homes of my Chilean hosts. My first worship service here was a startling experience, to say the least, after the relative solemnity of the small New England churches in which I grew up! Some five hundred members gather every Sunday to worship, and on special occasions the church, which has a capacity of three thousand, may be full to bursting. Imagine that many people praying aloud, singing together, or bursting out with spontaneous cries of "Aleluya!" and "Glory to God!" throughout the service. At first the commotion felt like an intrusion (at home we expect respectful silence during the sermon), but I have come to appreciate the enthusiasm with which this community worships, embracing the exuberant invitation of the Psalmist to "make a joyful noise unto the Lord!" (Ps. 100:1)."

Alison Buttrick, Chile

I believe that viewing the Gospel in the context of this land does not occur simply by using the name Aotearoa, or referring to indigenous plants and animals, or even the tangata whenua, the Maori people, but by asking how is God present in this land and what can we learn from this presence.

This sacramental approach to reality does not have to invoke the presence of God with such phrases as 'Come, Lord Jesus, be present in this our land,' for it has discovered that God is already present; it is only we who are not aware of that presence.

Bill Wallace, Aotearoa/New Zealand

Times of Prayer

For a Quinceañera (Girl celebrating fifteenth birthday)

O Creator, God of the universe, we praise your holy name for the life of (Name).
We rejoice that she has come to that time in her life when she assumes new and
*   greater responsibilities. We affirm her at this time of joy and celebration.*
This is a time of thanksgiving for the past and visions and challenges for the fu-
*   ture. We acknowledge that this is a time of commitment, not only to the highest*
*   ideals of life but also to the saving grace and sovereignty of Christ in her life.*
Accept her life in true commitment and fill her heart with joy, and grant that your
*   peace may come to abide in her heart for ever,*
*   through Jesus Christ, our Sovereign and Savior. Amen.*

Roberto Escamilla (Hispanic), U.S.A.

Prayer Meeting

About prayer—what people commonly do whenever any of the household
is seriously ill is to invite a whole lot of friends for a prayer meeting. If the
evening is fine and warm we sit in the courtyard on rush mats, the men on
one side and the women on the other. The host will say what he has called
the meeting for, and while he is about it, he will add a number of supple-
mentary biddings—Mary is taking an important examination, Peter is away
catching turtle, Uncle is going for a journey, and so on. We start with a
hymn, a lilting ragtime sung to drum and cymbal. There follows the Bible
reading with a brief (or not so brief) sermon attached. Then begin the
prayers, the president first and then others, often repeating each other, and
the good Lord is informed of a lot of things that he knows very well already.
Then sometimes we go on far into the night with hymn after hymn. Usually
at about 1:00 or 2:00 a.m., the final prayer is said, some light refreshments
are served, and everyone trails off across the fields to their own homes.

Dacca, Bangladesh

Tongsung Kido (Pray Aloud)

In Korean congregations, among others, Tongsung Kido is a popular and impor-
tant part of prayer life. Usually the congregation is given a specific time period,
with a common theme of petition or supplication. Then all pray aloud at the same
time. The voices of others will not bother them when they concentrate on their
own earnest prayers, longing for the empowerment of the Holy Spirit.

Korea

Simultaneous Prayer and Intercessory Crying Service

In the United Congregational Church of Mozambique, there is an infrequent service focused on intercession and confession, and turning over of both personal and community burdens to the Lord. The worship leader will ask the community to all join in simultaneous prayer, and the sound of it is as a waterfall of voices in which each is bathed. Each person prays out loud with no attention whatever to anybody else. Many languages are used, not just the official common language of the church, for this prayer is for God, who knows all languages, and nobody else need understand. A couple minutes into this prayer time, anywhere from three to fifteen women will work their way forward to the center front of the church and fall to their knees. As they pray, they begin to cry and sob and wail. Ritually, on behalf of everybody present, they divest themselves of burdens that are indeed heavy, laying them before Jesus and pleading for mercy and for strength. It is a very special cathartic and cleansing time.

The experience closes when the pastor or lay leader starts the hymn. Slowly the bubbling of voices and the sobs of those crying subside and more and more join the singing, and soon glorious four-part a capella harmonies are wafting into the streets, proclaiming once again the faith of those within that, indeed, Jesus can and will hear their prayers and help and heal.

This service may be begun by a deacon or the pastor after a particularly inspiring sermon or dramatization at a regular Sunday worship service, but it also can be a scheduled special worship service, as at the annual regional women's meeting.

Ruth Brandon Minter, Mozambique

Greetings and Opportunities

Incidentally, the Pentecostal community has a wonderful tradition of sending greetings back and forth between churches with visitors. If, for example, I plan to travel to another city, I ask for greetings from my home church members, along with their prayers for my safe journey and return. They send those greetings with three "Glories to God," which I then present in the church which I visit: " . . . and I bring you greetings from our brothers and sisters in Curico with three 'Glories to God!'" At which point all stand and exclaim three "Glories to God!" Individuals may also greet congregations in this fashion when addressing them from the pulpit: "I greet you, as is the custom among Christians, with three 'Glories to God',"and the whole congregation joins in.

This happens quite frequently because the Pentecostal community is also accustomed to offering "opportunities" to church members to speak during worship

Conference of European Churches

services. Members may ask for opportunities to sing, to give thanks to God for a blessing received, to ask the congregation for prayers, or to give testimony to the presence of God or the Holy Spirit in one's life, to describe how one was called by Jesus Christ or how He responded to a particular prayer.

Of course, time is more flexible in Pentecostal services than in United Church of Christ services in New England; congregants in the Pentecostal Church of Chile don't blink an eye if a service runs over two hours because it has included several opportunities! I am particularly drawn to the musical offerings, sung by children, youth, adults, couples, soloists, groups—those with tremendous talent and those who can just barely hold a tune but who sing and play from the heart. All music is received enthusiastically by the congregation, viewed as an offering to God.

Alison Buttrick, Chile

The only dimensions of our liturgical practice here that are even remotely unique are the "Dialogues" and "Healing Services," which are regular fixtures in our worship—two of the former and one of the latter every month. The dialogue is in response to the sermon, and sometimes it is great and sometimes it is lousy.

The Healing Service is during a regular service of worship, and people either seek healing or to be the channels for the healing of others. I think I have tried doing it just about every way that is possible. We have sunk into a bit of a habit now, and I have people raise their hands if they wish healing, or to be a channel; then we all hold hands and prayers are said, and people respond after each prayer with whatever I ask them to say. One British woman claims to have been healed of stomach cancer in our healing service. (I'm skeptical, but God does wonders I do not understand.)

Richard Wilcox, Spain

Breathing

Breathing and Meditation

I enclosed liturgies that we have used in Bali on Agape Celebration. But the beauty of them must be seen when they are being practiced in Bali, because the dances and the breathing meditation cannot be expressed in this letter.

Most of our liturgies on special occasions use dances and Balinese music, as well as the architecture of our churches. We will be very happy if you could come and visit us, so that we can show you when they are used in practice.

I. Wayan Mastra, Bali

O, Lord my God have mercy on me
O Lord Je-sus love me
O Lord Ho-ly Spi-rit
Come and a-bide in-to my heart and
    let your love a-bide in my heart
    that we will be ruled by love and
    walk in love; to vibrate love to all
    crea-tures around.

I. Wayan Mastra, Bali

Breathing

In a short period of consciously controlled deep breathing we realise the link between our inner being and earth's essential being, thus reversing the process of our alienation from earth's life typical of our age. Sitting in a yogic posture for this period of attuning to earth's life and to God's presence is also necessary. "Prana," meaning life or breath, with controlled inhaling and exhaling, is central to the ancient, diversely interpreted, yogic system of India.

OM

As the culmination of our rhythmic breathing, the mystic sound OM is chanted in a long drawn-out note, beginning with a deep-throated tone and gradually transposing to a nasal hum. This is another ancient Indian symbol with diverse meanings. Being properly comprised of three letters (A-U-M), it can mean the three worlds, the three primary scriptures, the beginning, middle, and end of life, and so on. We chant this ancient mystic sound in this last sense, attuning ourselves to the "eternal sound" of our cosmic life.

Silence

Silence follows the "mystic sound." Creative sharing of silence is essential to the Indian worship ethos and is frequently included in these inter-cultural services. Here we listen to the sounds of our natural environment so that they are not interruptions to our worship, but create inner resonance, increasing our sense of sharing in earth's life.

Drum and Tabla

The drum is another primal symbol of earth, the drum's beat echoing the throb of cosmic life. Beginning with a very slow beat, there is a gradually increased tempo. Then we are called in a tribal language to be more attentive to and attuned to earth's life and her sounds, and to be controlled by the Power, the Spirit from whom all our life derives.

United Theological College, Bangalore, India

Celebrations

(Please see "Service for Day of the Harvest," in Chapter 10.)

I may have already described Pentecostal parades, during which congregants march to the church with instruments and song, sometimes pausing to preach in the street along the way.

One month ago, the IPC (Pentecostal Church of Chile) had its annual conference, a week long event which attracted nearly two thousand participants during the first days, and over ten thousand members from around the country by the final day of festivities! It was truly amazing to see the dedication and spirit that brought so many people together, riding, cycling, or walking for a full day or more, traveling in from north and south in the hot summer sun to participate in Sunday's parade, a conference highlight. Group by group, they presented themselves in the temple, instruments and voices lifted in song, a banner held high, each with their own uniform and music. I vividly recall the arrival of one group of cyclists who processed into church with their bikes, worn, weary, but with the carriage of those who have come home after a challenging three-day trip up from the southern city of Los Angeles.

Next came the celebration of the harvest, during which church members who had traveled in from the countryside, as well as from the many "locales" within Curico, paraded down the church aisle, each with an offering of thanksgiving slung over his back or hefted in her arms: huge sacks of potatoes, beans, and corn, live poultry (chickens, ducks, geese, turkeys), freshly baked bread (still hot!), monstrous hubbard squash, full bags of popcorn, crates of fruit, . . . and I watched in awe as the pile of offerings from the harvest grew and grew in front of the pulpits, until the plastic sacks formed a small mountain on which the children climbed and perched. Here was an incredible testimony to the spirit of gratitude among those who know the hardship of failed crops, poor business, and bad weather, as well as a striking symbol of community: the gifts that thus piled up would be divided among the pastors to distribute to those in need during the coming winter months.

A festive spirit filled the hall, and when Pastor Muñoz, the president, lifted up a thick, picture-book sized tortilla (a special Chilean bread), pulled fresh from the oven, one could feel the joy and appreciation ripple through the congregation. He invited pregnant women to come forward and share pieces of the tortilla, while kids toppled over one another for handfuls of popcorn and officials passed palm-sized fresh bread through the crowd. And so we all partook of the first harvest, the gifts of thanksgiving, and the Spirit manifest in the generosity of the community!

Alison Buttrick, Chile

Prayer for Peace

(This prayer is said immediately after the Lord's Prayer is sung, for the lighting of the peace candle during worship.)

Our gracious God, we come into your presence asking you to bless us with your peace and quietness. Make our hearts peaceful before you, as we accept from you the peace which passes all understanding and that peace which helps us to live in harmony with ourselves and with all humanity.

We pray for peace within our church, our community, and our country. We acknowledge that your Holy Spirit is able to perform mighty miracles when all of your children are in one accord, and we remember that it is a good and a pleasant thing for brothers and sisters to dwell together in unity.

Take from us our sinful pride as we pray for the peace of the world, and prepare us for the coming of your Realm by guiding our feet in the way of peace.

We ask all this in the blessed name of the Prince of Peace.

Patrick Munroe, Guyana

Church Anniversaries

In the rural evangelical/protestant churches of Mexico, the anniversary of the church is a very important event. It is a time of gratitude for the life of the church, and also a replacement for the traditional celebration of the patron saint of the village (of Catholic tradition). The anniversary usually marks the dedication of the building. All the other churches of the area, regardless of denomination, are invited to this big "fiesta" of the church.

The church building is decorated with bold colors; ribbons of colored tissue paper with cut out designs called "Xochiamate" (the Nahuatl word for "flowers cut in paper") are strung up on the rafters and walls. Decorative crowns made of the root of the maguey plant grace the entrance and the wall behind the altar. Palm leaves or corn stalks decorated with bright flowers adorn the sides of the entrance. Pine needles are strewn on the dirt floor like a carpet. The pulpit boasts a new hand-embroidered cloth with a Bible text and decorative flowers and animals. This decoration is to affirm that nature is present and participates in the fiesta.

Representatives are asked to sit at the front of the church. All who have brought instruments (guitars, accordions, trumpets, saxophones, bass viols, etc.) sit at the front, as well, to help accompany the many songs. Each visiting group is invited without discrimination to participate with greetings, songs, a Bible text or words of encouragement. An important leader from another church is asked to preach the sermon. The service ends after several hours (four to six) with communion.

All the members of the celebrating church cooperate to prepare and provide a special meal. The best products of their area are offered. Children are normally served first because they hold an important position, the future of the community, as well as the fact that by now they are very hungry. Afterwards, adults are served; sometimes it takes several rounds because plates have to be washed in between turns. Any leftover food is shared with everyone, including guests, to be taken home and enjoyed. Some churches also make little souvenirs with a Bible text, the date and name of the church on it, for attendants to remember the occasion by.

Olivia Juarez and Sara Larson Wiegner, Mexico

New Life in Liturgy

Many communities and groups have experimented with ways of celebrating their faith in which all participate, ways that are no longer centered on the celebrant, the leader, the coordinator. Today, instead of a leader there is an animator, a liturgical animator. And reference is almost always made to a collective form: the liturgy committee or animation committee. . . .

*Simple gestures. Daily gestures. From within life itself, in all its simplicity,
some gestures stand out over others, due to the new senses they point to, due to
the new sensitivity they bring about. Gestures that arise from a new way of
looking at and thinking of reality: the Good News, Gospel of Life, of the
Kingdom of God.*

*The liturgy attempts to place daily life on the stage, to draw it on the canvas.
Human beings become both actors, as well as spectators.*

Ernesto Barros Cardoso, Brazil

Remembering in Hawaii

Opukahaia Sunday

*Henry Obookiah's story (his name is written in Hawaiian "Opukahaia") is
one of the most remarkable in Christian history. The young Hawaiian lad of
seventeen arrived in New England in 1809, having sailed from the islands on
the ship "Triumph" with a Yankee sea captain who took him to New Haven.
There Edwin Dwight, a Yale student, later a Congregational minister, discovered Obookiah sitting on the college steps, weeping because, as he said, "No one
gives me learning." "Do you wish to learn?" Dwight asked him, to which
Obookiah replied, "I do." Dwight and other Yale students began to tutor him,
and Yale President, Dr. Timothy Dwight, outstanding Congregational minister,
took him into his own home. Students from Andover Seminary and people of
the New England Churches befriended the orphan boy. Under their tutelage, in
a single decade, Obookiah went from illiteracy to eloquence and excellence in
speech and writing. More important, "by the prayers and instructions of pious
friends, he became a Christian." He was the first Hawaiian converted to
Christianity.*

*Determined to go back to Hawaii to carry the Gospel to his own people,
Obookiah was preparing himself at the Foreign Mission School in Cornwall,
Connecticut, when on February 17, 1818, at the age of twenty-six, he died, a
victim of typhus fever.*

*After Obookiah's death, his early friend, Edwin Dwight, published the young
islander's "Memoirs" in the form of a brief biography. The little book so aroused
the interest of New Englanders in Hawaii as a field for missionary work that the
American Board chartered a ship and engaged a pioneer company to go to the islands. Two ministers, two teachers, a doctor, a printer, a farmer, and their
wives, plus five children and four Hawaiian youths were on the "Thaddeus"
when it left Boston, October 23, 1819. Obookiah's was the face—and the
faith—that launched that ship!*

*We encourage our people to observe the third Sunday in February as a day of
commemoration in honor of Hawaii's first Christian.*

In Commemoration of Queen Kaahumanu

Queen Kaahumanu, wife of King Kamehameha I, became "kuhina nui"—"guardian of the realm"—at the time of the king's death in 1819. Born in an era when idol worship and the "kapu system" were common in Hawaii, Queen Kaahumanu lived to see the kapus overthrown and the idols cast down; indeed, through her, Hawaii's kapus were broken and women were freed from a bondage that had placed them in a lowly position for many years.

Although she had been born in what was called "the time of dark hearts," Queen Kaahumanu lived to become a devoted friend and supporter of the Christians, both men and women, who came to Hawaii to teach the Gospel of Christ. By her personal example and devotion to the new faith, she was able to lead many of her people to turn from the old gods to the God and Father of our Lord Jesus Christ.

Kaahumanu Church, in Wailuku, Maui, is named for this remarkable Hawaiian queen. When you visit Maui, be sure to see it, and remember the important place Kaahumanu has in Hawaii's history.

Prayer

(Using these or other words suitable to the occasion and the mood of the group.)

We give thanks unto thee, O Lord, for Queen Kaahumanu. We praise thee for her aloha for her people; for her glad acceptance of her new faith; for her eagerness, even in old age, to learn new truth and walk in a new way, the way of Jesus Christ. We thank thee for the good influence of the Word of God on her life, and the good influence of her life and character on the people of Hawaii. As thou hast also given each of us a mind and a heart to know and love thee, so teach us also thy Word and let thy Word abide in us, until it has wrought in us thy holy will. In the name of Christ our Lord. Amen.

Edith Wolfe, Hawaii, U.S.A.

Multifaceted Worship in India

I shall first very briefly list the main features of these liturgies as a whole, noting also what we see as distinctive features in comparison with other indigenous liturgies, Catholic and Protestant, that have emerged in recent years in South India. We may note such general common features as:

1. The adoption of a more characteristically Indian worship posture, such as leaving footwear outside the worship place, sitting on the floor, prostrating at appropriate points, sitting in circular form, com-

municating "Peace" through the namaste gesture, and the use of a few other hand-gestures, for example in relation to the Light.

2. The use of Indian musical instruments, such as tabla, mridanga, tribal drum, cymbals, flute, sitar, and the now Indianised portable, one-handed harmonium.

3. The emphasis on lyrical singing, and on chanting of prayers, praises, etc., with a large number of sung responses. The "bhajan"* is especially prominent at the beginning of worship, usually taking the form of "nama japa" (also known as "namakirtana" or "nama smarana") often with an attitude of "saranam" (refuge) in response to the recalling of the divine titles. The ancient mystic syllable OM (or Aum) is also chanted at the beginning of some services.

4. Considerable significance is also given to the lighting of the lamp, centrally placed, as an initial act in almost all our liturgies.

5. There are frequent pauses for silent meditation.

6. Flowers are offered (as part of the main offering) as well as used with flower-petals and leaves to depict symbolic imagery specially significant for the concerned service.

7. Offerings also include fruit, broken coconut and camphor; incense, too, may well be burnt as part of our offering.

8. All worshippers bring up their offerings to the central space, or they may be placed in brass pots on entering the worship-building.

9. In some services, substances such as sandalpaste, ash, etc., may be applied to the forehead.

10. There is a general emphasis in most of these indigenous liturgies on awakened consciousness, illumined God-consciousness, as the aim of worship, this being seen as the creative source of commitment to social action.

*Shared praise

Then there are some features more distinctive of the United Theological College liturgies.

1. They are more inclusively "inter-cultural" in character, a point that will be discussed more fully below. Here we might note the following four examples of this:

a. There is an attempt to incorporate, in some services at least, a tribal or more primal dimension, such as in the use of the tribal drum, folk-dance, an explicit orientation to earth-life as well as to God and to fellow humans, the offering of plantain and coconut, etc., the use of a central clay-pot, etc.

b. Readings from religious traditions—Hindu, Sikh, Muslim, Buddhist, etc.,—other than Christian scriptures, thus expressing our dialogical pluralistic religious context.

c. The use of a number of the regional languages of India, as well as English and Sanskrit.

d. Willingness to include the contemporary cultural fusion we find in Indian life and consciousness, as well as the classical, "popular" Indian, and tribal elements. A few songs, for example, are in contemporary "pop" style.

2. In our appropriation of "classical" elements of the cultural/religious traditions of Hinduism, we have turned primarily to the "Prabandhic" tradition, i.e., that bhakti orientation which gives primary emphasis to the glory of the divine character and to what is expected by way of devotional and ethical response. (Some Catholic "acculturation" has turned more to the "Agamic" ritual traditions.)

3. There is a prominently festive character of celebration, seen in the decorating of the worship-place, in the frequently poetic and dramatic form of language used, and in the thematic content of the liturgies.

4. Perhaps most significant is the strong and explicit emphasis on the social commitment involved in true worship as a necessary concomitant to worship, though this is always integrally linked with the characteristic Indian emphasis on the awakened consciousness.

United Theological College, Bangalore

The Role of Music in the Context of Worship Service in the East Indian Churches

Music plays a vitally important role in the worship services of the Indian Church for it binds people together in genuine feeling of kinship with one another in Christ. It is a kind of community building before the formal service begins—at least for twenty minutes. Worshippers enjoy singing together, as their individual voices are blended in one harmonious whole, praising God, who is the center of their life and their very being. The place of worship comes alive with music and sung lyrics, be it a dirt-walled shelter with thatched roof in the down-to-earth small hamlet, or a grandiose-looking cathedral built by Westerners in the big cities. It is especially so when the congregation sings the lyrics in the local languages, written by local poets, set to Indian classical music to the accompaniment of Indian musical instruments like sitar, veena, tabla (drums), cymbals, bells, and flute, etc.

The singing of the lyrics in the native languages is a holistic experience, for the singers can articulate their feelings through the words of the lyrics—and, depending on its theme, bring much solace to their souls. Almost everyone feels privileged to sing praises unto God and to worship God—the Creator and Protector. It is indeed an ecstatic experience to be part of that glorious singing—a sublime feeling of being one with God in the awesome presence of God in the true sense of "Bhakti"—which is paying worshipful homage to God in reverence as a loyal devotee.

Sheila S. Rubdi, U.S.A./India

10 Worship Services and Baptism, Wedding, and Funeral Resources

The liturgies we include in the next several pages range widely—from the outline of an ordinary Sunday service in Ghana (note the drumming and dancing as an offertory) to unique worship such as "The Day of the Pastor" from Chile; from simple family vespers in Hawaii to the experimental liturgy of a medical conference in Brazil.

The second section of this chapter includes the resources and reflections our correspondents sent us on weddings, funerals and baptismal customs.

Water into Wine, He Qi, China

Ghana

Evangelical Presbyterian Church Order of Worship

Procession (church choir, clergy)
Introit (church choir)
Call to worship (leader)
Opening hymn
Greetings/exhortations
Hymn
Prayers:
   Thanksgiving
   Confession
   Grace
   Supplications and petition

Creed
God's Will (the ten commandments/beatitudes)
Song (church choir)
First and second readings from Scripture
Hymn
Sermon text
Sermon
Offertory (drumming and dancing)
Dedication of offertory
Closing prayer/benediction
Closing hymn

Mabel Morny, Ghana

Bali

Artists' Experience in Bali, Dhyana Pura, Kuta Beach, Bali

February 12–22, 1989, Liturgy of Agape Feast

Call to worship:

Leader: Let us worship God.

Congregation: Jesus said, "I am the light of the world; he who follows me will not walk in darkness, but will have the light of life." (Jn 8:12)

Dance of praise: "The coming of the light" (Jn 1:1–14)
Song of praise
Silent meditation:

Leader: Let us have a moment of silent meditation, to prepare our hearts to hear the Word of God.

Congregation: (Breathing with the spirit of Jesus loves me.)

Scripture lesson:

Leader: "For God so loved the world that he gave his only son, that whoever believes in him should not perish but have eternal life." (Jn 3:16)

Women: "Christ Jesus, who though he was in the form of God, did not count equality with God a thing to be grasped, but emptied himself, taking the form of a servant, being born in the likeness of men. And being found in human form, he humbled himself and became obedient unto death, even death on a cross." (Phil 2:5–8)

Men: "Therefore be imitators of God, as beloved children. And walk in love, as Christ loved us and gave himself up for us, a fragrant offering and sacrifice to God." (Eph 5:1, 2)

Song of praise
Sermon in dance: "New Born Dance" (2 Cor 5:17)
Prayer of dedication:

Leader: Let us turn to God in prayer

Congregation: O Lord of light, in this hour of worship, in this beautiful place of Dhyana Pura, make pure our hearts, and we shall see thee, reveal thyself to us, and we shall love thee. Strengthen our wills, and we shall choose the good from the evil, and day by day manifest in the world the glory and power of thy blessed Gospel, which thou has made known to us through thy Son Jesus Christ, who taught us to pray: (Lord's Prayer)

Celebration of Agape Feast
Dance of praise: (1 Tm 6:12; 2 Tm 4:7)
Song of praise
Consecration of life:

Leader: Our Lord Jesus Christ said, "You are the light of the world. A city set on a hill can not be hid. Let your light so shine before men, that they may see your good works and give glory to your Father who is in heaven." (Mt 5:14, 16)

Congregation: "Here I am, Lord, send me." (Is 6:8)

Leader: "Go therefore and make disciples of all nations, baptizing them in the name of the Father, and of the Son and of the Holy Spirit, teaching them to observe all that I have commanded you, and lo, I am with you always, to the close of the age." (Mt 28:19, 20)

Song of praise
Benediction:

Leader: "Now may the grace of our Lord Jesus Christ, the love of God and the fellowship of the Holy Spirit be with you all." (2 Cor 13:13)

Congregation: Amen.

I. Wayan Mastra, Bali

Protestant Christian Church in Bali

Hawaii

Ohana: Devotions for the Family, Small Groups or Individuals

(It has long been a custom among Hawaiian Christians for the family—often including neighbors, guests, and friends—to join in devotions at the beginning or the close of day. Ohana may be held in a church or chapel, around the family table, in the living room, on the lanai, at the bedside of a shut-in, or outdoors under the Hawaiian moon and stars. Sometimes music is furnished by a piano, organ, guitar, or ukulele; more often, the family hymns are sung without any accompaniment except the trade winds blowing or the distant sound of the sea.)

Suggested Order I

- The family will sing a hymn. Each member of the family may take a turn choosing the hymn to be sung. Or the family may sit in silence until someone begins to sing, and then the others may join in. Or the members of the family may choose a special "family hymn" as a kind of "call to worship." When that hymn is heard, each member of the family begins to sing, wherever he may be in the house, and, still singing, joins the family as they assemble.
- The head of the house will read Scripture passage and perhaps give some explanation or ask some questions.
- Family conversation about the day's activities. This might include each telling of some special joy or achievement of the day. There may be shared some news of an absent friend or member of the family, a letter or picture.
- Memory verse by each in English or Hawaiian, or a Psalm, spoken together.
- Prayer by head of the house or by one designated. Sentence prayers if desired.
- Closing hymn.
- Benediction or the Lord's Prayer by all.

Suggested Order II (at the close of the day)

· A favorite hymn
· A litany for the family (adapt to fit members)

Father: Jesus said, Where two or three are gathered together in my name,

All: There am I in the midst of them.

Mother: O thou, who didst call Mary, Mother,

All: Come now into our midst, we pray.

Son: O thou, who were a boy like other boys, who grew in wisdom and stature, and in favor with God and man;

All: Come now into our midst, we pray.

Daughter: O thou, who had sisters and brothers and lived under a common roof and shared a common life with them,

All: Come now into our midst, we pray.

Mother: O thou, who were the son of a poor family, with love as its wealth and faith as its furnishings,

All: We ask thy blessing upon our family, here and everywhere.

Grandmother (or other person present): We give thee thanks, Lord Jesus, for all under our roof this night; for our family and our friends, wherever they may be. We remember especially now those whose names we say in our hearts before thee: (Here may be made mention of any special need or concern for members of the family at home or away.) For the aloha which binds us together with thee and with one another, we praise thy name. On all families, known to us or unknown, we ask thy fatherly blessing, now and forever. Amen.

Edith Wolfe, Hawaii, U.S.A.

Conference of European Churches

Chile

Day of the Pastor (from the Pentecostal Church of Chile)

(*Contributor's Note*: "I was truly struck by the spirit of giving and gratitude present in the sanctuary during this celebration. Members of the congregation filed up front to pile package upon package on the floor in front of the pulpit, all gifts purchased especially for the pastor—it was like a big birthday party!")

Introduction

Today we celebrate the day of our pastor. We understand that s/he has the great responsibility of leading us, God's flock, along the path revealed to us by the Holy Scriptures. It is fitting that we remember that Jesus, our Lord and God, is the Pastor of all Pastors to whom we give thanks and that we pray that all pastors be for us disciples of Christ, guiding Christ's flock.

Suggested Readings
Jn 10:11, 16
1 Thes 5:12
1 Cor 16:18
Phil 2:29
1 Tm 5:17
Heb 13:7

At this point in the service, various members of the congregation might be invited to express their gratitude to God for having given them a pastor and guide.

Prayer

After these members have taken part, the following prayer is offered:

¡Oh Dios! Nuestro buen Padre, te pedimos que bendigas a nuestro pastor, como asi mismo a su familia, y a nosotros que somos miembros de esta Iglesia, ayudanos para serte fieles y agradecidos por tu amor para tus hijos aqui en la tierra por el Nombre Maravilloso de Jesucristo Nuestro Señor te lo regamos.

(English translation)

O God! Our good parent, we pray that you bless our pastor, along with her/his
family and all of us who are members of this church. Help us to be faithful and
to be thankful for the love that you have for all of your children here on earth.
In the marvelous name of our Lord Jesus Christ we pray.
Members may now come forward to present gifts to the pastor, after which an appropriate hymn is sung.
The pastor gives the blessing to conclude this service.

Alison Buttrick, Chile

Day of the Harvest

(from the Pentecostal Church of Chile)

(*Contributor's note:* Although the introduction suggests decorating a special box to receive the
thanksgiving offerings, there is no way that a box could have contained the quantity of food
that church members brought forward when we celebrated this holiday on May 1! The sacks
of produce created a virtual mountain in front of the pews—an awe-inspiring sight!

The products of this celebration, all of that produce, gets divided up among the pastors to give
out as needed during the difficult winter months. So, although many U.S. churches in towns
and cities would not have fresh produce to offer during such a festival, they could certainly
maintain the spirit of the festival by taking a collection of gifts for the needy. A seamstress
might donate clothes; a baker, fresh bread; or a grocer, nonperishable foods, for example. The
idea is to capture the spirit of gratitude and joy that we give to God for each year, during each
harvest.)

Introduction

This spiritual fiesta is celebrated at the conclusion of the harvest
(May 1), an opportune time for members of the congregation to present fruits of the harvest in the church as offerings of Thanksgiving
to God. This service might be focused around a collection box especially prepared beforehand to receive gifts of the faithful on the Day
of the Harvest.

Suggested Readings

Praises to the Creator: Ps 8:1–4; Ps 45:1–6.
Praises to the Lamb: Rv 1:5, 6; Rv 19: 1.
Praises through song: Ps 42:10–12; Ps 98:1–9.
Praises with joy: Ps 47:1–7; Ps 65:1–4; Ps 95:1–7.
Praises that witness to the world: 2 Sm 22:47–51; Ps 96:1–16.
Praises throughout the nations: Psalm 66: 1-4; Psalm 67: 3-7.

Music

The Pentecostal hymns sung during this celebration take their imagery from Gal. 6:7, "You reap what you sow." I include here a poetic translation of one such hymn, to provide a flavor! (This might be shared as a poem in an English-speaking congregation.)

If you sow the land with flowers
Along the paths of flowers you'll go;
If from your hand tumble thistles
You will reap that which you sow.
  You will reap that which you sow,
  You will reap that which you sow,
  Surely, when harvest time comes
  A harvest of thistles you'll show.
If blessings you give in your travels
You'll be blessed wherever you go;
But if your words are deceitful,
You will reap that which you sow.
  You will reap that which you sow,
  You will reap that which you sow,
  Surely, when harvest time comes
  A deceitful harvest you'll show.
If your seeds are those of mercy,
You'll be pardoned wherever you go;
If to others you don't give forgiveness,
You will reap that which you sow.
  You will reap that which you sow,
  You will reap that which you sow,
  Surely, when harvest time comes
  A bitter harvest you'll show.

If in faith you scatter God's message,
The memory of the faithful to grow;
Jesus will note your fine farming and
With joy you will reap what you sow.
  You will reap that which you sow,
  You will reap that which you sow,
  Surely, when harvest time comes
  A harvest of gladness you'll show.
If your lips proclaim, "Christ is
  Risen!"
You, too, will be praised when you go;
If you sow your life in the Spirit,
  Life eternal with God you will
  know.
  Life eternal with God you will
  know,
  Life eternal with God you will
  know;
  For surely when harvest time comes
  Salvation's the harvest you'll show.

  Alison Buttrick, Chile

India

Sharing Earth's Life

(An intercultural celebration that may be held outside under trees. In a central place a large decorated clay pot is set, surrounded on the ground by a tree-pattern of leaves and petals. The tree contains a cross-shape, with red blossoms like drops of blood, signifying the wounding earth endures and our hope of wholeness. Musical instruments play. As far as possible, all sit on the ground.)

I. *Realizing Our Being as Earth-Sharing*

Leader: Our breath is our life, our prana.

By our inbreathing we share earth's life.

We live by earth's life.

As we together breathe in this life, deeply and slowly, with our outbreathing we join in a drawn-out chanting of the ancient sound that echoes our cosmic life.

All: (Following the leader, after a period of slow, deep breathing): OM, OM, OM.*

(Silence as we meditate on the source, sustaining power and end of all life, and listen to the sounds of earth's creatures.

The drum is a primal symbol of the earth. As earth's heart beats, first softly, then more loudly and insistently, in a tribal language we are called to listen to earth's sounds and to live in tune with her ways, and then to seek to know earth's eternal Power, her Creator. A tabla joins the drum-beat and the lamp is lit.)

Lighting the Lamp

(As the lamp is lit we begin a Kannada bhajan or some similar bhajan. A bhajan is shared praise, especially prominent at the beginning of worship.)

Saranam, Saranam (2)
Divya-jyotiye, Saranam,
Jiva-kantiye, Saranam,
Tejo-rupave, Saranam. Saranam, Saranam, Saranam.
Dari-dipave, Saranam,
Priti-sarave, Saranam.
Atma-nivasaye, Saranam. Saranam, Saranam, Saranam.

(Meaning: "We take refuge in the Divine Light," and so on.)

*OM: As the culmination of our rhythmic breathing, the mystic sound OM is chanted in a long drawn-out note, beginning with a deep-throated tone and gradually transposing to a nasal hum. See definition of OM, chapter 9, page 174.

II. Sharing God's Joy in Creation

A Ballad of Creation

(Sung with guitar, etc.)

1. Before God shaped the earth and sky,
Earth had no form, was empty.
Upon the deep, thick darkness lay,
Earth had no life, no plenty.
God's Spirit brooded like a dove.
God's Spirit hovered, full of love;
Then light was born, and land, and trees,
With insects, birds, beasts, fish in seas;
All creatures living by God's word.
He saw that all was good, so good,
For all that lives is God's.
2. God's action then was very bold,
From dust he shaped the human—
Those earthlings frail, and for their good,
As partners, man and woman,
With love shaped them his work to share,
Breathed spirit in the earthling pair;
And so gave power to stand on earth,
Like God to name, to see the worth,
To care for all creation.
That all may say: How great our God,
How good this earth he's given.

(Before the next stanza, the singer may say the following, or may invite all to join in this dance of creative joy.)

Singer: A story is nothing unless we become part of it.

A song is lost unless the listener dances to its tune.

As we now sing of God's dance of bliss, some of us will dance a simple folk-dance. Others may join in if they wish but we can all clap to the rhythm of the dance.

3. Then God rejoiced with all the earth,
God's dance more worlds created;
God's bliss brought countless stars to birth,
God's fullness undepleted.
Now join the cosmic dance of bliss,
Step gladly for the rhythm's his.
All earthlings in one life must share,
All bound as one in mutual care;
Drawn by the drum-beat of God's love,
We in God's dance so freely move. For all that lives is God's.

Leader: (vigorously) The earth is God's;

Congregation: And all its fullness too is God's.

III. Sharing Earth's Pain

Voices from the Press

Leader: Now let us listen to the state of our environment today.

(Brief cuttings from recent newspapers describing environmental crises)

(Silence, then a flute plays plaintively)

Earth's voice (read by a woman): I am Earth, mother Earth, and my body bleeds
   in pain.

The aggressive ways of humans disrupt my rhythms,

destroy more and more of my life.

Reckless technology poisons my waters, my soil, my air,

and kills the children of my womb.

Industrial man seeks only to 'master' me, and 'exploit' me,

as though I had no value in my own right.

For greedy gain my motherly body is wounded,

stripped, raped,

the body without which no earthling can live,

the body that gives habitat

to countless vulnerable creatures.

A Tribal's Voice: I am one of Earth's children most close to her.

Our tribal body bleeds too with earth's destruction,

When forests are hacked down for industrial profit;

When huge projects are built,

the result for us is life-dislocation,

the death of our kinship with nature.

The trees, our life-support, are robbed.

The soil of the hills is then washed away,

and the children of the earth are the first to suffer.

Woman's Voice: How will those who have lost touch with earth's life

share earth's plenty with their fellow-humans?

Will not those who rape the earth rape her children too?

Confession

Leader: Having listened to these diverse voices in judgment of human destructiveness, let us confess our part in this threat to earth's future.

All: Forgive us, holy Father, good Mother, our one great God, that we have failed to live as your true children.

Men: We have despoiled the life of nature with our violence and wasteful ways; Nature, by whose sustaining bounty we live.

Women: We have not risen up, like our Chipko sisters, to protect nature from destructive hands, to help lift earth's burden of suffering.

Men: We have denuded the earth of her covering of trees, destroyed her precious soil and thousands of her creatures, disrupted the delicate balance of her life.

Women: We have passively watched the poisoning of earth and her children, the polluting of her waters and her air. We have closed our eyes to the wounds inflicted on our mother, thinking we have enough pain of our own.

Men: We have plundered earth's resources, without the restraint we need for our own freedom.

All: Forgive us, holy Mother, good Father, our one great God,
that we have not lived in tune with you and with your world;
we have failed to be your earth-carers;
we need your healing, your wholeness, your peace.

(The following may precede the declaration of forgiveness.)

Ballad of Creation *(continuation of previous verses)*

Our great Creator, we recall,
On earth a tree once planted;
A tree of life, whose leaves would heal
The ills of all, was granted.
A tree whose arms out-stretched above,
Stood as a sign of painful Love.
Though humans, plundering its fruit,
Fell from their innocent estate,
Hope now lies in the cross-shaped tree,
And blood-red blossoms point the way
To life again, to glory. To life again, to glory.

Leader: God has shown us that in Christ he shares even our estranged life, and bears the pain. His healing hand, his Cross, shall be our hope. He speaks to us: your faith makes you whole. Amen.

IV. Witness to Wholeness
Witness of scriptures:
(Readings from Veda Gathas, Qu'ran, Granth Sahib):
Biblical Witness:
Reflection (a meditative talk)
Affirmation of Faith

(There is a period of silent reflection between each section.)

Leader: We have faith

Congregation: in One God, one Source of all life,
One Ground of the whole earth, with all her creatures.

Leader: And thus we have faith

Congregation: in the goodness of earth's life,
in the innate worth of all her dependents,
in human partnership in the life of nature.

Leader: And we have faith

Congregation: that in Christ we have been shown the special role of the human
race to bear God's likeness, in working and caring for the earth, in seeking to
understand her mysteries and powers, in gently working with these powers
for the well-being of all children of the earth.

Leader: And we have faith

Congregation: that God's Spirit will lead us to sensitive closeness with earth's life,
to that meek, unselfish and compassionate life-style by which the earth is inherited in peace, by which her life is transformed for all creatures to share
justly in her bounty.

So be it, Amen.

*(A Lyric is sung in one of our languages. This can be a paraphrase of the above
Affirmation and in its place.)*

V. Commitment to Wholeness

Praying for Wholeness

(Chanted in four representative languages of India)

We pray for a new vision of our life with nature; that the Church in India may awaken to its task of earth-caring; that we may all work unsparingly for restrained use and just sharing of earth's bounty.

We pray for all agencies for environmental protection; for those struggling for a more appropriate rural technology; for the Chipko movement in the Himalayas; for the Appiko movement in the Western Ghats; for environmental groups in Bangalore.

We pray for our country and its leaders, especially for Rajiv Gandhi and his Government; that new policies may soon make environmental impact; that there may be wise control of industrialists and contractors, and commitment to local development, bringing wholeness to our people's life.

We pray for the leaders of the nations, that industrialised nations may cease their violent, selfishly unjust, wasteful exploitation of earth's resources. We especially pray for reduction of blasphemous nuclear arms that threaten to destroy all life.

(Response—sung after each prayer:)

God, our Creator, hear our heartfelt prayer.

Self-Offering for Wholeness

(In the offerings brought up there are: flowers, fruits and plants, as signs of the bounty and beauty of earth; gifts of money, as signs of human industry and interhuman relations; fire [burning camphor] as sign of energy, human and cosmic.)

Commission

Leader: Having committed ourselves to solidarity with earth's life, as a sign of this earth-sharing life, members from among us will now receive plants and saplings to be planted in our environs, and cared for by us.

(Representative members come forward and receive the above.)

Leader: Go to a life of sharing with earth's life, to a life of caring for each other as for all creation, for the God of earth's wholeness goes with you. Amen.

United Theological College, Bangalore, India

Brazil

(Worship Services of the Christian Medical Commission (CMC) at its
Fourth Commission Meeting in Salvador, Bahia, Brazil, May 22–26, 1989)

Second Worship (of Five)—Liberated Bodies

The Idea

Free to grow and multiply, to dominate nature and obtain from it what is
needed for life. This is how, in Genesis 1, the Old Testament addresses man
and woman and explains the relation they could have in God's purpose.

However, this is not how life takes place every day. There are obstacles and
bonds, often invisible, that keep life from developing, from expressing itself,
from fulfilling its potential. Our bodies are oppressed in many ways.

This worship is to live these bonds, this imprisonment, liturgically. The tangled
string signifies the forces that stifle life. Thus the worship begins with low
lights, murmured songs, the knots of the string like those forces that entangle
the participants.

The second part is the experience of collective seeking to overcome these forces.
There is more light, more colour, songs of hope. Bodies meet, affirm each
other, support each other, find joy together. An affirmation of life, against all
that oppresses it.

The Space

The worship place is prepared beforehand. Place a circle of chairs around the
table spread with the cloths for the first and second day. Place the candles and
the string on the table, unwinding the string from the table and winding it
around the chairs. Intertwine various photos or objects in the string between the
table and the chairs. Place a strip of coloured cloth on each chair.

Material:
- Red cloth for the table
- Cloth from previous day
- String
- Photographs of everyday situations (families, work, school,
  play, etc.) or objects that signify these situations, such as
  tools, office supplies, toys, books, etc.
- Two candles
- 10 x 100 cm strips of coloured cloth or paper—one for each
  participant

Order of Worship:

- Begin the worship with the lights dimmed.
- Sing "Come, Holy Spirit" while lighting the candles.
- Read the Bible texts, with various participants reading from various selections.
- Talk about how human life is abused and violated, about the prisons, bonds and fetters that prevent people from fulfilling the purpose of God to make human life free and full.
- Ask the participants to disentangle the photographs or objects from the string and pass them around, while visualizing people and situations that are unable to experience even the simplest activities and possibilities of life freely and fully.
- Sing "Kyrie" while the participants are still holding the photographs and objects.
- Ask the participants to return the photos and objects to their original places—entwined in the string—emphasizing that even though you are all aware of them, the bonds are not broken, especially those that are invisible.
- Read "The Body,"* a prayer that reminds us of our resistance to domination and affirm God's purpose for our bodies and lives. At this point, the lights should be turned up.
- Sing a song.
- Invite each participant to pick up a strip of paper or cloth and mention words that signify attitudes or values that can overcome the bonds of oppression. The coloured strips of cloth or paper symbolize the ties of solidarity we need to help break these bonds. Tie or fasten them together into one long strip.
- Sing while the group embraces with the coloured strip wrapped around them.

*"The Body," by Simei Monteiro, is found in Part V, "Resources to Quicken the Heart," p. 206.

Third Worship—Fertile Land

The Idea

And space to live?
It is impossible to speak about human life, about caring for the body, without remembering that space is one of the basic needs of life.
Although this worship is about land, it is not restricted to liturgically exploring the relationship between people and land. Rather, beginning from this, it reflects on that which is the source of life—people's vital space for work, play and living. It celebrates our joy and concern with space to live in.

Many people today do not live in or have a direct relation with land, in the countryside or rural areas. They survive among buildings—concrete, asphalt and glass. However, everything that touches the land—its distribution, concentration, monopoly, etc.— affects the lives of individuals and the community (lifestyle, migrations, urban tensions, hunger, violence).

How can we care for the land?

Where can we find the promised land?

The Space

Identify an area out of doors, surrounded by plants, flowers or trees. Put the cloth for the day on the ground, and place the bowl of dirt on it. Later, place a tray of dark flowers or plants, wrapped with a large chain, on the cloth.

Material:
- A brown cloth
- A bowl of dirt
- A tray of leaves/dry or dead flowers mixed with garbage
- A chain

Order of worship:
- Gather the participants at the place of worship.
- Read Bible texts.
- Sing the chorus of "How Great Thou Art" while carrying in the tray of dry flowers and leaves, mixed with garbage and wrapped with the chain, to the center of the circle. Place it on the cloth.
- Talk about how we can please and praise God throughout creation at the same time that we can see the disastrous results of human action on creation. The devastation and abuse of the sources of life are more evident every day (as represented by the things in the tray). The earth is enslaved (represented by the chain) by greed and by the desire for profit, power and control in the hands of a few. Land is still a symbol of struggle and violence, as people are willing to die and kill for it (represented by the bowl of dirt).
- Pass the chain around, involving all participants in an act of confession and intercession. At the same time, remember the people and cultures that have been massacred in acts motivated by the desire to dominate and possess land.
- Allow a few minutes of silence.
- Mention how, in spite of everything, earth has still nourished—a free source of energy and life, and a dream—the production of culture and art. That is how it has been possible to resist in the midst of captivity.
- Sing a song.

Ernesto Barros Cardoso, Brazil

Baptism, Wedding, and Funeral Resources

Baptisms

At the Cidade Congregational Church of Maputo, Mozambique, baptism is followed by giving a lighted candle to the person baptized, one more symbol of their acceptance of Jesus Christ as the light for their lives. If several are baptized together, those baptized usually also prepare and sing a special song related to their new commitment to the faith. It is common for many to be baptized the same day and the parents of those too small to sing for themselves also to participate in the singing.

Ruth Brandon Minter, Mozambique

Resources for Infant Baptism

Proclamation of the Mystery

Before the child is baptized the minister or priest may hold the child up for all to see, saying: "The miracle of life renewed for us all." The congregation responds, "All life is holy, all life is one."

Prayers for the Child

Leader: . . . is an important part of this interwoven universe.

All: Help us to care for . . . and for all life.

Leader: No person is an island, we all belong to God's family.

All: Help us to respect all people.

Leader: We are amazed at the possibilities of . . . 's life.

All: Help us to enable people to achieve their potential.

Leader: We surround . . . with our love.

All: Help us to show understanding and acceptance to all.

The Peace

Leader: God's justice is our peace.

All: The peace of God be with us all.

Bill Wallace, Aotearoa/New Zealand

(For additional material on baptism, see "Sonia's Baptism" in Chapter 11, pp. 110–11.)

A Popoloca Wedding

Conference of European Churches

The Popoloca people are a small indigenous group who live in the Tehuacan area of Puebla, Mexico.

The church is decorated with bright colors (not white). The bride wears a red dress and a silk rebozo (shawl) over her head. The groom wears the traditional white homespun shirt and pants with huaraches (sandals) and a straw hat.

The groom and his family and guests walk to the bride's home to walk her to the church. The procession is led by children with flowers in hand and accompanied with songs and music (guitars and accordions). The flowers are placed at the entrance of the church.

Before entering, the bride and groom are given advice by their parents and grandparents. Then the music announces the entrance of the couple, and the congregation stands as the couple takes their place before the altar.

In a neighboring village, the custom is for the bride to prepare hand-embroidered clothing for members of the groom's family. This is her way of saying she is willing to share what she has with them.

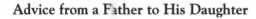

Advice from a Father to His Daughter

(The following are excerpts from Nahuatl codexes.)

Here you are, my daughter, my necklace of fine gems, my plumage, my human likeness, the one born from me. You are my blood, my color, my image is in you.

Now receive, listen: you live, were born, our Lord sent you to this earth, the Owner of things near and beside, the maker of people, the inventor of humans.

Now that you see life for yourself, be aware. Here it is like this: there is no happiness, no joy. There is anguish, worry, tiredness.

The old ones say: "So that we won't always be groaning, so that we won't be full of sadness, Our Lord gave humans laughter, sleep, food, our strength and robustness and finally the sexual act, through which we sow more people."

But now, my daughter, listen well, and observe carefully. Here is your mother, your lady, from her womb and her breast you broke off of, you budded. As if you were a small plant, that is how you sprouted. Just like the leaf, you grew and flowered. As if you were asleep and you woke up.

Listen: I have taught you that you are noble. You are precious, even though you are only a young woman. You are a fine gem, you are turquoise. You were forged, hewn, you have blood, color, you are bud and thorn, hair, a piece; you are of noble lineage.

Do not dishonor yourself, or our leaders and princes and governors, those that went before us. While you live on this earth, beside your people, always be truly woman.

Here is your vocation, what you will have to do: during the night and during the day, consecrate yourself to the things of God, think much about the Night and Wind. Make supplication, invoke, call, plead much when you lie down. That way your dreams will be pleasant. May you be happy and may our Lord bless you.

Olivia Juarez and Sara Larson Wiegner, Mexico

Continuing Christian/Buddhist Dialogue Discusses Rituals

(from *Occasional Bulletin*, September 1992)

Professor Chang, a member of the Academy's Ethnic Research Department pointed out that today's extravagant wedding and, especially, funeral rituals were a marked contrast to the traditional Taiwanese custom and culture. He also noted a book published by the government, Model Rituals for Country People, a sort of guidebook, misguides people by adding many confusing and unnecessary details. He urged people not to resort to unneeded or needlessly extravagant rituals.

In the last decade, Taiwanese weddings often include ten-course feasts, four or five changes of bridal gowns, and even dancing girls. Funerals have also taken on a more extravagant air. Family members of the deceased hire professional mourners and even strip-tease dancers to "please the departed."

Chin Iau, the Buddhist priest, emphasized to the listeners that having a faithful mind and serious approach to the event was more important than adhering strictly to proscribed rituals, especially since many of the ceremonies have become very superficial.

Rev. Wang reminded the audience that, just as Taiwan's society is changing, so the people's lifestyle also changes. If people do not adjust their wasteful excesses, Wang specifically mentioned the practice of burning "spirit money" and using oversized caskets for burials, Taiwan's environment will suffer.

All three speakers agreed that wedding and funeral rituals need to be updated to make them more suitable to contemporary society.

Sent by Virginia Thelin, Taiwan

Funeral Resources

(These attempt to relate to the wide variety of beliefs held by people in New Zealand about God)

Prayer of Approach

Let us be silent and reflect on our shock, pain and loss at the death of . . .
In the mystery of love,
Life springs out of death.
Let us remember that tears are for the washing away of grief, hope is for the
    building of dreams, and love is the tender life-force which conquers
    death.
In the mystery of love,
Life springs out of death.
There are many things in life which we cannot understand
many things we must accept. May the power of love enable us not to suc-
    cumb to bitterness or pointless questioning, but rather grow to live life
    with more tenderness, courage and purpose than ever before. May this be
    for us all,
for in the mystery of love,
Life springs out of death.

Prayer of Reflection, Thanksgiving and Commitment

Let us reflect on the pilgrimage of life; on how we all come from the earth
and all return to its womb.
    In death as in life,
    We are all one family.
Let us acknowledge that we share this experience with all living creatures
through the unity of nature.
    In death as in life,
    We are all one family.
Let us give thanks for the life of . . . , and for all the memories that his/her
death brings to mind.
    In death as in life,
    We are all one family.
In the strength of (God's) love, let us determine to keep alive in us those
qualities which we admired in . . . , for
    In death as in life,
    We are all one family.

Through the Rivers of Our Tears

(hymn for a child's funeral)

1. Through the rivers of our tears,
Through our anger's bitter pain,
Through depression, shock and
  fear
God we cry, we cry to you.

2. Why should life so near to birth
End in such untimely death?
Why this child of all on earth?
God we cry, we cry to you.

3. Help us bid this child farewell,
Loose our hold upon his (her) life
But retain in memory's well
Smiles and tears and tender touch.

4. If we mourn with all our heart
As we journey through our grief,
Tears will work their healing art
And release new inner strength.

5. God you show us in Christ's
  Cross
You are sharing all our pain,
Help us find, beyond our loss,
Love that celebrates again.

Bill Wallace, Aotearoa/New
Zealand

Leave Taking

(All standing)

We take our leave of our sister/brother, . . .
*We acknowledge the great gap which his/her death leaves in the lives of those
  who mourn.*
*We commit ourselves to helping each other work through the process of grieving,
  to new life beyond our shock, anger, guilt and tears.*
*May healing flow from sorrow, hope emerge from darkness, and memories be-
  come even more precious, so that past and present be as one in the mystery of
  (God's) love.*

The Committal

*In the presence of the living and the dead, we commit the body of our
sister/brother to be reunited with the ground/elements, earth to earth/ashes to
ashes, dust to dust, confident of the final victory of (God's) love over suffering,
injustice, ugliness and death.*

Benediction

*May the love which is stronger than death and which binds us together in the
unity of life, energize our spirits with divine stillness, now and forever. Amen.*

Bill Wallace, Aotearoa/New Zealand

Mozambique Flower Service

*A service that was new to us when we came to Mozambique is a "Flower
Service." This is a memorial service that is followed by putting flowers on a
grave. Flower services are almost always held eight days after a death (the funeral having been conducted twenty-four hours after the death). It is also quite
common to have flower services forty days, six months, and one year after a
death. They also may be held on any anniversary of a death. This custom may
have come into our church from a tradition in the Catholic Church. When he
saw what an important service this was in the life of our church, here in
Mozambique, Rev. Lawrence Gilley and several Bible School students worked
long and hard to develop a liturgy for this memorial service.*

*I include here an English translation of the words chosen to express the sig-
nificance of the flowers used in the memorial service.*

The Words about the Flowers

Jesus reminds us that flowers are more beautiful than Solomon in all his glory. The creator of flowers is also our creator and redeemer. All that is beautiful comes from God the creator. Jesus said, "Do not worry about your life. Your heavenly Father knows all the things that you need. But strive first for the kingdom of God and his righteousness and all these things will be given to you as well." (Mt 6:25, 32, 33)

As flowers last only a short time and then wither; we are born, we grow and serve the Lord. After a short time, we pass from the earth. The prophet Isaiah says: "All people are like grass, their constancy is like the flower of the field. The grass withers, the flower fades, but the word of our God will stand forever." (Is 40:6–8) Therefore, let us seek the word of God and his eternal kingdom while we still live. "Because whether we live or whether we die we belong to Christ, the Lord of the dead and the living." (Rom 14:8–9)

The flowers are brought to the early morning service in the big enameled basins and placed in front of the communion table. After a biography of the deceased, the sermon and prayers, the deacons bring the flowers to the pastor or leader of the service who takes a handful, holds them up for the congregation to see, and reads or recites the above words of explanation. Then follows a prayer:

Lord God, life, death, and eternal life are in your hands. Lord, our Preserver, we thank you that you have given us the flowers which beautify the world as a parable of our life. Help us to beautify the world while we live, and at the time of our death to look to you of the encircling arms. Through Jesus Christ, who taught us when we pray to say, "Our Father in heaven. . . ."

A blessing and dismissal follow, after which the deacons carry the flowers at the head of a procession to the grave. Hymns and choruses are sung. There are a few additional words about the flowers before they are passed around the congregation. People then come and place their few flowers on the grave. There is a concluding prayer and benediction.

There is usually a meal at the house following the service. It is expected that all go to the house and there is a good deal of pressure to participate in the meal. The memorial service starts at 6:00 a.m., and it may be 9:00 or 10:30 before the meal has been served. Large numbers of people will have been involved for twenty-four hours preparing food, and many people will remain at the home for the better part of the day. Memorial services are a major part of our religious life. They take precedence over almost all other activities. Our Regional Council voted an instruction to the churches a couple of years ago that memorial services must not be held on Sunday morning or be allowed to interfere with Sunday morning worship. I would guess that most congregations average almost one memorial service a week.

Carol and Lawrence Gilley, Mozambique

I I *Youth Offerings*

Rini Templeton, U.S.A./Mexico

With delight we received worship offerings from young people—often in their own handwriting. We have added these to some resources about youth and children. Among the resources included in this section are prayers from high school students in Zimbabwe, reflections of Japanese university students and liturgical materials prepared by the World Student Christian Federation in Geneva. Resources by youth and about youth issues appear elsewhere in the book, particularly in the section on affirmations of faith which concludes this chapter.

Praise Given by Students

February 9, 1992, World Day of Prayer for Students; Journée Mondiale de Prière pour les étudiants; Dia Mundial de Oracion par los Estudiantes

From down deep, O Lord, we call to you. From down deep in our lives, where our thoughts become contradictory and we are naked, stripped from the masks of hypocrisy. It is there that we praise you.
We praise you from the student desks, in the classrooms, in daily life, in sports and recreation.
We praise you as student workers, in the midst of our efforts and sacrifices to work and study at the same time.
From down deep in our hearts we cry out: may everything that breathes praise the Lord!

World Student Christian Federation, Geneva, Switzerland

Prayers from High School Students from Chikore, Zimbabwe

(Written at a worship workshop in 1991 led by Geraldine Abbott)

Closing Prayer

Mighty God, we come before your throne of love. We thank you for leading us through the whole service. We also thank you for speaking to us. May your word find a fertile place in our hearts and may we walk in the Spirit throughout the week. May the devil find no place in our hearts through the power of the blood of Jesus. Amen.

Closing Prayer

Mighty God, now that we are leaving your room, help us to put your word into practice. May your Holy Spirit be with us always, for the world is ever hungry to receive us back. Amen.

General Prayer

O wonderful God, we have been hearing the works of your Holy Spirit. Now we ask you to shower it into us as we are studying for our exams. May the Holy Spirit maintain peace in our country. May this very Spirit guide our staff and give them power to feed us academically. Amen. (By Daniel, Adam, Rachel, Phillimon)

General Prayer

Mighty, merciful God, we pray that your loving Holy Spirit may liberate those who are in trouble. We bring to you those who are victims of hunger in the whole world. Send your angel of harvest to relieve them from their trouble. We seek your love and peace in the community we live in. In your name, we pray. Amen.

Offering Prayer

God of all good, our gifts we give to you.
We pray that they may multiply and be blessed, as the fish and the loaves were. May they be tokens of our love to you. We all had wishes to show our love, though some could not, but down in our hearts we are all thanking. Little maybe our offering is, but meaningful in love, may it be. Amen. (By Shami, Betty, Sandra, and Patience)

Geraldine Abbott, Chikore, Zimbabwe

Examination Answers by Japanese University Students

(John Moss, Teacher)

As some of you know, I go to Niigata University each week on Wednesday morning to teach a course in the Bible in English. It is in the Education Department. The students are upper-classmen preparing to become English teachers in Japan's high schools. This is the thirty-fifth year for me to teach this course. Two professor friends in this department were students in this Bible course many, many years ago.

Very few of the students have had previous contact with the Bible—except to know its importance in Western history, thought and literature. As it is a gov-

ernment school, direct evangelism is not permitted. Nevertheless, the Bible speaks for itself. Through the lectures and personal fellowship with these students, they are sometimes influenced a great deal. If they ask me, I can introduce them to a church and, at the end of the year, I urge them all to continue their spiritual quest.

Three times a year, they hand in essays in English expressing their thinking about some questions I assign. I thought you might be interested in some excerpts from their most recent papers. Our course this past year centered on the Old Testament. Some of their mistakes in grammar were corrected by me.

I chose excerpts from their answers to my last question: "What are some important things you have learned from this course?"

When I read the scene of God's creation, I felt God is like a child playing in a sandbox or playing with clay. I saw God enjoying creation! For example, "I want light." (There is light.) "Yeah, that's good, . . . very nice!" I've heard that there is a computer game about God's creation of the world. So creation must be so enjoyable that such a game was made. (By Yoshiaki Arai)

We were created in the image of God because God hoped that we would govern this world with love and justice. So we must make an effort to realize the world of God and have a brighter future. Now we forget our original role and pursue profit and make war, but we should remember the significance of existence. As long as we live in the world, we should worship our Father, God. I'm going to worship God, not because I want the blessing of God, but because I'm grateful for God's creation. (By Ayumi Imai)

First, I noticed that there is much avarice which is born of human ego in everyday life. I felt that this class where we learn to read the Bible was like an oasis for my mind. I step out of the world which is covered with human ego like filth, and could become a brand new one like a pure baby, I felt.

Second, in daily life, there are few people who have a sense of thanksgiving, I feel. From this class, I thought we should do the basic human way like saying "Thank you" for the help or kindness of other people. (By Hiroaki Susai)

We are often disappointed with our power and come to a deadlock. But that's the very time when we can have open eyes to the (Bible's) teachings. Nobody knows what will happen in his future. I know only how I have lived so far, my own history. In it, not only good events but also unpleasant events, and not only success but also failure happened. But I think there are no meaningless things in my life. So I have come to think that God guards me behind these hardships. I think it's important to realize about God's love to us. (By Mitsuko Fujinami)

John Moss, Japan

Prayers from Students at Mt. Silinda High School, Chipinge, Zimbabwe

(Jeffrey Phillips, Teacher)

General Prayer

Lord we thank you that you have all gathered us, and we thank you for the words that have been delivered to us. I pray in the name of Jesus that you may be with the blind, the poor, the destitute, the hungry, the refugees, and those with tormented souls. May you instill your spirit within us that we may all praise you and know you. May your spirit continue to be with us as we carry on with our studies, so that we may all succeed and be all prosperous in our work. Lord, I also pray that you be with those in hospitals and journeys, and I pray all this in the name of our Lord and Saviour, Jesus Christ. Amen. (By Simbarashe Kutywayo)

Offertory Prayer

Let's Pray!

Thank you Lord for gathering us this evening, as you gave us sense of thanksgiving we have to give to you. We do this to have peace and justice. To all those who have tried by all means to offer to you, let them be blessed, and to those who didn't, give them time and a chance to do the job for you. Lord help us in all our doings and give us the faith to know that we have to offer to you. For all I have prayed, I put them in your hands. Amen. (By Perperstina Dhliwayo)

General Prayer

Our mighty God, we come to thee Lord with thanksgiving. We want to thank thee Lord for thy Love. We also kindly ask thee for thy guidance. Let the eyes of the blind open, so that they may know your kingdom. We also pray for the sick, the poor, and those facing different crises. We, again, ask you to guide us in our studies so that we may achieve our goals. Be with our teachers, as well as the headmaster, so that whatever they teach may sink deep in hearts.

We all pray this through our Christ. Amen. (By Phillip Makamu)

An Offertory Prayer

Lord, we thank thee because you give us many things in life, though we are not free to give freely and wholeheartedly. We know that we (Zimbabweans) are too stingy to give, but we ask you to bless the little we have offered so that it will benefit those who are in need. Help the poor, hungry, disabled, deaf and blind with these offerings, Lord. Help those who have failed to give today so that they will give tomorrow, for it is more blessed to give than to receive.

We offer unto you at this hour of prayer, all the refugees we are sheltering here in Zimbabwe. Give them food and clothes, O Lord. We submit also into thy hands the misfortunate ones in Zimbabwe—

that is, those who are crippled and all the disabled who are kept in the Jairos Jiri Camps of Zimbabwe. We offer unto you, Lord, the street kids of our country, Zimbabwe. Most of them are orphans; may you give them all what they need. Help them, for you know what they need. Amen. (By Lydia Mlambo)

Prayer of Confession

Dear God, stretch your holy hands of grace and peace over us, to all the corners of the earth and beyond; that we may find thy salvation in your Son, Jesus. Pick us off the hands of Satan. Cast thy bright light over us and reign over us, too. Our security is in you, therefore, show us thy grace in thy Son, Jesus. Amen. (By Solomon Siyakisa Mlambo)

Offertory Prayer

Blessed are they who give today the products of their sweat to God so that the poor may also be satisfied, and that God's purpose may flourish on earth as it has been fulfilled in heaven. The little that thy people can get is what they have offered. May their love and compassion feed their needs in the name of Jesus. Amen. (By Solomon Siyakisa Mlambo)

Offertory Prayer

Almighty God, your creation is big, with some people going without anything sufficient for them every day. We give this little in remembrance of them. Multiply it, and give us light and strength to give more in the future. Also work with this little for your service in the world. Through Jesus our Lord let it benefit your people in all the nations. Amen. (By Solomon Siyakisa Mlambo)

Jeffrey Phillips, Zimbabwe

What Is the Future Worth?

But for now, I want you to imagine for a moment that there is a child seated right there. Color the child red or white or black or brown or yellow. It makes no difference. Imagine that this child is the valued prize in a spirited auction. This child is not only loved by parents, but also wanted by many forces in society.

The distiller would like to make that child dependent on alcohol. The dope peddler would like to make that child the victim of a needle. The fashion industry and the world of entertainment would like to make that child a faithful customer. The world of sports would like to make that child a fan. The world of food would like to make that child a gourmet. How much are we willing to bid to make that child a Christian?

If we believe that that is what ultimately matters, and matters most, how much is the future worth?

Janet Ross-Heiner, U.S.A./Nicaragua

Keep the ocean clean
Keep Palau clean
Keep the air clean
Keep your air.
Leave us alone so we can stay alive and happy.
Leave the ocean so the fish can survive and we people can survive.
Keep the nuclear waste out of the ocean.

Fifth-grader, West Caroline Island of Palau

Youth

Youth, a divine treasure, . . . Our great poet, Ruben Darío, had reason when he defined with beautiful words the most marvelous phase of the people: the youth.

One phase where the life is wonderful, intense, safe and trusting.

The youth are profound idealists, they love the truth, the sincerity, and freedom.

We, the young people, dream for a better world, a world of progress, peace, justice and love.

But, what is our reality in youth? In many countries the youth are exploited in many forms; prostitution, neglect of the right to education and medicine.

Many youth live in the streets, unemployed, addicted to drugs and abuse. They live without hope.

*The politics, the imposters, the religions utilize the force, the vigor, the work of
the youth, and in return the youth receive lies, frustrations and vicious
deaths.*
Why do they insist on terminating the dreams of our youth?
Why can't they leave us live in peace?

Tatiana Martinez Parrales, Nicaragua

" . . . exactly at this time,
there is a child in the street,
there is a child in the street."
"Boy, kid,
mysteries in your eyes,
you live by the skin of your teeth . . .
The magic of childhood has lost its place
to an adult-child who seeks to find
peace to live, peace to dream,
peace to smile and love. . . . "

Xico Esvael, Brazil

Sonia's Baptism

*It was six o'clock in the morning on February 28, 1983. We found shelter by
the side of a creek in a deep ravine. We had been walking since the 25th, fleeing
the bombing. On the afternoon of the 25th, a 250-pound bomb killed a woman
who was carrying her baby girl. The father pulled his two-month-old daughter
from the dead mother's arms and had been carrying the child for the last three
days.*

*We gathered in the shadow of the trees to baptize the infant. José, a seminar-
ian, spoke: "We are going to participate in one of the most beautiful acts of our
Church—baptism. We will give a name to this little girl who three days ago lost
her mother.*

*Christianity has humble origins. But Christianity has been betrayed because
at times the Church has been, and still is, characterized by wealth and pomp.
This is because of King Constantine who gave the Church great power so that it
would support him. The Church thought that having power and wealth and
great cathedrals and schools would build the Kingdom of God. But if we go back
to the origin of our faith and to the life of the one who is our friend, the founder
of our Church, our companion and our older brother, Jesus Christ, we see that
he was poor, like us."*

*Then Father Tilo added, "As José has said, I invite you to share in this beau-
tiful ceremony. We are going to use the symbol of water. But first let me ask
you: Who knows the value of water? What does water mean to you?"*

*One person answered, "Water is essential to life. We can go for days without
eating, but if we don't have water, we will die."*

Father Tilo continued, "That's right. The river has given us life for the past three days. Now it is going to be a symbol of the life we are giving to this little girl as we receive her into our community. During these past three days, when one person has eaten, everyone has eaten. When one person has had water to drink, everyone has had water to drink. Today we are not only going to baptize this little girl, we are also going to make her a member of our community. She will suffer what we suffer. She will struggle as we struggle and win the same freedom as all of us on the day of our victory. What name are we going to give her?"

Her father answered, "Sonia."

"On behalf of Sonia, on behalf of all the children, on behalf of all the orphans, on behalf of all the baptized, we are going to pray to you, Lord, the prayer of all your children, the Lord's Prayer."

Before pouring the water, Father Tilo reminded us, "Let us remember that in a liberated community, all of us are the child's godparents. It is the community which takes care of Sonia and of all the children in the world. We are making this revolution for them. A revolution would not be worth the sacrifices if it were not for the children."

And this is how Sonia was baptized, with water from a stream, as a community gathered in the ravine. (April 1983)

El Salvador

Universal Day of Prayer for Students (February 1994)

Call to Worship

Leader: We have chosen to be here, forming one body out of many.

Congregation: We are one in the Spirit; we are one in Christ.

Leader: With us are those we see and those who share our vision but are scattered across creation.

Congregation: We are one in the Spirit; we are one in Christ.

Leader: We share a vision of students of differing experiences, men and women, rich and poor, of many races, creeds and cultures being one with us in this moment.

Congregation: We are one in the Spirit; we are one in Christ.

Conference of European Churches

The Prayers

Leader: God's spirit is with us in our community and in communities of people all over the world: Jesus Christ lives in the actions of those who reach out to touch others with unselfish caring: the Holy Spirit lives when we are givers and receivers of grace.

Let us now pray for all of Creation, in the spirit of universal concern which we have witnessed in the life of Jesus.

We pray for the students, faculty, administration and staff on our campus, that this place of instruction may be a place where the objectives of learning and education are always held in balance with a concern for the dignity of all people and the integrity of creation.

Congregation: God, in your mercy, hear our prayers.

Leader: We pray for those who are students around the world, realizing that life on campus holds significant challenges for every person, that there are stresses and anxieties that only those who share in the experience can easily understand. Help us separate performance from worth, and to remember that no matter what we achieve, God loves us.

Congregation: God, in your mercy, hear our prayers.

Leader: We pray for our members who work in the fields, offices, churches, factories, stores and institutions that form a reality often considered separate from the campus life. Help us to find ways of finding a common bond where the world wishes to create division.

Congregation: God, in your mercy, hear our prayers.

Leader: We pray for our local communities, knowing that the campus is a mirror of the wider community but with unique privileges. We pray for those who will sleep on the ground tonight, who will go to sleep hungry tonight, and who suffer from injustice and oppression.

Congregation: God, in your mercy, hear our prayers.

Leader: We pray for your creation, full of promise and yet full of the reality of suffering and abuse and pain. We pray for the renewal in ways of thinking and acting among all the peoples of the world; that we may become partners with you in the healing of the sufferings we create with thinking that is parochial and exclusive.

Especially, we pray that the religions and beliefs of the world will bring peace and unity rather than war and separation, and that the message of Christ will liberate us from all that divides us from the world around us.

Congregation: God, in your mercy, hear our prayers.

Leader: We pray for the church in all nations and our part in it; for the ecumenical ministry which brings us together; for the spirit of people in the international community and for the World Student Christian Federation within which we find expression of the oneness of the faith.

We especially pray for the WSCF today in its preparation to celebrate 100 years of service and mission.

Congregation: God, in your mercy, hear our prayers.

Leader: As the prayers of the community are also the prayers of the people of the community, let us offer up our prayers of concern and thanksgiving.

Congregation: God, in your mercy, hear our prayers.

Leader: We offer up our hopes and fears and praise, confident in your mercy. As members of the World Student Christian Federation, we know that we are not alone in prayer or in purpose. And so, in remembrance of the one who brought us together in this way and continues to guide us through our journey of faith, we pray the prayer that Christ taught us:

(The Lord's Prayer).

History of the Universal Day of Prayer for Students

The Universal Day of Prayer for Students was first celebrated on Sunday, 13 February 1898, following a decision made in July 1897 at Williamstown in the United States, on the occasion of the second General Committee of the World Student Christian Federation. The participants of the ten member countries worldwide believed that "only a Christianity which has as its central thought the purpose of God for the whole world can claim to be the religion of Jesus Christ." Believing that intercessory prayer should be a vital ingredient in the life of a worldwide body of Christian students, these early WSCF leaders called Christian students on college and university campuses around the world to join together on the second Sunday of February each year for observance of the Universal Day of Prayers for Students.

For nearly one hundred years, the international student community of the WSCF, which today comprises movements in over ninety countries, has observed the Universal Day of Prayer for Students as a symbol of their Christian commitment to be faithful witnesses to the message and work of Jesus Christ in the world. It also symbolizes the profound and steadfast conviction that prayer is central to the life of the Christian community. The Universal Day of Prayer for Students serves as an annual reminder that the student Christian community receives its life as a gift from God, and calls upon Christian students from around the world to offer prayers of praise and thanksgiving for God's love and the gift of life. It is also a time for students to remember the needs of others and to hold in prayer the students, faculty, and administration of their college or university, the international student community, the people of their community and nation, and all members of God's human family throughout the world.

World Student Christian Federation

(Other resources from the World Student Christian Federation are found throughout Part I, "Resources to Lift Up Our Voices.")

12 *Affirmations and Statements of Faith; Prayers of Commitment and Dedication*

Resurrection, He Qi, China

The final section of "Resources to Join Hands Together" is, indeed, its logical conclusion. Whether the words are "I believe . . . ," "we believe . . . ," "we commit ourselves . . . ," "we hear the cry . . . ," "give us courage . . . ," or "we greet the God in you . . . ," and whatever the language in which they originated, when we bring affirmations and prayers into our own worship context, we walk hand in hand with the faith of a global community.

Affirmations and Statements of Faith

Earth Credo

I believe in the sacredness of the earth,
the integrity of the whole of creation and dignity
of all people and creatures.
I believe in a gracious God who created humankind—
male and female, and gave them the responsibility
to take care of the earth. We need to care.
I believe we human beings have failed God and ourselves.
In the name of greed and development
we have dominated the earth.
The people and creatures destroyed the forest,
polluted the air, river and seas and have sacrificed
the future of our children. We need to repent.
I believe that when we destroy the earth,
we eventually destroy ourselves.
We must protect and preserve the earth not
only for our own survival but for the sake
of our mother earth. The time to change is now.
I believe we need to change our ways, values, lifestyle
and ways relating with creation.
Repent, fast and pray. Consume less, waste not.
Work for justice and peace.
We should not covet our neighbors' timber butterflies,
white sand beaches, nearly extinct animals nor cheap labor.

We should not oppress children, indigenous people,
women, the homeless, refugees and victims of war.
We need to live in the sense of people and creation.
For I believe in the interwovenness of life.
Creator and Creatures. Cosmic and Individual.
West, North, East, South. Rest and Prayer.
Food and Freedom. Theology and Ecology.
I therefore commit myself, together with you,
to take care for mother earth.
To advocate for peace and justice.
To choose and celebrate life.
These things I believe. Amen.

       Elizabeth S. Tapia, Philippines

We believe in you, O God, for you have made the suffering of humanity your suffering. You have come to establish a kingdom of the poor and humble. Today we sing to you, because you are alive, you have saved us, you have made us free.

    Cuba

Affirmation of Peace and Justice

All: I believe in God, who is love and who has giveth the earth to all people. I believe in Jesus Christ, who came to heal us, and to free us from all forms of oppression. I believe in the Spirit of God, who works in and through all who are turned towards the truth. I believe in the community of faith, which is called to be at the service of all people. I believe in God's promise to finally destroy the power of sin in us all, and to establish the kingdom of justice and peace for all humankind.

Reader 1: I do not believe in the right of the strongest, nor the force of arms, nor the power of oppression

Reader 2: I believe in human rights, in the solidarity of all people, in the power of non-violence.

Reader 1: I do not believe in racism, in the power that comes from wealth and privilege, or in any established order that enslaves.

Reader 2: I believe that all men and women are equally human, that order based on violence and injustice is not order.

Reader 1: I do not believe that war and hunger are inevitable and peace unattainable.

Reader 2: I believe in the beauty of simplicity, in love with open hands, in peace on earth.

All: I do not believe that suffering need be in vain, that death is the end, that the disfigurement of our world is what God intended. But I dare to believe, always and in spite of everything, in God's power to transform and transfigure, fulfilling the promise of a new heaven and a new earth where justice and peace will flourish.

    Indonesia

Affirmation

Reader 1: I believe in God: creator and farmer, lover and friend, challenger and enabler; wellspring and womb of purposeful living.

All: We believe in God.

Reader 2: I believe in Jesus Christ: compassionate and wounded healer, wise-one and fool; liberator from oppression.

All: We believe in Jesus Christ.

Reader 3: I believe in the Spirit: go-between and negotiator, inspirer and encourager; barrier-breaker, community-maker.

All: We believe in the Spirit.

Reader 4: I believe in the community of faith: alive in the aliveness of Christ, prophetic in its solidarity with all who suffer, celebratory in its hope, its work, its witness.

All: We believe in the community of faith.

Reader 5: I believe in God's commonwealth: beckoning and burgeoning, dynamic and harmonious, present and future; in which we glimpse:

· the satisfaction of our deepest longing,

· the healing of our painful rifts,

· the forging of justice, peace and integrity.

All: We believe in God's commonwealth.

Kate Compston, England

The Creation Covenant

Reader 1: The universe in its awesomeness, reflects the loving, dreaming and shaping of the Divine Artist, who looks upon what has been created, sees how good it is and celebrates its life.

Reader 2: Scripture affirms the value of human beings, within nature's intertwining tapestry, for we who are formed from the cosmic dust, have the breath of God within us.

Reader 3: Each of us is Adam and Eve, responsible for nurturing the life and resources of this greening planet.

Reader 4: Each of us, like the woman and her husband Noah, is entrusted with the survival of the species.

Reader 5: Each of us in the spirit of Tāne* and Tangaroa is called by God to nurture and protect Aotearoa's sacred soil, water and bush for generations yet unborn.

All: We commit ourselves

To join with you, O God,

To nurture

The plants and the animals,

The elements,

The sacred womb of sea and soil.

We offer to you,

Our ability to create and

Our potential to release

People's loving energies

For the benefit of all creation.

We sing with you the song of the universe!

We dance with you the dance of life!

We are yours,

And you in us are hope

For the renewing of nature

Through the healing of the nations.

May Aotearoa* be bread and wine for us all.

*Tāne is defined in chapter 18, page 209. Aotearoa is defined in chapter 5, page 41.

Bill Wallace, Aotearoa/New Zealand

I am a Woman
I believe
that women are equal in ability
to men;
I believe
that just because my mother
    accepted
a subservient role it does not
    mean
that I must too;
I believe
that if I do not fight for the rights
of my sister, then she will always
    be
oppressed;

I believe
that limitless horizons lie before
my daughter, not just a few
traditional choices;
I believe
that I have much to contribute
to the world, and I alone possess
    my
particular talents and abilities;
I believe
that each woman is an individual,
not a stereotype.

Rene Parmar, India

Rini Templeton, U.S.A./Mexico

Conference of European Churches

Renewal of the Covenant

Leader: And now, as one people within the household of God,

in the unity of the faith,

in the communion of saints,

in love and goodwill to all,

let us in the presence of our Lord Jesus Christ

give ourselves afresh to him and to one another

in joyous covenant:

promising to walk together

with God and with one another

in all the privileges and duties

of our high calling in Christ Jesus.

Congregation: We believe in God, Our Heavenly Father;

We confess Jesus Christ as Lord and Saviour;

We depend on the guidance of the Holy Spirit;

We seek to live in God's presence

According to all he has made known

And will make known to us.

We covenant to Worship, Work and Witness together

In the Fellowship of the

United Congregational Church of Southern Africa,

For the building up of the Body of Christ

And the manifesting of the Kingdom of God on Earth.

All: Alleluia, Amen, Alleluia, Amen, Alleluia, Amen,

Alleluia, Amen.

Silver Jubilee Service, 1992, The United Congregational Church of Southern
Africa

Profession of Faith of the Christian Base Communities

(Christ the Saviour Church in the Zacamil district of San Salvador was bombed in 1980 and remained closed for four years. In November 1989 the church was desecrated again by army troops, who violated the tabernacle and scattered the Blessed Sacrament on the floor. The following prayer was offered by the people of the parish on February 12, 1984, to commemorate the fifteenth anniversary of the Christian base communities in Zacamil. The church was decorated with red flowers in memory of the 623 martyrs from this parish. The Eucharist was celebrated by a thousand people, among them twelve priests and the Archbishop.)

We believe in God, who created us free and walks with us in the struggle for liberation.

We believe in Christ, crucified again in the suffering of the poor, a suffering which calls out to the conscience of people and nations, a suffering which ends in resurrection.

We believe in the power of the Spirit, capable of inspiring the same compassion which has led our best brothers and sisters to martyrdom.

We believe in the Church, called forth by Jesus and by the Holy Spirit.

We believe that when we gather, Jesus is with us, Mary, our Mother, is at our side, a sign of faithfulness to the Lord.

We believe in the Christian community where we proclaim our ideals, through which we practice our Christian faith.

We believe in building a Church where we pray and reflect on our reality, and share in the prophetic, priestly and pastoral mission of Jesus. In this way we make the Kingdom of God present on earth.

We believe in unity in the midst of differences.

We believe that Christ calls us to communion and to live as sisters and brothers.

We believe that we need to love one another, to correct one another compassionately, to forgive each other's errors and weaknesses.

We believe that we need to help one another recognize our limitations, to support each other in the faith.

We believe that the poor, the illiterate and the sick, the persecuted and tortured, are closest to the Gospel of Jesus. Through them, Christ challenges us to work for justice and peace. Their cause is our cause.

We believe that Christ is also present in those who are slaves to their passions, to vices, lies and injustice, to power and money.

We commit ourselves to never give up hope in the possibility of their conversion, to love them even though they slander, persecute and kill us; to pray for them and to help them so that one day they may live simply and humbly in the way that the Gospel calls all of us to live. Amen.

El Salvador

I believe in our responsibility for
creation, the trust
of every mountain range
of every forest
of every harbour
of every plain
of every plan
to build a future
as Eves and Adams of today.
I believe in our hopes for a great
human family as Christ wishes it;
in hopes fostered by memories
and banishing from the land of the
Holy Spirit the stupor of despair.
I believe in myself
in mobility that God
has bestowed on me
to experience the greatest of all
joys, to give myself
on the road to Emmaus and
Jericho.

Gerald O'Collins, Australia

Affirmations of the Asian Methodist Youth Seminar, March 1993

Asian Methodist Youth Seminar Statement

We, the Methodist Youths from the Philippines, Korea, Malaysia and India, have gathered together in our desire to be in solidarity with one another.

Through the Asian Methodist Youth Seminar, we believe that God is in our midst, in our lives, in our work, and in our ministries. We also believe that God is with the people of the Philippines. We saw God suffer with the women who needed to sell their bodies for daily bread, we saw God starving with the farmers who lost their land, we saw God walking alongside the street children. We saw God angered and saddened by such injustices. And we heard the divine call for us to walk with the people and walk with God.

We, the participants of the Asian Methodist Youth Seminar, have resolved to answer this call. We will strive to transform the church so that youth, women and laity will be empowered. We will also strive to transform the society so that the oppressed who have nothing will be empowered. We will strive to co-create God's reign in each of our homelands while integrating our efforts for the common struggles in Asia.

We believe that God calls Asian Methodist Youth to be in solidarity. So we raise our drooping shoulders and hold each other's tired hands. And we must now decide the direction as we walk together.

We part for now with the promise to meet again in the near future. May God guide us and be with us in our struggle.

The Social Creed of Methodist Youths in Asia

We the Methodist Youths of the Philippines, Korea, Malaysia and India, through common sufferings and struggles believe that we have inherited the tradition of the Exodus. Our national identity, culture, languages, and rights have been taken away from us. But we do not believe that God wants us to suffer in this way. We believe that God is with us to live in a free and peaceful world, and calls us to co-create God's reign here on earth.

To pursue this goal we must:

> Transform the society and the Church;
> Educate ourselves and others;
> Be in solidarity with women, children, laborers, peasants and
>   the urban poor;
> Resist imperialism, militarism and unjust economic systems;
> Preserve the environment;
> Strive for racial harmony, and
> Preserve our Asian heritage.

In spite of our calling, we confess that we often do not respond to social injustice. but we will no longer turn a blind eye nor be drowned in self pity. We will rise and join our hands in our struggle. God will lead us with pillars of cloud and fire and guide us into the Promised Land. God will deliver us.

Affirmation of Our Discipleship

Leader: We are called to proclaim the truth. Let us together this day proclaim the truth about human worth and dignity. And let us believe: It is not true that this world and its people are doomed to die and to be lost.

Congregation: This is true: there is future for the children of today.

Leader: It is not true that we must accept inhumanity and discrimination, hunger and poverty, death and destruction.

Congregation: This is true: the Sovereign Lord will wipe away the tears from all faces and will remove disgrace of people from all the earth.

Leader: It is not true that violence and hatred should have the last word and that war and destruction have come to stay forever.

Congregation: This is true: the Lord foils the plans of the nations and thwarts the purposes of the peoples, but the plans of the Lord stand firm forever, the purposes of the heart of the Lord through all generations.

All: So let us dream, let us prophesy, let us see visions of love. And let us seek peace and justice with humility, with joy and faith, with courage.

Asian Methodist Youth Seminar

Prayers of Commitment and Dedication

An Indian Prayer

O Great Spirit, Whose voice I hear in the winds, and whose breath gives life to all the world, hear me! I am small and weak, I need Your strength and wisdom.
Let me walk in beauty, and make my eyes ever behold the red and purple sunset.
Make my hands respect the things You have made and my ears sharp to hear Your voice.
Make me wise so that I may understand the things You have taught my people.
Let me learn the lessons You have hidden in every leaf and rock.
I seek strength, not to be greater than another, but to fight my greatest enemy—myself.
Make me always ready to come to You with clean hands and straight eyes.
So when life fades. as the fading sunset, my spirit may come to You without shame.

Native American, U.S.A.

The Star Light of Commitment

Far and bright is the light of the
    small star
Shining in the sky
Like the golden lantern shimmer-
    ing in one's heart,
Like a banner leading us out of
    misery.
When thundering storm comes,
Heavy clouds blacken the sky and
    moon;
But the star of commitment shin-
    ing above
Still lights and strengthens our
    hearts.
Scorn all hardships!
The people remain firmly stand-
    ing,
Distinct and daring.
Though the sky is dark and the
    moon is gone,
The shining star of commitment
    stays on:
It will glow until sunrise.

    Thailand

แสงดาวแห่งศรัทธา

พร่างพราวแสงดวงดาวน้อยสกาว

ส่องฟากฟ้าเด่นพราวไกลแสนไกล

ดั่งโคมทองผ่องเรืองรุ่งในหทัย

เหมือนธงชัยส่องนำจากห้วงทุกข์ทน

พายุฟ้าครืนข่มทุกคาม

เดือนลับยามผ่านธินีคมมน

ดาวศรัทธายังส่องแสงเบื้องบน

ปลุกหัวใจ ปลุกคน อยู่มิวาย

ขอเยาะเย้ยทุกข์ยากขวากหนามลำเค็ญ

คนยังคงยืนเด่นโดยท้าทาย

แม้นผืนฟ้ามืดดับเดือนลับสลาย

ดาวยังพรายศรัทธาเย้ยฟ้าดิน

ดาวยังพรายอยู่จนฟ้ารุ่งราง

Star Light of Commitment, Thailand

New Responsibility

Great Spirit,
    still brooding over the world—
We hear the cry of the earth,
we see the sorrow of the land
raped and plundered in our greed
for its varied resources.

We hear the cry of the waters,
we see the sorrow of stream and ocean
polluted by the poisons
we release into them.

We hear the cry of the animals,
we see the sorrow of bird, fish and beast
needlessly suffering and dying
to serve our profit or sport or vanity.

Please teach us

    a proper sensitivity
    towards your feeling creation

    a proper simplicity
    in the way we live in our environment

    a proper respect
    for the shalom of the universe.

We turn from our arrogant ways
to seek you again, Creator of all life.
Redeem us—and redeem your world
and heal its wounds and dry its tears.
May our response to you bear fruit
in a fresh sense of responsibility
towards everything you have created.

    Kate Compston, England

Conference of European Churches

O God, our Saviour, in whose paths of love is the secret of all of life and the hope of
    every person, give us courage, give us peace to confront this day and hour. We did
    not choose to be born nor to live in such a time as this. Permit us, however, to be
    challenged by the problems, to draw hope from the discoveries, to be filled with
    anger at the injustices, to be inspired by the responsibilities, to be renewed by your
    strength, through the love of your Kingdom.
O God, we thank you for the glorious opportunities we have to build a new society
    of peace, justice and love, where we can praise and worship you.
Help us, we ask, to stand courageously, to work with love and to live in hope,
    through the love of Christ. Amen.

    Ecumenical Circle of Prayers, Brazil

Our Prayer

Make us keep the sputtering lantern burning
and not to break a wounded reed.
Make us understand
the secret of eternal life
from the pulse of blood in our veins
and realise the worth of a life
from the movement of a warm heart.
Make us not discriminate
the rich and the poor,
the high and the low,
the learned and the ignorant
those we know well and those we do not know.
Oh!
A human life can't be exchanged for the whole world
this supreme task of keeping the lives
of the sons and daughters of God.
Let us realise how lovely it is
to feel the burdens of responsibility.

By a worker of Peace Market, Korea

All: God of all tenderness we rejoice that you see good in all people. Help us to
be like you, for it is only through seeing you in all things that we and this
world shall be saved. Amen.

*(The following may also be used. Each person turns to the person next to them, affirms
them by telling them something good about them and then, touching them in some
appropriate way, says:)*

I affirm you my sister/brother—

I affirm your value and your potential—

I affirm God's love in you.

(As an alternative one or the other of the following may be used.)

I see the God in you.

I greet the God in you.

Bill Wallace, Aotearoa/New Zealand

Call to Commitment

Leader: Christ has come to bring peace anchored on justice and genuine love, to offer us renewed vision of transformed persons and communities.

Congregation: Christ calls us to become channels of peace based on justice.

Leader: With open eyes, let us seek truth . . . with eyes of love, let us perceive the suffering of people in all nations, and claim their aspirations, their struggles and their victories as our own. Let every fiber in our body become a string of harmony, devotion and commitment to the dreams and vision of all struggling people.

Congregation: Lord, make us channels of your peace.

Leader: What is peace? It is never given away. It is fought for with utmost courage by a people who dare to cross the crucible of suffering and determination.

Those who are to harvest the fruit of sacrifice must cultivate in their lives the communal responsibility to the blood once shed for the life of the world.

Congregation: We believe that peace can never be attained by empty silence and outstretched hands of mercy.

Leader: In humility, let us commit ourselves to the pursuit of God's promise of life abundant, life with dignity and worth, life with justice and peace for our brothers and sisters in our neighboring countries, who amidst their pain and suffering, continue to hope because they struggle.

Congregation: We offer ourselves to always seek peace and affirm justice for all people: choosing struggle rather than indifference; choosing to be friends of the earth and of one another, not enemies; choosing to be peacemakers rather than peace keepers; choosing life, not death, for all creation.

Leader: Let us pray . . .

All: (We pray The Lord's Prayer in our own language.)

   Asian Methodist Youth Seminar

Conference of European Churches

Offering of Our Life and Labours to God in Gratitude and Praise

(The offerings of the people are received as the choir sings an anthem. The offerings are brought forward. As they are presented to God, the people rise and sing:)

As one family we bring
these our gifts to God, our King;
who in love has made us one
in the Church of Christ, his Son.
Use us and our gifts, good Lord,
in the service of the world.
Hope to all your people give
as we to your glory live.

(The congregation is seated. Small groups then come forward with a symbolic offering representing the contribution made to the UCCSA, the Region Synod, and local church over the past twenty-five years. When they have presented their gift, they form themselves into a human cross on the stage. Then, the children come forward.)

Leader: For our children, in the home, the Church and Sunday School, and for all the solemn hopes which gather around them.

Congregation: Siyabonga (3) Nkosi Yam (sung).

(Young people come forward, some dressed casually, others in Brigade uniforms.)

Leader: For the energy, enthusiasm and hope of our young people and for their desire for faith in action and fuller participation in the life and work of the Church.

Congregation: Siyabonga (3) Nkosi Yam (sung)

(Families come forward.)

Leader: For the many families which make up the household and family of God in the United Congregational Church, holding young and old together in love and mutual support.

Congregation: Siyabonga (3) Nkosi Yam (sung)

Leader: For the commitment, dedication and loving service of the Women of our Churches.

Congregation: Siyabonga (3) Nkosi Yam (sung)

(Soldiers of Christ and Broederbond come forward.)

Leader: For the zeal of the Soldiers of Christ and the Broederbond in proclaiming the Gospel.

Congregation: Siyabonga (3) Nkosi Yam (sung)

(Ministers come forward.)

Leader: For the worship of God in Word and Sacrament, and for the fellowship of praise and prayer, enabling us to grow in grace and equipping us for service in the Church and in the world.

Congregation: Siyabonga (3) Nkosi Yam (sung)

(Deacons come forward.)

Leader: For the comfort given to those who mourn, the counsel offered to those in need, and the light shown to those who seek the way.

Congregation: Siyabonga (3) Nkosi Yam (sung)

(Builders come forward.)

Leader: For the Churches built to your glory and the halls and centres erected for the service of the community during the past twenty-five years.

Congregation: Siyabonga (3) Nkosi Yam (sung)

(Community workers come forward.)

Leader: For the outreach of our Churches into the communities in which they are set through social and personal services which minister to people's total needs.

Congregation: Siyabonga (3) Nkosi Yam (sung)

(Administrators come forward.)

Leader: For those who administer the affairs of the United Congregational Church at local, regional, synodical and denominational levels, for their dedicated efficiency, their tireless patience and hard work.

Congregation: Siyabonga (3) Nkosi Yam (sung)

(Political prisoners and concerned Christians come forward.)

Leader: For the commitment of the United Congregational Church to justice and peace in the midst of oppression and strife, and for those of our number who have shown courage and never lost hope as they endured suffering, humiliation, banning, detention, exile, injury and death because they stood for the truth.

Congregation: Siyabonga (3) Nkosi Yam (sung)

(The Bible and newsvendors come forward.)

Leader: For God's living word in the Bible—speaking to us through the events of our time and place as clearly as in ancient times—challenging us to see, judge and act, transforming individuals, the Church and Society and giving hope to all God's people.

Congregation: Siyabonga (3) Nkosi Yam (sung)

(The congregation stands.)

Leader: For this time when we celebrate our life together in the United Congregational Church of Southern Africa for the past twenty-five years.

Congregation: We worship and praise you for our fellowship, witness and service.

Leader: For this time when we rejoice in our unity with the Holy Church in all the world and our partnership in mission with all your people.

Congregation: We worship and praise you for the privilege of sharing in your mission to the world.

(Singing:)

Now to the God whose power can do
more than our thoughts or wishes know
be everlasting honours done
by all the Church, through Christ his Son.

Silver Jubilee Service, 1992, The United Congregational Church of Southern Africa

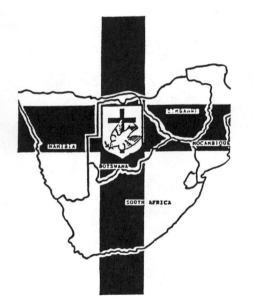

Silver Jubilee Symbol, The United Congregational Church of Southern Africa

Prayer for Dedication of a Bible

Leader: Be a blessing O God, on this Bible and on everyone who hears it read.

Congregation: Open each ear,
each eye.

Leader: The Gospel of the God of life

Congregation: to shelter us,
to aid us.

Leader: The Gospel of the beloved Christ and Holy Spirit

Congregation: to keep us,
to guide us,
to empower us for service.

Leader: The Word of the God of mercy

Congregation: to give us hope,
to give us strength.

Leader: The Word of the God of power and gentleness

Women: to companion us

Men: to encourage us when we are in fear and doubt and pain

Women: to convict and challenge us

Men: to disturb our complacency.

Leader: The Gospel of the God of life be a blessing

Children: on our prayers in this place
on our hymns in this place
in our listening here
in our speaking here.

Leader: May every word from this Book spring forth in creative power and joy and might

Congregation: illumining each face, each soul, each heart.

All: God to enfold us.
God to surround us.
God in our worship here
God in our journeys from this place.
God in our homes
God in our hearts
Now and forever.

Leader: Be a blessing, O God, on this Bible and on everyone who hears it read.

Congregation: Open each ear,
each eye.
Fill us with your fullness.

Kathy Wonson Eddy, U.S.A.

Robert Eddy, U.S.A.

PART III

Resources to Walk the Sacred Seasons and Holy Days

This part of our book, focused on the church year, includes worship resources—calls to worship, prayers, litanies, benedictions—and general resources—poems, art, stories, and brief descriptions of worship. The definition of each chapter is broad. In Chapter 13, "Advent, Christmas, and Epiphany," the themes are waiting and expectation, the birth of Christ into contemporary mangers of rejection, and the incarnation and manifestation of God into all the human communities of the earth.

Resources in Chapter 14 are divided between the Lenten season of profound reflection and the celebration of Easter; a bridge is formed by the four Good Friday pieces on the Cross and the Easter Eve traditions which witness to the simultaneous experience of crucifixion and resurrection in our world.

In this part, we share resources of a family. From India, Savithri Devanesen sent her husband Chandran's poems, written before his death, as well as her own poetry, which continues his tradition of annual Christmas poems. She also sent poems of their son Dayalan Devanesen from his medical school days. Dr. Devanesen is now a doctor among aboriginal people in Australia.

Chapter 15, "Pentecost, Saints, and the Marking of Seasons and Sacred Days," has its own introductory note.

Annunciation, He Qi, China

Waiting

Life is painful
because of the ones who have
    died.
Joy is painful
because of the ones who are
    crying.
Love is painful
because of the ones who hate.
And while I am loving, laughing
    and crying,
I am waiting for you, my Lord!

    Julia Esquivel, Guatemala

Advent Wreath Liturgy

Reader 1: What does this Advent wreath mean?

Reader 2: The circle says God's love and care are eternal. The green leaves say that God's love and care are renewed every day. The cheerful light of the candles is like the brightness of Christian hope. Let us pray:

(First week of Advent)

All: God of hope, we thank you for the hope you gave the Jewish captives in Babylon. The hope of a Messiah who would bring peace, joy, and righteousness. We thank you for the hope you have given us. It makes our lives bright. We look forward to the celebration of the coming of the Messiah. Help us to share the Good News with our neighbors. Amen.

(Second week of Advent)

All: God of hope, we thank you for the hope of the Messiah. We thank you for Zechariah and Elizabeth who trusted and hoped in your promise to them. Help us to trust and hope in your promises to us. We need to be reassured every day. We rejoice in the joy of hope you bring us. Help us to understand something of the mystery of the Messiah and to share hope with someone who is hopeless. Amen.

(Third week of Advent)

All: God of hope, we rejoice in your presence and live in hope because you are with us. We thank you because you gave Mary the courage to accept the mystery of her vision. Often we do not understand—how can we understand the mystery of Jesus, the Messiah? Give us courage to live in the light of hope. Let us share the joy of the mystery of God with us. Amen.

(Fourth week of Advent)

All: God of hope, we live in the line of those who had great hope: the captive Jews in Babylon, Zechariah and Elizabeth, parents of John the Baptist, Mary and Joseph, parents of Jesus the Messiah. The light of the hope of the Messiah shines out on all people. We thank you for ancestors who help us find the light and joy of hope in the Messiah. May we be the ancestors of other people of hope. The time of our celebration of the coming of the Messiah is near. May we celebrate in a way that is suitable for remembrance of this great event. Amen.

(Christmas Eve or Christmas Day)

All: God of hope and joy, we sing for joy because you have given us hope and joy. Our world is full of problems, yet the coming of the Messiah is reason for hope. We have come to worship in your special presence. Give us wisdom as we go to our places in daily life. Teach us and guide us as we deal with the problems of our world. Thank you for Jesus and hope. Amen.

Thomas McNair, Taiwan

Leader: Remember not the former things.
Do not consider the things of old.
Behold I am doing a new thing;
Now it springs forth—do you not perceive it?

Congregation: Lord, we await.
Do a new thing among us.

Leader: I will make a way in the wilderness
and streams in the desert.
Every valley shall be exalted
and every mountain and hill made low.

Congregation: Lord, we await.
Do a new thing among us.

Leader: In the wilderness prepare the way of the Lord;
Make straight in the desert a highway for our God.
Here is my servant, the one I have chosen;
I have filled him with my Spirit—
He will not lose hope or courage;
He will establish justice on the earth.
Distant lands eagerly await him.

Congregation: Lord, we await.
Do a new thing among us
and establish justice on the earth.

Leader: Sing a new song to the Lord, sing the Lord's praises, all the world.
Praise God all you people,
let those who live in distant lands
give praise and glory to the Lord.

Conference of European Churches, 10th Assembly, 1992, Prague

A Celtic Rune of Hospitality

(English)

I saw a stranger today
I put food for him in the eating-
    place
And drink in the drinking-place
And music in the listening-place.
In the Holy Name of the Trinity
He blessed myself and my house
My goods and my family.
And the lark said in her warble
Often, often, often
Goes Christ in the stranger's guise
Oh, oft and oft and oft,
Goes Christ in the Stranger's
    guise.

Gedicht über Gastfreundschaft

(German)

Ich habe einen Fremdling gesehen
    am heutigen Tag,
ich gab ihm zu essen, wo man isst,
zu trinken, wo man trinkt,
Musik, wo man hört.
Im heiligen Namen der
    Dreifaltigkeit
segnete er mich und mein Haus,
mein Gut und meine Familie.
Une es sang die Lerche:
oft, oft, oft geht
Christus im Kleid des Fremdlings;
oft, oft, ja oft geht
Christus im Kleid des Fremdlings.

Rune d'hospitalité

(French)

Aujourd'hui, j'ai vu un étranger
J'ai mis de la nourriture au lieu o—
    l'on mange,
Et à boire là où l'on boit,
et de la musique là où l'on écoute.
Au nom de la sainte Trinité
Il m'a béni, moi et ma maison,
mes biens et ma famille.
Souvent, souvent, souvent
Le Christ vient sous l'habit de l'é-
    tranger.

Celtic Traditional, Conference of
European Churches

Stranger at the Door

Tinsel sways like ghosts
in the half light and bitter
wind of opening door,
candles flicker, too.
Another stranger has come
seeking money
in the cold Advent night.
Hard times drive many here
to the parsonage door.
Some, ashamed to beg, first time,
but hungry and too poor
for Christmas, please,
my children are crying,
please, lady.
Others have grown smooth,
rehearsed pleas, tough
against denial, damning
gratitude, never enough,
angry at me
for my home,
more, lady.
Others, weak or drunk,
exhausted by want,
mumble words, words,
it doesn't matter, look at my face,
knowing I'll give
or not—
give so I can
shut the door
on the cold,
give, lady.
The bell rings again.
Another stranger has come
in the cold Advent night—
I search the face
for Christ.
Yes, yes—
there he is,
there he is,
there he is.

Maren C. Tirabassi, U.S.A.

Unto Us a Son Was Given

The year was the decade-maker,
    1970—
Along a German street, head down,
    stomach empty,
walked a young man totally alone.
"Who are you, young man?"
"I am Mudeer, I fled Pakistan to es-
    cape—
I was turned back from England where
    my sister lives.
I cannot speak German and I am
    afraid."
"Come home with me. You need have
    no fear.
Let us first get you something to eat":
Unto us a son was given!
Later two grandchildren call us, "God
    Parents."
Mudeer is a Muslim, and I am a
    Christian,
and in the universe somewhere
God is smiling.

      Richard Wilcox, Spain

Felix Navidad y Una Vida Digna, Rini Templeton, U.S.A./Mexico

Antiseptic Words

The Emperor Augustus called it a "Census."
Joseph and Mary knew it to be "enslavement."
Hitler called it "The Final Solution,"
my generation knew it was "The Holocaust."
Milosevec has called for "Ethnic Cleansing."
but for Muslims it is another "Genocide."
Jesus said, "If thine eye be single,"
and we cannot help but know his meaning—
"Be forever done with using words to forge lies!"
Messiah comes to bring truth and justice
to a people who walk in darkness still.
So the world waits for truth to be spoken to power!

      Richard Wilcox, Spain

Las Posadas

(Service of Shelter for the Holy Family)

May the very special spirit of Christmas extend to all of you and be shared within the vision of peace during the New Year. During the first week of December we celebrated the Purisima. It is the most focused celebration of the year here in Nicaragua. The people share in the visiting of families and friends and in giving thanks.

Here the families give fruit and sugar cane to the children. The adults pray in faith and hope for peace and goodness toward the coming of the new year. Most families adorn their houses with the shrine of the virgin Mary laced with plants, flowers, candles and lights. During the evenings of celebration one's sleep is interrupted due to the fiesta of firecrackers. It sounds very similar to the fourth of July night skies.

Janet Ross-Heiner,
U.S.A./Nicaragua

In the Hispanic tradition of Latin American countries, especially in Mexico, one of the oldest celebrations is Las Posadas. It was created by the Augustinian Father Diego de Soria about 1587 to introduce Christianity to the New World, and now is revised by United Methodists Carlos Avendano, Raquel M. Martinez, and Roberto Escamilla. This celebration takes place during Advent, from December 16 through December 23. It is a preparation for and anticipation of the birth of the Savior, commemorating the nine months when Mary carried the infant Jesus in her womb and emphasizing his coming again and the need of all persons for repentance and God's mercy. Las Posadas is a Christian, biblical, and evangelistic service out of the Hispanic culture.

Well ahead of time, eight homes of church members are chosen in different areas for the eight nights prior to Christmas Eve. These homes should be willing to have a house party, including a piñata to be broken by a child. The piñata represents the devil, who cannot be recognized, and therefore the child is blindfolded. The child is fighting against evil with the rod of virtue, symbolized in the stick provided to break the piñata. When the child perseveres to the end, the glory of God will come down on everyone, as shown by the candy hidden within the piñata. The homes may also offer cups of hot chocolate, coffee, apple cider, or punch; buñelos (thin fried pastry); tamales; hot doughnuts; sweet rolls; all kinds of avocado and other dips; or other refreshments. Each family should also visit neighbors and invite them to Las Posadas.

On the appointed day, people meet at the corner near the home to be visited. In small communities this procession of pilgrims would walk from one home to another, but in large communities it could be a car caravan. Traditionally, persons carry lighted candles and sing as they walk. In the lead may be Mary, seated on a donkey, with Joseph. Children, possibly dressed as shepherds and the magi, accompany the procession. Then, in procession, the people approach the darkened house and proceed with the following service:

(Knocking on the door, a person begins:)

Listen! I am standing at the door, knocking; if you hear my voice and open the door, I will come in to you and eat with you, and you with me. (Rev 3:20)

(People outside the home say:)

Who will give lodging to these pilgrims who are weary of traveling the roads?
We have come exhausted from Nazareth. I'm a carpenter, by the name of
   Joseph. In the name of the heavens, I beg you for lodging, my beloved wife
   can no longer travel.

(People inside the home answer:)

Although you tell us that you are weary, we do not give lodging to strangers. We
   don't care what your name is; let us sleep. We are telling you that we will not
   let you enter.

(People outside say:)

He was in the world, and the world came into being through him; yet the world
   did not know him. He came to what was his own, and his own people did not
   accept him. But to all who received him, who believed in his name, he gave
   power to become children of God. (Jn 1:10, 12)

(People inside say:)

Who are the children of God?

(People outside say:)

All who are led by the Spirit of God are children of God. (Rom 8:14)

(People inside say:)

To what does the Spirit of God guide us?

(People outside say:)

You shall love the Lord your God with all your heart, and with all your soul,
   and with all your mind. You shall love your neighbor as yourself. (Mt 22:37,
   39)
The fruit of the Spirit is love, joy, peace, patience, kindness, generosity, faithfulness, gentleness, and self-control. (Gal 5:22–23a)

(People inside say:)

How do we know we love the Lord and have faith?

(People outside say:)

What good is it, my brothers and sisters, if you say you have faith but do not have works? Can faith save you? If a brother or sister is naked and lacks daily food, and one of you says to them, "Go in peace; keep warm and eat your fill," and yet you do not supply their bodily needs, what is the good of that? So faith by itself, if it has no works, is dead. (Jas 2:14–17)

(People inside switch on all the lights and say:)

Lodging we will give you with much happiness; enter, good Joseph, enter with Mary.

(The doors of the home open and all enter. People inside say:)

Enter, holy pilgrims. Receive this corner not of this humble home, but of our hearts.

(Host family offers the following prayer:)

God all-powerful, grant that we may rid ourselves of the works of darkness, and that we may invest ourselves with the weapons of light in this life to which your Son, Jesus Christ, with great humility came to visit us; so that in the final day, when he returns in majestic glory to judge the living and the dead, we shall rise to eternal life through Jesus Christ, who lives and reigns with you and the Holy Spirit now and forever. Amen.

(A member of the host family or another person reads Psalm 80 and one of the following:)

December 16: Mal 3:1–6a, Mk 1:1–8
December 17: Mal 4:1–6, Lk 1:5–17
December 18: Is 62:1–12, Lk 1:26–38
December 19: Is 11:1–10, Lk 1:39–56
December 20: Is 35:1–10, Lk 1:57–66
December 21: Is 42:1–9, Mt 3:1–12
December 22: Is 9:2–7, Mt 1:12–17
December 23: Zep 3:14–20, Lk 1:67–80

(The host family now serves refreshments, and the piñata may be broken.)

Mexico

Nativity, Midori Shibata, Japan

God of God . . .

Only the sound of an infant
crying in the night,
a familiar, homely, human sound
like the sound of hooves on flagstones,
like the rattle of chains tethering cattle,
like the crunch of straw in the mouths of oxen,
like the rustle of hay tossed into a manger.
Light of light . . .
Only the light of a star
falling on an infant in a crib
like the light in a shepherd's lantern,
like the light in the eyes of a mother,
like the light in the learning of wise men,
like the light that lightens each dawn.
Very God of very God . . .
Only a pillow of straw
and an infant in rags and tatters
like the weather-worn blankets of shepherds,
like dusty, travel-stained garments of travellers,
like old cloths stuffed in a stable window
to keep the draught out and cattle warm.
God is with us,
terribly, simply with us.
And the shadows of men
with arms outstretched to take Him
fall across the manger
in the form of a cross.

Chandran Devanesen, India

If Mary and Joseph had arrived at an African village (almost any village in Sierra Leone) they would have found a place. Someone would have given Mary a mat by the cooking fire, and there would have been grannies and aunties to help her with the birth. The men would have made room around the rice bowl for Joseph to dip his hand in while he told his story. Angel visitations, dreams, and signs in the sky would have called forth awe and wonder but no surprise, for here the spirit world is fully as real as the physical one.

Dorothy R. Gilbert, Sierra Leone

Christmas/Navidad

The day when my eyes see light
In the eyes of a campesino
In the heart depths of a dictator
In the smile of a stable child
That day is Christmas

The day when my ears hear the
    Messiah
In the chirp of a sparrow
In the dim of the market place
In the lullaby of a young mother
That day is Christmas

The day when my hands touch the
    body of the Savior
In the wounds of a refugee
In the picking of coffee in the
    mountains

In the toes of a new born
That day is Christmas

That day when my tongue tastes
    the sweetness of God
In the honey of a bee
In the rice and beans of the people
In the tortillas of covenant and
    communion
that day is Christmas

The day when the heart finds peace
In the struggle and vision
In the tall palms gentle waving in
    the distance
In the swaddling clothes of
    Bethlehem
That day is Christmas

> Janet Ross-Heiner,
> U.S.A./Nicaragua

Christmas Litany

Leader: This is the season of celebration.

Congregation: What are we celebrating?

Leader: We celebrate the birth of Jesus.

Congregation: Why? Our stores are burned down in the riot. We are hated just
    because we are Koreans. The world ignored our cries and anguish.

Leader: We celebrate the birth of Jesus who came as a savior.

Congregation: Why? Movies portray us as Scrooges. Universities refuse to accept
    our children because they are Asians. They make us feel guilty when we eat
    Kimchee.

Leader: We celebrate the birth of Jesus who came as a savior for all of humanity.

Congregation: Why? We are ridiculed for our accents. We face glass ceilings on
    our jobs. We are voiceless in this society.

Leader: We celebrate the birth of Jesus who came as a savior for all of humanity
    so that peace and justice will reign throughout the world.

Congregation: Then we can celebrate in the hope that someday peace and justice
    will prevail.

All: Let us celebrate this season because the Hope came to us when there was no
    hope. We can now dream about the future when people of all races can live
    together in harmony and love.

> Keith Hwang, U.S.A./Korea

Christmas Prayer

O Holy One, Word made flesh, Eternity captured in a life within time, heaven laid in a manger stall; You, the Light dipped down into our darkness: we pray that you will forgive our sins and make us clean and open to receive you at your coming. Loose us today from our treacheries toward you and our cruelties toward one another.

Now we have come again, dear Lord, to the time of the Morning Star, to yourself moving as azure blue into our contamination; as open touch to our fisted exclusiveness; as a carol sung to our meagerness; as Rose to our bitterness; as love to our emptiness. You are upon us as sky, hands, songs, garlands, tastes . . . making us yours in joy. We marvel not that angelic hosts sang and shouted for joy. Amen.

Richard Wilcox, Spain

Christmas 1988

Lord,
there is enchantment in the air
tonight
casting a mysterious spell
of expectancy on all creation
fulfilling the promise
of the birth of God
on earth
as a human child.
And as I watch with trembling
    hope
the wondrous pageant pass by
of poor shepherds
and powerful kings—
the radiant serenity of the night
is suddenly broken by a storm
of power-drunk winds
spewing bullets of hatred,
hurling stones of violence
on men and women
on frightened children
all fleeing

from the grips of oppressive
structures,
from bondage of sorrow and
    broken
lives,
from explosive knowledge
which has not yet solved
the problems of hunger and
    poverty,
from crumbling values
which confuse the mind,
from death itself . . .
searching for the manger
where God's love and goodness
for all humanity
blossoms in the heart of a Babe
and lets us know anew
this Christmas morn
all people
as our brother,
as our sister.

Savithri Devanesen, India

Christmas 1992

Lord,
This Christmas I wonder at the
   artistry
of your glorious creation
this beautiful planet
draped
in gossamer mists
with shy opal dawns,
with vibrant sunsets,
and night skies hung
with a myriad lamps.
Yet I want to lie
comfortably enshrined
in my insensitive tomb,
closing my heart
to suffering humanity,
human faces disfigured
by hunger and disease,
conflict and intrigue,
by unjust laws and crippling
   systems

tearing apart
the fabric of dreams.
It frightens me, Lord.
Somewhere I hear the cry
of a child!
Is it the cry of god?
calling me out of my complacency
to become an architect
for the temples of
love and care
where a new humanity
can be born
as one family,
to work together,
to understand together,
to suffer together,
to chant together
the divine ragas
of Love and Peace.

Savithri Devanesen, India

Christmas

Each church has its own tradition for celebrating Christmas. The following traditions come from different sources but are pretty typical. In general, Christmas is a church celebration not so much a family tradition. The celebration at church would include not only a service but also a time of fellowship and fun for everyone.

Each family would prepare and bring a piñata to contribute to the celebration. The church would be decorated with greens and natural flowers available locally. Children would paint peanuts to put on dry tree branches. Small bags filled with sweets and surprises are prepared for everyone too.

The service would include a program of poems, songs and dramas done by children and adults. The live nativity scene would include real lambs from their farms and typical dress from there. A message or homily is also included.

Afterwards, all enjoy the traditional tamales (cornmeal wrapped in husks and then steamed) and atole (a hot drink made from cornflour, brown sugar, cinnamon, and water). Everyone participates in the breaking of the piñatas and other games. Some places exchange gifts which are always some product from their farm like a squash or a chicken or a handmade item like a basket or embroidery work.

Olivia Juarez and Sara Larson Wiegner, Mexico

Living Water

One who said I am the eternal
    water
Dwelt among us
Living with us
Sustaining us
This is Christmas.

To receive a cup of living water
Is not only to cleanse ourselves
But also to cleanse all the waters.
River and well, lake and ocean,
And to share them with all.
This is Christmas.

      Masao and Fumiko Takenaka, Japan

Living Water, Fumiko Takenaka, Japan

(Other Christmas illustrations can be found on pages 221, 225, and 228)

Epiphany

Leader: We glorify you, O Master, lover of humankind, almighty, pre-eternal King.
We glorify you, the Creator and Maker of all.
We glorify you, O only-begotten Son of God, born without father from your Mother, and without mother from your Father.

Congregation: Light from Light, we glorify you.

Leader: In the preceding feast we saw you as a child, while in the present we see you full-grown, our God made manifest, perfect God from perfect God.
For today the time of the feast is at hand for us: the choir of saints assembles with us and the angels join in keeping festival.

Congregation: Light from Light, we glorify you.

Leader: Today the grace of the Holy Spirit in the form of a dove descended upon the waters.
Today the Sun that never sets has risen and the world is filled with splendour by the light of the Lord.
Today the moon shines upon the world with brightness of its rays.
Today the glittering stars make the inhabited earth fair with the radiance of their shining.

Congregation: Light from Light, we glorify you.

Leader: Today the earth and sea share the joy of the world, and the world is filled with gladness.
The waters saw you, O God, the waters saw you and were afraid.
The Jordan turned back, seeing the fire of the Godhead descending bodily and entering its stream.
The Jordan turned back, seeing the Invisible made visible, the Creator, made flesh, the Master in the form of a servant.
The Jordan turned back and the mountains skipped, looking upon God in the flesh; and the clouds gave voice, marvelling at him who was come, the Light of Light, true God of true God.

Congregation: Light from Light, we glorify you.

Leader: For today in the Jordan they saw the triumph of the Master; they saw him drown in the Jordan the death of disobedience, the sting of error, and the chains of hell, and give to the world the baptism of salvation.

Congregation: Light from Light, we glorify you.

Orthodox

Conference of European Churches

Leader: We offer you, O Ruler of men and women and of heavenly beings, the *gold* of our costly service. Take the labour of our hands, the skill of our minds, the power of our organization. Purge us of pride, and stir us from sloth, that we, being refined by your grace, may become better servants of your kingdom, now and hereafter.

Congregation: Amen.

Leader: We offer to you, our Lord and our God, the *incense* of our worship and our prayer. By the gift of your Holy Spirit, you have hung forth a star in the lowly heaven of every Christian soul; grant us with eager feet to follow wherever it leads, until our searching souls are blessed with the vision of yourself, who are our heaven and our home, for ever.

Congregation: Amen.

Leader: We offer to you, O Man of sorrows, the *myrrh* of your church's sufferings. When we have nothing else to give, this offering remains. Where you are on the cross, there also may your servants be. May your perfect sacrifice avail to make our light affliction redemptive in the world, that sharing the fellowship of your sufferings we may rejoice in the power of your resurrection, now and for ever.

Congregation: Amen.

Ghana

Flight into Egypt, He Qi, China

From the East

Christ, the savior of humankind, is the great light which shines upon all peoples. But the very first to be called to worship the holy infant were the wise men from the East. Why them, in particular? Was it that the ancient cultures of the East had received more of God's revelation and were thus better prepared to accept Christ? Or was it that the East stood in greater need of Christ because of the endless river of tears which is its history? I do not know. Perhaps the answer lies in the star that lit their path.

What I do know is that the East, in its recent history, has been hammered on the anvil of extreme adversity, there forged and tempered for over a hundred years. Precisely because of this, should not the East be able to offer up an even more refined gold when it worships Christ? Out of this pain and agony, should not the East be ready to bring forth even more fragrant frankincense and myrrh?

The wise men have already returned home, because people from the East have a deep sense of attachment to their native places. And yet, they haven't really gone far from the manger. Don't you see them still, kneeling over the infant?

Wang Weifan, China

Carrying the Cross, He Qi, China

Lent, 1991

(During Lent, 1991, the United States was engaged in conflict with Iraq in the Persian Gulf area.)

Lent comes.
We draw a holy comma
in rushed and busy lives.
We follow down
old scripture words
the journey to Jerusalem.
We stumble into prayer again
and whisper soft
the dearest, fearest
of our thoughts.
Lent comes.
Last year's palms
crumble into ashes.
Last year's peace
weeps into war.
We sing of Gethsemane
amid new tears, new bleeding.
The screaming bombs
burn crosses in our hearts—
this too is God's story.
Lent comes,
but also Ramadan's fast,
Passover's freedom memory,
Easter's crazy contradiction.
Faith is born of prayer
and sings with courage,
while all the children
of the earth
shelter in the wings of God
awaiting our embrace.

Maren C. Tirabassi, U.S.A.

O Christ, as the spear opened a passage to your heart we pray that you would ever keep a way open to the hearts of your people everywhere. . . .

Ecuador

Yisu ke pichhe main chalne laga, na lautunga, na lautunga. . . .
I have begun to follow Jesus, no turning back, no turning back. . . .

Source unknown, Pakistan

As the needle naturally turns to the north when it is touched by the magnet, so it is fitting, O Lord, that your servant should turn to love and praise and serve you; seeing that out of love you were willing to endure such grievous pangs and sufferings.

Raymond Lull, Bugi, Algeria
(stoned June 30, 1519)

Benediction

Leader: Sisters and brothers, let us claim the freedom Christ gives us by his self-giving on the cross.
　　　May he enable us to serve together in faith, hope and love.
　　　Go in peace and serve the Lord.

Congregation: Thanks be to God.

　Source unknown

Handwashing Ceremony for Maundy Thursday

St. Merri, Centre Pastoral Halles Beaubourg, in Paris, is a church renowned for spiritual vitality and vibrant worship. Each week a group of lay volunteers works with the priest to plan worship. The following is part of a Maundy Thursday service planned by lay volunteers:

During the Maundy Thursday worship in 1994, the congregation was asked to rise from the sanctuary and walk to the side chapels. There, tables had been covered with cloths and set with a bowl of water and a reader at each table. Congregants went two by two to the bowls and as they washed and dried each other's hands, the reader read the passage from John's gospel where Jesus washed the disciples' feet and called them to service. (The pace was slow and meditative, so that sometimes the reader read the passage twice through as each pair washed hands.)

After the handwashing, people returned to the sanctuary. Children carrying potted plants processed to the front and constructed a "Garden of Gethsemane" in the area in front of the altar. The congregation came forward and stood in the "garden" as the priest spoke quietly about how the garden was a time of waiting and darkness. To end the service, the congregation simply experienced this waiting in silence, leaving one by one as each person was ready.

　Gretchen Amussen, Paris, France

Arising from the Ashes

Guarjila and many other villages in the Department of Chalatenango were forcibly depopulated by the Armed Forces' bombing and ground incursions in the early 1980s. Most of the survivors fled and sought refuge in camps in Honduras. Seven years later, the refugees organized a repatriation to repopulate their abandoned homes in El Salvador. In the following selection, a North American priest writes about his visit to Guarjila during Holy Week in 1988:

" . . . I also remembered what I had seen that morning. We had walked to San Antonio de los Ranchos, a small community hidden in the hills of Chalatenango. The day before, a battle had taken place between the Army and the guerrillas. The village looked like a ghost town. The church had been bombed, houses were destroyed, and the plaza had been turned into rubble. Many other small villages suffer the same violence.

This is the fundamental mystery of Christianity—the emergence of life from death. The people understand this mystery.

Perhaps some light can be shed on this by describing what happened on Holy Thursday. On this day the Church commemorates the Christian commandment to love and serve one another in the washing of the feet. Here in Guarjila, however, the people used another symbol. An old man gave a young widow an armful of firewood, and she gave him some tortillas. These gestures expressed service to one another. This new symbol of firewood and tortillas added an important element: the mutuality of service and the giving and taking which builds community.

This is how they expressed their faith: To go from death to life is to grow from individualism to community. These people who pray for their dead, also pray for their oppressors. We prayed for their 3,000 murdered family members and also for the soldiers who committed these crimes. Then one woman said, 'May we always be able to love, to hope and to forgive.'

During the Holy Week, I became convinced that sharing is a great truth that cannot be concealed. The oppressors will not triumph over the victims, just as they did not triumph over Jesus. From Guarjila, a thousand men, women and children proclaim to the world that they have not been vanquished. They proclaim a new way to live, oriented toward community service, work and hope. They speak of a new way to die and of resurrection."

El Salvador

Nama-Kirtana

(This Sapta-Ratnavali, or "Row of Seven Jewels," is a reflection on the names of Christ, through which we see his commitment to a needy world. We take refuge in him as he moves on towards the cross in his ministry. In each stanza, the opening titles are chanted. Other lines are sung. All join in the "Saranam."*)

1. Nazaretha-Pravadi, Prapanca-Jyoti:
(Prophet of Nazareth, Light of the World)
You have pointed to God's new world soon to arise;
Saranam, saranam, saranam.
You have shown up our false life, our darkness, our lies;
Saranam, saranam, saranam.

2. Abhishikta Natha, Davida-Kumara:
(Anointed Lord, Son of David)
Though anointed as prophet, as priest and as king;
Saranam, saranam, saranam.
In your lowly compassion your triumph we sing;
Saranam, saranam, saranam.

3. Dina-Naraputra, Loka-Vimochaka:
(Humble Son of Man, World Redeemer)
Your own life given gladly the whole world to free;
Saranam, saranam, saranam.
Your new cov'nant gives hope that a new life will be;
Saranam, saranam, saranam.

4. Isvara-Sevaka, Prema Svarupa:
(Servant of God, Embodiment of Love)
Till on earth for all people true justice is found;
Saranam, saranam, saranam.
By deep love and its dharma* you ever are bound;
Saranam, saranam, saranam.

5. Daridra-Upachara, Badhita-Bandhu:
(Minister to the poor, Brother of the oppressed)
Till your life's awful travail bears fruit for the lost;
Saranam, saranam, saranam.
You'll not give up, nor lose heart at seeing the cost;
Saranam, saranam, saranam.
You will never break the weak, crushed reed,
Nor snuff out the flickering flame that stands in need,
Till all the poor are saved from evil greed;
Saranam, saranam, saranam.

6. Pradhana-Yajaka, Visva Madhyavarthi:
(High Priest, Interceder for all)
From God's worship to drive out corruption you dare;
Saranam, saranam, saranam.
God's house now is a place for all people to share;
Saranam, saranam, saranam.
King of the meek ride on in lowly power,
Riding on your donkey to the final hour,
Ride on through treachery, through sweat and prayer;
Saranam, saranam, saranam.

7. Papi-Mitra, Dukha-Purusha:
(Friend of Sinners, Man of Sorrows)
By the wounds you receive we have all been made whole;
Saranam, saranam, saranam.
By your life of compassion for us a new goal;
Saranam, saranam, saranam.
Lamb of God, you take away the whole world's sins,
Lamb of God, your suffering mercy each heart wins,
Lamb of God, your love our service now constrains;
Saranam, saranam, saranam.
Saranam, saranam, saranam.

*Saranam—refuge.
*Dharma—the basic principles of cosmic or individual existence.

United Theological College, Bangalore, India

Palm Sunday, He Qi, China

Ideas to Celebrate the Passion and Resurrection

(During the Latin American Art and Liturgy Seminar, held in Rio de Janeiro, February 1993, one of the workshops was in charge of developing liturgical resources for Easter. The results of this group's work are presented in the following memoir of the seminar. This material was used by the participants in their own communities.)

Passion and Resurrection

(The first group was to experience the Passion and Resurrection as "carrying equal weight." This idea arose because many communities meet only on Easter Sunday, often without taking into account the Passion. The Passion and Resurrection are inseparable, even though we might want to live the intensity of each day separately. However, on Good Friday [Passion], it would be impossible not to live the certainty of the Resurrection. Nor can the Resurrection be celebrated on Easter Sunday in the attempt to eliminate all the suffering Jesus experienced. Here, the key word is "contrast.")

Suggestions for the Celebration

At the beginning of the worship service, there are no flowers on the altar. A Salvadoran cross is placed on the altar, back to front. The chairs or benches are arranged in such a way that two corridors are formed, in the shape of a cross. As a sign of Christ's suffering and of our sins, a large crown of thorns is placed on a table. This introduces the moment of confession, which takes place with the lights turned down. Still in darkness, small candles decorated with symbols/Bible verses/words that represent signs of life, are distributed. At that same time, a group of persons moves into the corridors in the shape of a cross. These persons are dressed with long flowing clothing, tied with sashes that can be embroidered or painted with symbols of life (fruit, fish, flowers, joyful colors, instruments, light, etc.). However, no one can see them yet, since the light is off.

The instruments begin to play an Alleluya. One person comes in with the Paschal candle, which has been lit, moving with liturgical gestures and showing the light to all present. The instruments could also be brought in, moving forward from the back, and come into the church with the Paschal candle.

The person carrying the Paschal candle walks to the crossing of the two corridors, and makes a long and slow movement toward each one of the cross's "arms," as if showing the light to the four corners of the earth. After this, the candle of the person standing in the middle of this cross-corridor is lit, and the Paschal candle is taken up to the altar.

After his or her candle is lit, the person in the center of the cross also makes liturgical gestures, as if showing the light to everyone, and the four candles closest to it are lit, while the Alleluya is sung. The rest of the candles within the cross corridor are lit, in sequence. As each person's candle is lit, he/she makes gestures showing the lit candle (at the same time showing the symbols of life on their clothing), continuing to sing the Alleluya. When the entire "cross" is lit, the people within it begin to light the candles of the congregation, until all the candles have been lit and the entire church is singing the Alleluya. The Salvadoran cross is turned to face front and lilies are brought up to the altar. At another point (departure, blessing), these lilies could be given as a token to each person.

Sunday—The Sound of the Stone Moving

(The second group worked on the sound of the tomb opening on the Sunday of Resurrection. This idea, however, could also be adapted to end the celebration on Friday, remembering the closing of the tomb.)

(Reproducing the sound of the stone moving:)

The sound should begin very low, increase gradually, and stop suddenly (for this there should be a leader). The movement should always be vigorous. While sitting, some people begin to stomp their feet on the floor, in quick movements. One person should begin this movement, and others join in gradually, until the noise is really loud. At a sign from the leader, the movement is suddenly stopped.

Suggestions for the Liturgy

The worship service begins with the door closed, while people gather outside the church (expectation, waiting). From inside the temple, the sound of the stone moving is heard, and the door opens slowly. Three women are standing before the altar, and say, "Christ has Risen!" The choir or community responds, "Truly, Christ has Risen." The congregation enters, singing the Alleluya (or another song). When everyone is in place, the community may express the mystery of the Resurrection through a suggested gesture (or a spontaneous one).

Each of the women standing before the altar has an object in her hands (for example: a cocoon, a seedling, an Easter egg). One after the other, they explain the meaning of their symbol with regard to the Resurrection, while placing it on the altar. (For example: In the same way as this cocoon is the sign of a new life that will spring forth, we also wish to be the sign of a new world of justice.)

Good Friday—The Sound of Nails

(This group wanted to plan a celebration that would reflect our daily problems. The ideas was based on the seven words or phrases spoken by Jesus on the cross, expressed through the stations and the sound of the nails hammered into Jesus' hands and feet. The proposal is to have a procession in the church or outdoors. For a church in a large urban center, it could be possible for this procession to take place by bus, selecting points in the city as stations for reflection [hospital, jail, orphanage, rest home, school, government building, etc.]. Good Friday . . . Friday of Passion: silence, death/execution, suffering of the people/injustice, mourning, starkness/take down decorations, blindness/perplexity. . . .)

Suggestions for the Liturgy

The entry is closed and the people gather at the door. The chairs or benches have been arranged in such a way that the procession can walk between them. In each station, there is an unlit candle on the floor, and a person (or people) standing there, representing an issue (for example, women, street children, racism, margination, workers, the problems of a peasant family, violence, human rights, housing, etc.). The altar is prepared beforehand.

The church opens and the congregation is invited to visit the seven stations. The musicians (who walk along with the procession) lead music, and the procession begins carrying a wood cross and a hammer, which are passed from one person to another.

At the first station: while everyone listens to the reflection at the station, one person places the cross on the floor and begins to pound nails into it. The candle is lit and the person representing this station joins in the procession. Everyone continues to walk on, singing along the way.

This is repeated at each station. After each one has been visited, the procession moves up to the altar, and the seven candles are placed on it, one after the other. While placing the candle on the altar, each person says a brief prayer of intercession for the theme he/she has just presented to the community.

From Thursday to Sunday: Continuous Sequence

(The last group worked on the idea that it is impossible to separate Thursday, Good Friday, Saturday, and Easter Sunday. The experience of the Paschal mystery involves a celebration that encompasses all these days, considered as a whole.)

Thursday (Solitude/Solidarity/Solitude)

In the center area set aside for the liturgy, there should be some red cloth with the elements for communion. The chairs are arranged around this altar, with their backs turned to it. People come in and sit down. Each person is facing in a different direction: we aren't completely present. Each person brings his/her own worries, concerns, problems. . . . They sit there immersed in their own individuality (solitude).

After leaving our worries outside this circle, we can meet and share together. We turn our chairs around, look at each other, and begin to share the Lord's Supper (solidarity).

During Jesus' last meal with his disciples, there is some selfishness and betrayal. There is also a farewell, a sense of holding on to each other desperately before the catastrophe. After communion, we replace the red cloth with a black one. Or, we can place the black cloth on top of the red one, or use one that is red on one side and black on the other and simply turn it over. A single candle is placed on the altar. The chairs are turned to their original positions (with their backs to the altar), and we listen to Jesus' prayer in Gethsemane (Lk 23:41–44) (solitude).

The feet-washing ceremony could take place on this day, especially with groups that are discriminated against in society or with community leaders. This ceremony could try to portray or contrast those people towards whom Jesus showed his solidarity, and those who abandoned him.

Good Friday (Suffering and Mourning)

The lights should be dim. The furniture should be arranged in such a way that it expresses sadness. In front, there is a dark cloth with one single candle. Everything in the temple (altar, cross, pulpit, candelabra, pictures, musical instruments, etc.) should be covered with dark cloths, with rope wrapped around them. A person could also be tied up with rope. This rope expresses the violence of Christ's death. A sword, spear, hammer and nails could also be placed on the altar. The liturgy ends with Psalm 22, beginning with the words, "My God, my God, why have you forsaken me?" The candle is put out.

Saturday

The place should be arranged in such a way that it expresses absence, nostalgia, memories. During the worship, the lights start dim and go up gradually. By midnight, the temple should be completely lit. A circle can be formed, with people sitting on the floor. Silence is the tone for this celebration of anticipation. A photo album can be circulated, with photographs of people who have left the community or of events in the community's life. This suggests a moment for memories. Everyone should look at the album in silence. The color: ash gray.

Sunday

The altar should be decorated with bright colors, flowers, the elements of the Eucharist, cultural objects (typical food, musical instruments, etc.). White should be the outstanding color. The worship service could begin by removing the dark cloths from the furniture and exchanging the dark cloth on the cross for a white one.

The space should be well lit, as a sign of feasting and hope. The crown of thorns and bitter herbs should remain on the altar as a reminder of Christ's suffering and the pain of the community, not so much as a negative sign but rather as the hope of salvation. The Eucharist should "close" in the form of an agape.

This celebration could also take place outdoors, at daybreak on Sunday morning.

Silvana Cesar Vargas, Latin American Council of Churches

O Majesty, O Magnificence, O Mystery, come!
Be hammer, and break our indifference.
Be sun, and splinter our shadows.
Be wind, and scatter our despair.
Yea, in the dry country of our souls,
Let thy grace rain;
So that we take root in thee, and grow.
Make of us trees strong in all seasons,
Bearing good fruit,
Giving shade to all weariness
And shelter to them that are lost.
So we pray to the glory of Jesus Christ
Who made the crosstree
Green and flourishing forever.
Amen.

Arnold Kenseth, U.S.A.

Bill Wallace, Aotearoa/New Zealand

Your Cross

When I think of Good Friday
I think of your cross.

Today I see crosses
In chapels and churches
Surmounting steeples
On altars.
Brass crosses. Silver crosses. Gold.
Some studded with jewels
All surrounded by walls.

When I think of Good Friday
I think of your cross.

It was out on the open highway
And stood between thieves.
Soldiers. Gamblers. Drunkards.
All sorts of people.

Suddenly I feel something is
    wrong.

        Dayalan Devanesen, Australia/India

The Cross

Leader: The cross . . .

All: We shall take it.

Leader: The bread . . .

All: We shall break it.

Leader: The pain . . .

All: We shall bear it.

Leader: The joy . . .

All: We shall share it.

Leader: The gospel . . .

All: We shall live it.

Leader: The love . . .

All: We shall give it.

Leader: The light . . .

All: We shall cherish it.

Leader: The darkness . . .

All: God shall perish it.

Amen.

        John L. Bell, Iona, Scotland

Crosses

Almost all the crosses
I have ever seen
seem much the same
despite their differing
size, shape, texture—
some are empty
others bear
cosmetic
Christs
but few
if any
present
the crosses
of our world
crosses of plants and animals
under threat of extinction,
crosses of people suffering
unjust imprisonment,
starvation, torture,
personal and institutional
violence.
Sometimes I wish
I could place
real bodies
upon these crosses
bodies of dead whales
dead native birds and trees
bodies of dead, dying, emaciated
and mutilated people;
for at the intersection
of the horizontal
and vertical
elements of life
there is always
a body
and in the body of Christ
I see
all the bodies
of this world.

        Bill Wallace, Aotearoa/New
        Zealand

(Milton Lopez is a five-year-old Nicaraguan who was seriously injured by a Contra mortar attack.)

Who will speak my words now
and ask my questions?

I have no words to tell my story,
but there must be a way to make the world listen,
even though I am five years old
and speak only Spanish—

if I could speak,
but I am missing half my jaw.

Who will speak my words now
and ask my questions?

My family is poor,
and with those who were starving,
went to cut coffee in the mountains,
where fighting began before I was born.

The scream of mortars was not known to us
before I fell slower than the rest—
but not as slow as the fire against my face.

Who will speak my words now
and ask my questions?

When was the decision made
that I would never shout with joy or anger
and sing psalms in church
or disturb the priest's homily?
What were you thinking when you fired the shells,
when you shipped the weapons,
and when you signed the order that destroyed
all the words I want to speak,
all the questions I need to ask?

I am not a story.
I am not a debate.
I am a prayer.

Who will speak my words now
and ask my questions?

Amaya Lopez (Milton's mother), Nicaragua

Rini Templeton, U.S.A./Mexico

Holy Saturday/Easter Eve

In Maputo Region, the United Congregational Church has a custom of holding what is essentially an all-night Easter Vigil. It begins in the late evening of Saturday with prayers, singing, scripture and continues all night until at the earliest morning light the women join those of other nearby churches, spilling into the streets banging rhythm instruments or pans and singing loudly throughout the neighborhood "Jesu Kristu i vukile" (Jesus Christ is risen)—reliving the tremendous excitement of the women who went to the tomb and then had to tell the world what they found. By the time the sun really rises, they are back at the church for the main worship of Easter Day. Although a service is held later at the regular hour it is quite anti-climactic and poorly attended.

Ruth Brandon Minter, Mozambique

In the Fields Where Rice Is Planted

In the fields where rice is planted in the water's womb,
Or where cattle gasp and die upon the parched earth's tomb,
Within the peasant mud or bamboo dwelling place
God is found in the people of the land:
In their songs of pain and joy,
In their dreams and dark despair
Bethlehem and Calvary are unfolding everywhere.

Where the butterflies take wing and highrise buildings soar,
Or where poverty and wealth destroy both rich and poor,
Within the celebrations of this Asian soil
God is found in the people of the land:
In their songs of pain and joy,
In their dreams and dark despair
Bethlehem and Calvary are unfolding everywhere.

Bethlehem and Calvary are not the final page,
Empty tombs and broken chains announce the Gospel age
When all oppression, greed and war flee ravished lands
Giving space for a just and loving peace:
In their triumph songs of joy,
In their dreams beyond despair
Resurrection shall be shared by the people everywhere.

Bill Wallace, Aotearoa/New Zealand

Midori Shibata, Japan

Easter

Worshippers gather before dawn Easter Sunday and go to the local graveyard by candlelight to look for Jesus' body. They don't find it, so they all return to the church joyously singing, "He is risen, He is risen, our Savior is risen," in the local language. By this time dawn has broken, and they have a sunrise service at the church.

   Nancy Lightfoot, Liberia

Swiss Easter Sunrise Celebration with Bonfire

(This tradition of lighting a bonfire on a hill on Easter morning is growing in Switzerland. Esther remarks that once she had to return to the parsonage to care for her baby after the sanctuary part of this service. Standing at the window she saw the torches moving up the hill and found it very moving to hear the trumpets' traditional Easter hymns ringing out over the hills.)

- At 5:30 a.m. the congregation meets in the dark church; each is given an unlit candle.
- Call to Worship—Ps 121
- Taizé song: "Im Dunkel unsrer Nacht, entzunde dein Feuer das niemals verloscht" (In the darkness of our night, light a fire that never ends) is sung one time here.
- Reading of the crucifixion and resurrection from Luke, in four parts, with meditations in between. After each meditation, the congregation sings, "Im Dunkel unsrer Nacht," one more repetition each time. (Instead of the Gospel of Luke, the readings from the classical orthodox Easter service can be used: Gn 1, Ex 13 and 14, Ez 37, and Jn 1.)
- Prayer
- Children carry the Easter light they have lighted in the cemetery in front of the church into the sanctuary, and light the altar candles with it. While the Easter candle is being brought into the church, someone sings "Christus Licht der Welt" ("Christ, Light of the World"), and the congregation answers, "Dir Sei Lob und Preis" ("We praise and adore you").
- Choir anthem about the Resurrection or light. (There is beautiful orthodox music for this.)
- The Easter light is passed to each member of the congregation until the candles of the worshippers are all alight.
- Prayer
- Resurrection hymn with organ
- Lit on the Easter light, a torch carries the light outside. A procession forms to walk up the hill with many torches. At the top, a pile of wood has been laid previously. With the torches and candles a big Easter fire is lit. Trumpets proclaim the Easter message. Easter songs are sung to praise God, and there is a prayer in which everyone can join.
- We return to the church to have a wonderful Easter breakfast together. Afterwards, each denomination has its own Easter morning service.

Dieter and Esther Bühler-Weidmann, Rorbas, Switzerland

Resurrection

I am in love with life,
the sun, the howling of mountain
   winds,
the storm, the clap of thunder,
the songbirds' joyful singing,
the rabbits' delight,
the barking dogs,
and the promenade of the snails
after the rain.

I am in love with life,
the deep chant of rebel gypsies,
ancestral lament of the flute,
the violent dance of the Russians,
shy smile of the Indian children.

I am in love with life,
dark skin or white,
the shine of Black cheeks,
hair the color
of cornsilk.
I love the ants that never rest,
the lowing cows

and the sound of their bells
clanging in the Alps.

I am in love with life,
the buzzing of gluttonous bees,
the mischievous squirrels,
the fox's wonderful fur,
the musk deer's beautiful form
and the gallantry of the horse
with his mane to the wind.

I am in love with life,
the plain little violets
appearing like a miracle
defying even the winter's ice,
the tiny yellow primroses,
delicate, fresh anemones,
luminous narcissus
and the wonderful aroma
of lilies pouring in through my
   window.

     Julia Esquivel, Guatemala

A Special Easter Prayer

Creation's Lord, I give my silent thanks:

- for the times I have been startled by the world's beauty,
- for the selfless love I have found in others,
- for the humble people of courage who labor on with little freedom but with incandescent inner joy,
- for the peace that pervades my life and others,
- for the myriad omens of impending new life I encounter every day.

Amen.

Richard Wilcox, Spain

In Thy Hand

In thy hand, we see the whole cos-
    mos,
Heaven and earth reflect
the mystery of thy handiwork.

In thy hand, we see a little child,
Men and women are recaptured
by the event of Bethlehem.

In thy hand, we see the scar of the
    cross.
Sin and death are vanquished
by thy suffering on Golgotha.

In thy hand, behold a new light,
Day and night are transformed
in the glory of Easter morning.

> Masao, Fumiko, Makoto, and
> Yukako Takenaka, Japan

Collect

Risen Lord,
You walk through this earth
using the feet of very imperfect disciples;
may every race and generation take time to
look up and see you,
draw nearer, listen and worship,
and turn to follow you.

Congregation: Amen.

> Australia

Sharing through Interceding

(A sung litany with spoken specific concerns after each two verses.)

Leader: Risen Christ Jesus, risen from your dark tomb
    Death could not bind you, you broke out as from a womb.

Congregation: Share through us your presence, risen Christ today.

Leader: Light of the whole world, you leave no one in despair,
    Strengthen weak faith, that we with you great deeds may dare.

Congregation: Share through us your presence, risen Christ today.

Leader: Chief Shepherd of us all, you gave your life for the lost
    Help us guide the scattered; no careful counting of the cost.

Congregation: Share through us your presence, risen Christ today.

Leader: Jesus the joy of life, now begin your dance of bliss,
    The whole world rejoices, tune each heart to ways of peace.

Congregation: Share through us your presence, risen Christ today.

Leader: Companion of the needy, always near to those who seek,
    Use us as your body to bind the wounds of all the weak.

Congregation: Share through us your presence, risen Christ today.

Leader: Head of God's new creation, every creature now is called
    To live in your freedom, men and women, young and old.

Congregation: Share through us your presence, risen Christ today.

Leader: Strong Hero of the lowly, may all oppressed find hope in you;
    Turn every life to loving, your cross for us is powerfully true.

Congregation: Share through us your presence, risen Christ today.

> United Theological College, Bangalore, India

Story for an Easter Sermon

As I was skimming through some reading material the other day, the word "ritual" came into focus. Ritual is something that as a society we can not get away from. I remember years past when one of my anthropology professors gave us a tribe to study. The Nacirema were a people of puzzlement to me.

These Nacirema people used daily water ceremonies; some of the women of this group baked their heads in ovens, painted their faces and toes; the elders were known to place drugs down into a swirl of water to be carried away somewhere underground. Nearly each morning these people would ingest a white liquid into their bodies for strength.

The Nacirema is American spelled backwards. "I wonder what others think of our rituals and culture?" May we find meaningful rituals in prayer and expressions of love this Easter Season and move aside the stones that need to be moved. Who will roll the big stone aside? Do we know what the big stone is (what is the obstacle?)? Who will roll away the stone for us from the entrance to the tomb?

Janet Ross-Heiner, U.S.A./Nicaragua

Leader: Let us pray for the whole world, for which Jesus lived and died and rose again.
In your mercy—

Congregation: Risen Lord, hear our prayer.

Leader: Let us pray for growing unity between the churches.
In your mercy—

Congregation: Risen Lord, hear our prayer.

Leader: Let us pray that this Easter may be a time of reconciliation for all who are estranged or at enmity with each other.
In your mercy—

Congregation: Risen Lord, hear our prayer.

Leader: Let us pray for those who live in fear and doubt, that they may be comforted.
In your mercy—

Congregation: Risen Lord, hear our prayer.

Leader: We pray that by our words and in our lives we may be pointers to your living presence in the world.
In your mercy—

Congregation: Risen Lord, hear our prayer.

Source Unknown

Strong and gentle Christ,
Our deaths are part of your death,
Our resurrections part of your resurrection,
Our hopes part of your hope.
Holy Spirit, baptize us with fire,
purge us and enliven us that your
passion for Justice, Peace and
Community may burn within us
and set the whole world alight.
Parent, child and creative spirit,
all radiance and mystery are yours,
here and everywhere, now and forever. Amen.

The Proclamation of the Mystery

(*A candle is held up for all to see.*)

Christ is the light of the world.

(*A container of water is also held up.*)

Christ is the water of life.

Bill Wallace, Aotearoa/
New Zealand

Messenger of Marvels

(This can be sung to the tune Noël Nouvelet.)

Messenger of marvels, challenger of sleep,
Light is born—and quickens life within the deep.
God, quicken us, empower and set us free:
Light is come, like treasure salvaged from the sea.

Truths, obscured and buried, speak in language plain;
Old wells are unstopped, and water springs again.
Once locked in folly, now we find the key:
Truth is come, like treasure salvaged from the sea.

Beauty's gold is rescued, dross is skimmed away;
Hoards from secret places shine anew today.
Give we our hearts to God's fierce alchemy:
Beauty comes, like treasure salvaged from the sea.

Love of Christ, rejected, buried in the tomb,
Now is resurrected, leaps the prison-room.
Called out* from death, Christ's living Body, we:
Love is come, like treasure salvaged from the sea.

Secret, silent Kingdom—jettisoned, denied —
Rises from the deep and dances on the tide:
In and around us, waiting patiently:
Kingdom come! like treasure salvaged from the sea.

*"Ekklesia" [Church] is that which is "called out."

Kate Compston, England

Easter

We do not make Easter happen,
nor do we cause the sun to shine.
God does it all—
God made our Savior rise!
By dawning light
While God takes towel in hand
to dry the dew,
We sing our glad "Hosannas,"
While darkness gives way to light,
And death itself, by Easter magic,
becomes the doorway to eternal life.

Richard Wilcox, Spain

And the Waters Will Flow from Your Altar, Lord

And the waters will flow from your altar, Lord
And flood the earth.
And we will be like a garden watered,
cared for,
exposed to life.

Oh! let these waters come,
Impetuous and pure,
and destroy the powers
and clean the paths
which my people will take,
which my people will take,
singing and rejoicing
in an endless celebration,
the Word, Life, Freedom
and the Resurrection!

And the waters will flow from your altar, Lord,
and clean away the debris
and we will have courage to act,
to serve,
to change the world.

And the waters will flow from your altar, Lord,
life will be rekindled,
And we will see the new creation,
act,
of your love.

      Simei Monteiro, Brazil

Conference of European Churches

15 *Pentecost, Saints, and the Marking of Seasons and Days*

Spirit, tongues, witness. Remember, martyr, witness. This chapter includes resources for the festival of Pentecost and for "saints" or remembrance occasions. The worship experience of both of these involves a similar expression of honor for those who have shared their faith and commitment to carrying it forward. Saints' days are various—All Saints' Days of November 1 and 2; the Latin American and Caribbean solemn commemoration, on October 12, of the invasion and conquest of their land; the August marking of the first use of nuclear weapons; the anniversary date of Wounded Knee or of Archbishop Oscar Romero's murder; Memorial Day; Holocaust remembrance; and the Martin Luther King, Jr., holiday. Any of these may be the occasion for recollection and recommitment.

We live in the natural rhythms of earth, and we are shaped by the seasons and delight in their changing beauty. The last resources of this chapter celebrate the seasons, both the great turning of weather patterns and the social rhythms of our communities of faith.

Pentecost, Zhang Guijie, China

Pentecost

The Hope of the Coming of Christ

We hope you come like the wind
At this time of despair
And that with you bring
A breath of fresh air.

We hope that you clearly say
To this poor human race,
The ancient, the beautiful,
Words of truth and grace.

We hope that you see now
True acts of friendship
And that you be the joy
Of a new human fellowship.

We hope that you come soon,
To falseness overcome,
the watchword of promise
hands open and free.

Jaci Maraschin, Brazil

Pieces

Pieces
A world in pieces
A life in pieces . .
We want to live new times, Lord God.
We want to see flourishing signs of hope
that we may put the pieces together
and rebuild a united world.
We cry out for the Spirit of Unity,
so that from the four corners of the Earth
the breath of new life may caress all beings . . .
Come, Spirit of God,
spread over nations in conflict in former Yugoslavia
spread over groups and factions in South Africa,
spread over gangs of Blacks and Hispanics in New York and L.A.
spread over . . .
May a new wind blow
to fill us with desire and strength
so the pieces may become one body
the world's body
the people's body
because you created us as one, and that is how you want us to be.

Ernesto Barros Cardoso, Brazil

Alpha and Omega, Midori Shibata, Japan

Come, Holy Spirit

Lord, Holy Spirit,
You are as the mother eagle with her young,
Holding them in peace under your feathers.
On the highest mountain you have built your nest,
Above the valley, above the storms of the world,
Where no hunter ever comes.
Lord, Holy Spirit,
You are the bright cloud in whom we hide,
In whom we know already that
the battle has been won.
You bring us to our Brother Jesus
To rest our heads upon his shoulder.
Lord, Holy Spirit,
In the love of friends you are building a new house
Heaven is with us when you are with us.
You are singing your song in the hearts of the poor.
Guide us, wound us, heal us. Bring us to God.

    James K. Baxter, Aotearoa/New Zealand

Come, Holy Spirit! (English)
Komm, Heiliger Geist! (German)
Viens, Esprit Saint! (French)
Ven, Espíritu Santo! (Spanish)

Open Your Hearts

The poet Li Si has said: "The mountain cherishes the soil which gives it height; the sea does not disdain the water which gives it depth." The boundaries of the realm of the Spirit depend on the narrowness or breadth of the heart.

If our embrace is narrow, we cannot put our arms about another. If we are partial to our own group or attack those who are different: this too is displeasing to God. If we take every small thing to heart, if we cannot forget past grudges, can our hearts be vast as the ocean?

The great land supports the myriad creatures. There is nothing that does not feel the warmth of the sun. But how narrow my heart, smaller than the chicken's roost or the pig's enclosure; empty but for ambition. How can it soar with the eagle or race with swift horses?

I pray God to open my heart. Only then can I find peace. May it be high as a mountain peak, deep as the sea—when, Lord, when?

    Wang Weifan, China

All Saints' Day, Days of Remembrance

The God of Columba

Leader: The God of Columba, the wandering one . . .

All: Stay with us now.

Leader: The God of Clare, the poor one . . .

All: Stay with us now.

Leader: The God of Luther, the reforming one . . .

All: Stay with us now.

Leader: The God of John 23rd, the enlightening one . . .

All: Stay with us now.

Leader: The God of Sojourner Truth, the free one . . .

All: Stay with us now.

Leader: The God of Bonhoeffer, the brave one . . .

All: Stay with us now.

Leader: The God of Martin Luther King, the just one . . .

All: Stay with us now.

Leader: The God of Teresa, the kind one . . .

All: Stay with us now.

Leader: The God of Desmond Tutu, the wanted one . . .

All: Stay with us now.

Leader: The God of Mohandas Gandhi, the peacemaker . . .

All: Stay with us now.

Leader: The God of the women of Greenham, the witnessing ones . . .

All: Stay with us now.

Leader: The God of George MacLeod, rebuilder of the common life . . .

All: Stay with us now.

Leader: The God and Father of our Lord Jesus Christ,
    Crucified, Dead, Risen, and Ascended . . .

All: Stay with us this night and every night.
    Amen.

    John L. Bell, Iona, Scotland

Sanctuary Prayer

Leader: We stand with Sojourner Truth and Harriet Tubman who followed the call of their conscience in freeing the slaves through the underground railroad.

All: Presente.

Leader: We stand with Rosa Parks who was imprisoned for demanding her right to sit in the front of the bus.

All: Presente.

Leader: We stand with Martin Luther King who was imprisoned for non-violent protests against laws of discrimination.

All: Presente.

Leader: We stand with Raoul Wallenberg who fought to save the Jews from Nazi death camps.

All: Presente.

Leader: We stand with Ita, Maura, Dorothy and Jean who were raped and killed for serving the poor.

All: Presente.

Leader: We stand with Oscar Romero who gave his life for defending the rights of the persecuted poor of El Salvador.

All: Presente.

Leader: We stand with Ivan Betancourt and companions killed at Olancho, Honduras.

All: Presente.

Leader: We stand with all the poor, the persecuted, the disappeared and the refugees of Central America.

All: Presente.

Leader: We stand with sanctuary workers all over the world who seek to give shelter to refugees.

All: Presente.

U.S.A.

Some Acts of Commemoration of Contemporary Witnesses

(One very informal service to commemorate the Communion of Saints used in Britain commences with a brief period of discussion naming some of the saints especially dear to those present, and singling out some of the qualities and gifts for which thanks are to be given and intercession made.)

All: We remember, O God, those through whom you have acted, in the world, in the church, and in our own experience. We invoke their names, that they may stand beside us and provide us with the insight of their lives and the encouragement of their prayers:

Leader: Great convert, Paul, missionary and "man in Christ":

All: Stand beside us.

Leader: Little poor woman of Calcutta, Mother Teresa:

All: Stand beside us.

Leader: John, exile on Patmos, with a vision and care for the seven churches of Asia:

All: Stand beside us.

Leader: For the faithful priests and pastors of our earlier years, whose teaching and example brought us here tonight:

All: Stand beside us.

Leader: Victims of Hiroshima, Nagasaki, and of the slaughter of the holy innocents:

All: Stand beside us.

Leader: Doctor and writer, St. Luke, who preserved for us the story of Emmaus and of a risen Christ who mysteriously walks with his people:

All: Stand beside us.

Leader: Neighbour, casual acquaintance, brother and sister in Christ, in all that you have been, all that you are, and all that you will be:

All: Stand beside us.

England

16670

The concentration camp number of Blessed Father Maximilian Kolbe of Poland focuses attention and prayer on all victims of conscience, past and present, including those many persons without a "number" who have "disappeared" in so many countries.

Poland

Remembering Archbishop Oscar Romero

(During his years as Archbishop of San Salvador, Monsignor Oscar Romero lived in a cottage adjacent to a cancer hospital staffed by Carmelite nuns. One of the sisters, a close friend of Monsignor Romero, was present at the Mass in the hospital chapel when Romero was assassinated on March 24, 1980. She offered this testimony about his life:)

Monsignor Romero's last homily was beautiful. He spoke as if he knew that he was going to be killed. He said several times that if a grain of wheat does not die, it cannot bear fruit. When he finished his homily, he walked to the center of the sanctuary. He died as Christ died. Today he intercedes for all the poor and for all his flock.

A journalist once asked Monsignor Romero if he was afraid when he denounced injustice and abuses. Monsignor said that he was afraid and that he knew what was going to happen to him. He also said that he forgave those who were going to kill him. He knew that he would be resurrected in his people.

We should all have this faith and hope and love.

We have already witnessed Monsignor's resurrection in the people's faith and in their hope that one day things will change.

The grains of wheat are bearing fruit. Monsignor suffered from seeing so much injustice, so much death, so much of his people's blood shed. He often felt powerless. But now that he is near to God, he is able to do much.

We must be patient, and have faith in God and the Virgin Mary, the Queen of Peace, to whom Monsignor was so devoted. We are sure that one day we will live in peace. Until then, we hope for the day when everyone will love each other.

"I solemnly assure you, unless the grain of wheat falls to the earth and dies, it remains just a grain of wheat. But if it dies, it produces much fruit." John 12:24

El Salvador

Our Ancestors, Presbyterian Church, U.S.A.

Christianity and Aizu

In 1590 Leo Gamo Ujisato became Lord of Aizu, the area in which we now live. He built a castle, renamed the city where it was located (Wakamatsu), and brought in new industry such as the making of lacquerware and pottery. He had been baptized about five years before coming to Aizu and introduced Christianity to northern Japan.

In 1595 while in Kyoto, Gamo died at the age of forty. On his deathbed he said, "If I recover, I will return to Aizu and spread the gospel of Christ, so that everyone in Aizu becomes a Kirishitan (Christian).

At that time, Hideyoshi, virtual ruler of Japan, had already issued an edict against Christianity, an edict at first not strictly enforced. But in 1597, six Spanish Franciscans and twenty Japanese converts were put to death on crosses in Nagasaki.

It is said that perhaps as many as two thousand persons in Aizu (three hundred thousand in all of Japan) were Christians at the time the great persecution gained momentum. In the early seventeenth century, Christians either gave up their faith or were killed. It is said that there were more Christian martyrs in Japan than in ancient Rome!

Thirty minutes from where we live is a stone memorial at the Kirishitan-zuka (burial mound of the Christians), where many Christians were beheaded or put on crosses to die. It is an inspirational, yet a humbling experience to visit the Kirishitan-zuka, where so many Christians became martyrs. Whenever we go there, we ask ourselves, "Would we have the courage to die rather than renounce our faith in God?"

At the same time, we Christians (missionaries especially) must be careful that we do not become religious imperialists. The stories of Columbus and of missions in Hawaii and also in Japan remind us that the complicity of "Christian" mission in Western imperialism has had a negative impact. Therefore we must continually be willing to learn as well as teach, to change and grow, to allow God to take the initiative, as a wonderful new variety of Christianity heretofore unknown develops in the Asian context.

Armin Kroehler, Japan

As I light this candle the flame burns in the spirit of unity and hope, courage and integrity with dignity for all people.

We are a country blessed with diversity, and not everybody walks the same way, not everybody talks the same way, but most of all not everybody worships the same way. We Native Americans have a saying, "Do not judge others until you have walked in their moccasins." The Mexican-Americans have a saying, "Dime conquien andas y te digo quien eres"; translated, "Tell me who you walk with and I tell you who you are." Whom do you walk with? The true answer lies in what we will give each other as we walk together.

Do we walk with the poor of this country who give the gift of humility? Do we walk with the Native Americans who give the gift of respect to Mother Earth? Do we walk with the Hispanics who give the gift of celebration? Are we walking with the Blacks whose gift is resiliency? Do we walk with the Asian-Americans who bring the gift of inner peace? Whom are we walking with and what are we giving?

The Mayan people wear their history, philosophy and religion in their weavings. They never had to wait for their trees to be turned into paper, or paper into books. Their textiles were their books and each one wrote their own.

Janet Ross-Heiner, U.S.A./Nicaragua

Remembrances

We remember this bleeding woman, blood made her an outcast.

We remember all unnamed women who have toiled in fields until hands and feet have bled.

We remember our grandmother slaves, whipped and raped by masters.

We remember our sisters who died given no opportunity to be priests or pastors in the church they loved.

We remember women healers—our midwives, our holy mothers and keepers of ancient secrets.

We remember the bleeding wounds of women working in factories or in brothels.

We remember all our sisters who are widowed and childless because of the violence of war and conquest.

We remember our sisters and daughters whose blood is tainted by AIDS.

We remember women, our mothers, our sisters and our daughters, bleeding in their homes, battered by husbands and lovers.

We remember this bleeding woman who touched Jesus deeply. We also have been touched by the blood of a woman. Jesus acknowledged this woman, gave her life and risked solidarity with her—alone, unclean and marginalized.

Take a red thread. This thread is the trail of blood of our grandmothers, mothers, sisters, daughters—all women. We need to become tied to this trail, but we cannot do this by ourselves. While a partner ties the thread on your wrist, remember a particular woman who has touched you deeply.

Art and Liturgy Seminar participants, Rio de Janeiro, Brazil, February 1993

Remembrance

In remembrance of those—
throughout time, all over the world—
who have died in war,
    we pray urgently today
    that children, women and men
    may become makers of peace.

We pray for children growing up
in violent surroundings
or thinking, talking and playing in warlike ways.
    God, give to your people a new challenge,
    new ways in which to test their strength—
    in sharing power and risking non-violence.

We pray for women who are silent
while their male partners engage
in any part of the business of war.
    God, give to your people a new courage
    to question accepted dogma,
    and dream about the things that make for peace.

We pray for men brought up to believe
that might is manly—and for men who think otherwise
and so are labelled cowardly or weak.
    God, give to your people a new determination
    to struggle for justice and peace
    instead of for "extra shares" and superiority.

O God, we pray for—
    new awareness of the battlefield within us
    new ways of channelling aggressive instincts
    new thought-patterns, language and ideas
    new appreciation of the world as one community
    new methods of dialogue and negotiation
    new attempts to befriend those different from ourselves
    new readiness to forgive and reconcile,
    new visions, new love, new hope . . .
and a new faith that the peace that passes understanding
can reach out from within us to embrace the world.

    Kate Compston, England

(For another resource for All Saints' Day, see Nid's poem in Chapter 18, page 208.)

Conference of European Churches

Marking of Seasons and Sacred Days

Canticles

Winter

O God, your gifts abound where we
are:
The dart and whirl of winter birds,
Snowfall on hills and drift in the val-
leys,
Children booting home from school,
Food and laughter at the table,
Hands that sew and bake,
Love walking toward us.

So much, so much, and everywhere
And everyday given over and over!
And yourself, in the midst of it all:
Calling our names,
Clearing the way,
And keeping the watch!
Amen and amen and amen.

Spring

Now come the jonquil days
And the airs for new hearts.
Winds look white
And branches toss
And hope is
In the up and down.

Everywhere, O everywhere,
Are grackle, cowbird,
Redwing, robin,
Blue jay, finches,
Purple, gold;
And morning waking
To the mourning doves.

O God, you come to us
In colors, skies,
The days, the nights,
In touch, dream, smile.
O marvelous, fabulous, great
Is your coming among us. Amen.

Summer

All summer the days come to us, various, wide,
From mornings of meadows
Into the green dark and the nightfall
of stars.

We heard the weather gathering,
coming and going;
Small birds were among the berries;
The grasses dried,
And we felt our hearts in their sway-
ing.

And, then, always the trees,
The great combs of shade in our yards,
And the hundred thousand leaves for
our watching.

All was good and gift and grand!
And the days come on; the gift is still
given.
Thy goodness stays. Thy grandeur
stands. Amen.

Autumn

O God, everywhere the gold has
shaken down;
And the walks are wanders and wonders
Of russet, of blaze, and of green.

You give fields
And the tawny grass catching the
winds.
You tangle cold in the orchards
And crisp the pumpkin heaps.

Surely your harvest is in our hearts;
And your joy is in us
Tumbled high, pressed down, and
running over.

Blessed are your hands upon us this
day
And blessed are all seasons. Amen.

Arnold Kenseth, U.S.A.

A God for All Seasons

Springtime God, coming alive within us, like pale shoots
         thrusting through frozen earth,
   we need your persistent love
   to disturb the impacted soil of our hearts' rigidity.
Summer God, growing luxuriously, blossoming with heady scents,
         holding us in your warm embrace,
   we need these times of perceived presence
   to draw upon in cooler seasons.
Autumn God, falling and dying in Christ,
         etched with the colours of vulnerability,
   we need the fellowship of your wounds
   to dignify our brokenness.
Winter God, dormant and distant,
         starkly challenging our self-absorption,
   we need your austerity
   to nudge us into a warm compassion for your suffering ones.

    Kate Compston, England

Mid-Winter

(The need to celebrate Mid-Winter is, I believe, an essential part of rooting the Gospel in the soil and seasons of Aotearoa (see chapter 5, page 41). While Christmas is the Mid-Winter festival in the Northern Hemisphere, there is no corresponding liturgical celebration of the winter solstice in our Southern latitudes. Indeed many of the gatherings which have resulted from the current resurgence of interest in celebrating winter have even been labelled Mid-Winter Christmas events! Such occasions often fail to address the urgent need to develop a contextual spirituality in which winter has a place in its own right. Especially in Southern Aotearoa, winter forces us to reflect on what God is saying to us through the reality of darkness, and poses the question "Can darkness ever be holy?")

A Bidding Prayer

Sisters and brothers in Christ, now that we have passed the Winter solstice, let us celebrate the lengthening of the daylight, looking forward with hope to the coming of Spring and the season of Advent.
Let us again reawaken our sense of wonder at God's greatness which far exceeds even the warmth, beauty, light, life and health radiated by the sun, that with saints, mystics, artists, prophets, scholars and all humble servants of God we may exalt the One who is the origin and creator of all light.
But first let us remember all who are afraid of darkness, all who have lost their physical sight, all who are blinded by prejudice and misconception, all whose hearts are frozen, all who can only see bleakness ahead of them, all who do not know the warmth that comes from accepting their God-given worth.

Scripture Readings

(On the theme of darkness and light)

Gn 1:1–5, God creates both the darkness and the light. It is out of the
 darkness that light is born.
Ex 20:21, God is present in the darkness
Dt 5:23–24, God speaks from the darkness
Ps 139:12, Darkness and light are the same to God
Am 5:18, God comes in darkness
Is 9:2, A light is promised to those who walk in darkness
Jn 1:1–9, God's light shines in the darkness
Jn 8:12, Christ is the light of the world
Lk 16:8, The children of the light have many lessons to learn
1 Jn 1:5–7, Living in the light produces good relationships
Rv 21:22–25, Both night and day are superseded by the brilliance of God's
 presence.

Bill Wallace, Aotearoa/New Zealand

Body Moments for the Other-Festivals

(a poem for Liturgical Dancers celebrating the Church Year)

Dance radiant Lucia—
on dark midwinter,
hair crowned with candles,
arm-gifts and miracle bread
for the hungry
stars of hope, and
very quiet
balance.

Dance martyr Stephen—
knees bent
into a body-comma,
stone-throwing elbows sharp,
hurt face raised into
forgiveness.

Dance Transfiguration—
linked fingers shield eyes from eclipse-bright holiness
then reach across to build
booths like London bridges . . .
falling down,
falling down.

Dance the Palm walk—
sweet slapping feet, loud
green claps, empty mouths
open with the echo
of Hosanna.

Dance Ascension Day—
lonely longing arms,
reach up,
reach up,
tiptoe . . . gone.

Dance Trinity paradox—
intricate pattern of weaving steps
and syncopated rhythms, above
some deep harmony of
chords.

Dance John's Midsummer—
baptism and bonfires,
a solstice tarantella
and waving evergreen boughs
with cool drops of
promise.

Dance Michaelmas—
angels and dragons,
the great, bold gestures,
acknowledging the battle
in autumn flame.

Dance All Saints'—
dance all the stories,
dance all the little lives,
dance the ordinary time,
dance the many
incarnations.

Then dance the holy
everymorning,
and dance the sacred
allnightstide.

Notes:
St. Lucia's Day—December 13
St. Stephen's Day—December 26
Transfiguration—last Sunday in Epiphany
Palm Sunday—first day of Holy Week
Ascension Day—forty days after Easter
Trinity Sunday—first Sunday after Pentecost
Festival of St. John the Baptist—June 24
Michaelmas—September 29
All Saints' Day—November 1

Maren C. Tirabassi, U.S.A.

Robert Eddy, U.S.A.

PART IV

Resources for Communion in the Body of Christ

The ultimate source of our human ability to lift our voices, to join our hands, to walk the journey of our years and days is the presence of the Body of Christ in our midst. The Body of Christ is the church; the Body of Christ is that which was broken in the Upper Room and on Golgotha; the Body of Christ is the sacrament we share around the table. We call it Eucharist, Holy Communion, Lord's Supper, and it binds us truly together.

The sacramental resources presented in Chapter 16 are about Body and Blood, but they are not only about sharing wheat and grapes, but about sharing tortilla and atole, lime juice and cassava, puto and salabat juice, rice, coconut, and coffee. Whatever the sacramental elements may be—the prayers, customs, and celebrations of hope from the Body of Christ throughout the world are profoundly similar in spirit whether the words are from the contemporary worship of the minjung house church in Korea or the ancient Teocualo of the Mexicas.

Along with the wonderful worship resources we received when we sought contributions for this book were straightforward requests for prayer. We are aware that, because of the time frame of this kind of project these prayer concerns may be no longer "current events," and other situations of danger, disaster, hunger, threat of war may fill the "news." Yet we have kept faith with these requests and include them in Chapter 17. Somehow these specific prayers have become representative of the universal specificity found at the table of our Savior where there is no "more urgent" or "more pressing"—no priority but Christ's love and care for all.

We ask you who pick up this book and plan worship for your congregation to pick up as well the current mission publication of your denomination . . . and to pick up the newspaper too. Thus we can all pray with others, not as an "exotic exercise," but as a life-changing experience that leads to a world-changing commitment.

Last Supper, He Qi, China

Eucharist

You emptied yourself completely
keeping nothing for Yourself.
Now naked, utterly stripped,
you give yourself to us as bread
which sustains us
and as wine that consoles us.
You are Light and Truth
You are the Way and the Hope
You are Love
Grow in us, Lord!

Julia Esquivel, Guatemala

Communion

(The coconut, marked with a cross and kicked, rolled, and finally hacked with a knife, is used as a moving commentary on Is 53 and 55 in a service that concludes with the water and meat of the coconut being used to celebrate the Lord's supper. It is perhaps the incorporation of this rather more painful aspect in the symbolism of the coconut palm which is to the fore in the minds of Christians in the Pacific in these troubled days.)

O Lord, our palm trees can no longer hide us from the world.
Strengthen our hearts that we may look with confidence to the future.

Tahiti

The Breaking of Bread

(Somebody will first pass a piece of puto to the person next to him or her. Each one will take it and pass it to the next until the last person in the line has taken it. The piece of puto will be altogether eaten.

The salabat juice will be placed in a big cup. Each individual will take a sip, wiping off the cup, then pass it to another. The cup will be passed on from one to another.

During the communion, hymns or psalms may be sung.)

All: Here are the Gifts of God for us. Let us take these in remembrance that
    Christ died for us and feed on him in our hearts by faith with thanksgiving.

Asian Methodist Youth Seminar

Communion

Some indigenous churches have begun to use elements more traditional to their culture such as tortillas for the bread and atole or pozol (a corn drink) or coffee for the wine. In the Nahuatl culture it is important to look each other in the eyes when sharing the elements because they reflect one's inner song. With one's eyes you can give a flower or a thorn. This act then demonstrates a person's sincerity in confession both of sins as well as faith.

Olivia Juarez and Sara Larson Wiegner, Mexico

Communion Reflection

(Read Jn 6:25–35, substituting the word "tortilla" for the word "bread.")

We have used the word "tortilla" instead of "bread" in the reading of this text because our food is not bread but tortillas. The tortilla is made from corn—corn that sprang forth from a seed sown in the plowed earth, labor done with much respect because the indigenous people respect the earth. The small corn plant (milpa) grew and gave fruit to this ear of corn and from an ear of corn we shell the grain with which we make our tortillas.

We will share this tortilla in this celebration which we call the Lord's Supper (Communion). It is a time to share our food, that which gives us life. In Exodus we read of the manna sent from heaven to feed the Israelites, but for us food is the tortilla. That is why we use tortillas and not cookies or bread made in fine bakeries. The tortilla is made by the hands of our sisters and the labor of our brothers.

Instead of wine or grape juice we are using atole made from the corn, pilon (raw sugar), and cinnamon, a drink that warms our bodies.

This is the food the Lord has given us from the land—the land in which we live, the land which bears many burdens because sometimes we do not respect it; the land which is so important to us, we refer to it as "our mother."

One of our ancestors wrote the following:

May the land endure!
May the mountains remain standing!
Said Ayocuan Cuetzpaltzin,
in Tlaxcala, in Huexotzinco.
Scatter about
flowers of toasted maize, flowers of cacao.
May the land endure!
If we want the earth to remain, brothers and sisters, we must be
    united, caring for the things that God has given us.

Olivia Juarez, Mexico

Eucharist

Lime juice and cassava—these ingredients from our lives and lands are Eucharist. In them we can give thanks to God for God's gift—that is the breaking down of all social, economic, and political barriers.

Indonesia

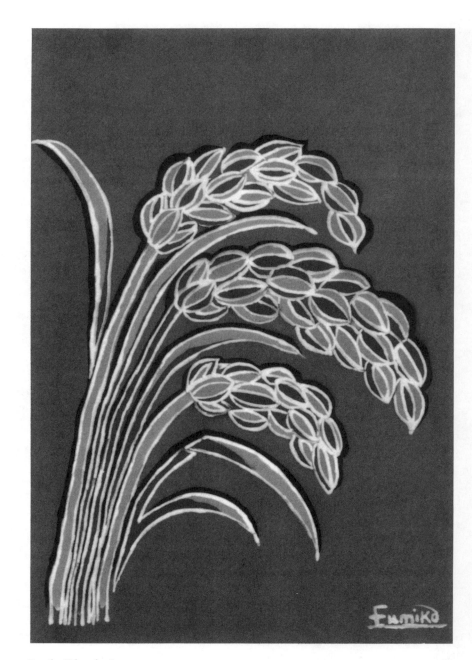

Fumiko Takenaka, Japan

God Is Rice

Rice is the symbol of our life
We eat rice daily
There are different kinds of rice
But we are one
as the rice-eating community
Rice is the symbol of celebration
We express our joy of harvest with
    it
There are many sufferings in Asia
but we anticipate the time of
    cosmic celebration.

    Masao and Fumiko Takenaka, Japan

Eucharistic Prayer

Introductory Dialogue

Leader: Did you take a meal with our Lord and your family in this morning?* Let us pray to God of daily rice who is in our daily sufferings and life itself. God be with you.

Congregation: And also with you.
We know God's love for us who are the oppressed, the estranged and weak.

Leader: You are the people of Yahweh. Yahweh always loves those like our community.

Congregation: Amen.

Preface

Leader: We are living in the suffering field. Day by day, we are laboring hard and long to have food, shelter, and clothing for ourselves as concrete facts. We are the powerless, the ignorant, and the poor, we are drenched with tears when we always remember our Lord's suffering.

We lift our hearts to the Lord.

Sanctus

Congregation: Holy, holy, holy suffering Lord,
you are surely the friend of us, the estranged.

Thanksgiving

Leader: What is showing thankfulness to our Lord?

Congregation: That is life itself.

Leader: What is graceful for you?

Congregation: Yahweh's love, which is like the endless cycle of transmigration.

Leader: What do you seek?

Congregation: It is the truth itself.

Leader: Where is that truth?

Congregation: In our rice, in our community, in our friend's voice, and in our Lord's suffering.

Leader: We thank the Lord who is the archetype of suffering.

Preliminary Epiclesis

Leader: O Lord, come and join the community that is thy people of suffering.

*In Korean customs, "Did you take a meal?" is one of the greetings like "How are you?" or "Good morning!"

Narrative of the Institution

Leader: We feel with passion thy saying on the night of betrayal and desertion:
"This is my body which is broken for you.
Do this in remembrance of me."
And "This is the new covenant in my blood.
Do this, as often as you drink it, in remembrance of me."
But we sometimes forget thy will like disciples who were ignorant of their teacher's words.

Anamnesis-Oblation

Leader: Remember, the Lord, the friend of sinners who were the oppressed, the estranged, the weak, the sick, widows, orphans, etc.
Remember, the Lord, the one disliking of the common structure and power.
Remember, the Lord, the one sharing of daily food is life.
Remember, the Lord, the one liberating from a dictator.
We remember thy suffering, O Lord, at thy Last Supper.

Epiclesis

Leader: The sky is gray and chilly, and the plain is frozen hard. The warmth of sunlight is gone from the barren and dark street of the poor. From where did they come, those drawn and haggard faces? For what are they searching, those eyes, those emaciated hands? O Lord, now come to us here, be with us together in this place.

Ah, this street, this lonely street where outstretched hands are rejected, this empty and dark street of contempt. Oh, where can it be, the kingdom of heaven? Can we find it in the thick clouds that hover over the place of death? O Lord, now come to us here, be with us together in this place.

Intercession and Doxology

Leader: Always suffering is close to the life of Christ. We always appreciate the Lord's suffering. We confess our suffering is weaker than the Lord's. We are standing in the Lord's suffering at the crossroad. So, we are happy because of this. O Lord, thanks to You we will attend your presence in suffering. We praise and glorify You for ever and ever. We believe, O Lord, Your suffering is praise and glory in itself in our beings.

Thanks be to God!

Amen.

Sung-Hwan Park, U.S.A./Korea

The Lord's Supper

The Invitation

*Partake of the bread and the wine, the ageless symbols of Christ's life given for
others.*

*Eat and drink because of your need and not because of some special goodness
you may possess or privilege you may feel.*

*Reach out to those near you and receive their friendship, reach up to receive the
friendship of God and be this day truly reconciled.*

Prayer of Consecration

*Eternal God, who has called us from the busy world to worship thee in quiet-
ness, we approach the table of thy Son unworthy even to be near it; for who of
us can say he has no need to ask the ancient question, "Lord, is it I?" Help us to
eat the bread in remembrance of the body that was broken for us, and, by the
drinking of the cup, to show forth the Lord's death til he comes again in glory.*

*Henceforth let that mind be in us which was in Christ Jesus, and grant also that
we may be in him. Consecrate now these emblems that they may be truly to
us the bread of heaven to succor us and the wine of joy to sustain us, and
grant us the comforting presence of thy Holy Spirit.*

In Jesus' name. Amen.

Richard Wilcox, Spain

Communion Prayer

(from workers in community soup kitchens in the shanty towns of Lima, Peru)

God, food of the poor;
Christ our bread
Give us a taste of the tender bread
from your creation's table;
bread newly taken
from your heart's oven,
food that comforts and nourishes us.
A loaf that makes us human
joined hand in hand,
working and sharing.
A sacrament of your body,
A warm loaf that makes us a family;
your wounded people.

World Student Christian Federation

From Agape Feast Liturgy, Bali

The Cross of Fruit and Flowers

Dear Friends:

In front of us there is a cross as the foundation of the tree of life—full of fruits, flowers, and drinks. They are symbols of God's love. God loves us so much that He left the glory of heaven to live among us, to humble Himself, to empty Himself by taking the form of a servant. And He even gave His life, to die on the cross for our salvation, so that we may live. He created the trees, fruits, flowers, and drinks to keep us alive. He gave us the Holy Spirit to lead us in our way. During His life, He had shown his love by feeding the hungry, healing the sick, and liberating people who were possessed by demons or evil spirits.

When we try to be His imitators, we must show our love to people who live around us. Let us go to the tree of love. Let us pick one or two fruits, flowers, and drinks. But we cannot pick them up for ourselves. Each one of us will pick for his or her friends, friends that he or she loves. After he or she has given something to other people, he or she must return to his or her place to wait for other people to come and give him or her something to eat and to drink. Let us start.

Meditation

Many times when we think about our life and think about our difficulties in our life, we tend to find scapegoats that we can accuse and we can consider as enemies. In that way, we always look at other people, other objects outside of ourselves. We seldom look at ourselves, the inner selves. We do not want to blame ourselves. Then we forget that our chief enemy is exactly within ourselves—the ego, the greed—the longing for our own comfort at the expense of other people. We surrender ourselves to our egos, to the desires of our egos, or to the desires of our flesh.

In Bali, we consider the desires of our flesh as the desires of our five senses: the desire of the eyes, the desire of the nose, the desire of the ears, the desire of the mouth, and the desire of the skin. Moreover, the Balinese compare our bodies to chariots which are pulled by five horses of five senses. That is why we need to be in control of the five horses or five senses, so that the chariot, or the body, will not go astray or fall into a ditch or tramp on something to be broken.

So we try to prepare ourselves, our bodies, to be dwelling places of Christ and the Holy Spirit. We let Him be the driver of our bodies, or the controller of the five senses. He will give us the right direction or motivation by love in all our actions. We try to focus ourselves to Christ, so that

with our eyes—we can see Christ who cannot be seen,

with our ears—we can hear Christ, who does not emit any sound,

with our mouths—we can answer Christ's calling, who does not say a word,

with our noses—we can smell the fragrance of Christ's word and deed,

with our skin—we can feel His touch, who does not touch us with His hand.

I. Wayan Mastra, Bali

Teocualo or the Communion among the Mexicas

The word "teocualo" literally means "to eat God," and it was an act of communion, a memorial, an act of hope for the people. It resembled very much the Christian Eucharist brought by the Spaniards.

Each sector of Mexica society had its beneficent protector deity and with Her/Him they practiced the Teocualo: the traders had theirs, the pulque makers had theirs, etc.; but the most important Teocualo was celebrated in the month of Toxcatl, and panquetzalisti to the image of Huitzilopochtli, the most ancient and important god of the Mexicas. He was the one who led the people from distant lands to a promised land, the one who made them into a great people, having been insignificant. Huitzilopochtli showed them the place where they were to settle.

The young people who were in charge of the cult to this god and his temple would grind and knead the grains of amaranth, combining it with corn and honey water. This dough was then sculpted into the image of the statue in the temple.

When the special day arrived, they broke the amaranth statue in two—one piece for the inhabitants of Tenochtitlan and the other for those in Tlatelolco. The priests and rulers ate first of the piece for their city, and the rest was broken into very small crumbs so that all could eat of it: children, young people, men, women, and old ones.

It was such an important rite for the people that before partaking they fasted and abstained from many comforts in order to acquire dignity and be able to eat of God, or celebrate communion.

The Teocualo was also an act of affirmation of the unity of the people—that is why all participated. It was an educational act, because even the children were invited to participate. All believed in Huitzilopochtli, all believed that he was the god that had brought them greatness, and therefore all should eat of him.

The Teocualo was a memorial because the people were to remember that the gods had sacrificed themselves to be the sun and the moon. To give life to the world they had to give up their lives, not just once, but just as the sun dies (sets) every day and the moon every night, the gods died and resurrected every day (a common theme in agricultural societies). In the communion of each celebration, Huitzilopochtli and the other gods gave up their lives in order to continue living, leading, and giving life to their people.

The Teocualo was the death of the god as well as the resurrection; if they didn't die they could not rise again. To die and resurrect was life for Mexicas; that is why their theology of sacrifice was to them a theology of life. They wanted to continue living and receiving the blessing of God in which nature greened again, the seed sprouted, the sun rose, the new fire lit a new life, but for this it was necessary to spill much blood, which is the life, that is what gives life.

The Teocualo was a theological concept. God must live with the people, in every person. God's energy must be transmitted to everyone, and this was done through the communion, the Teocualo. Those who did not participate in the Teocualo were not of the people, did not believe in Huitzilopochtli, were not grateful to him, did not have hope, did not believe in the resurrection of people and nature.

The Spaniards saw this, but never perceived that God was manifest and present in the indigenous cultures. On the contrary, they made a point to destroy and devalue indigenous theology even though there were many similarities with Christian doctrine and principles. They never understood that God was made manifest to them first because God was already present in different ways in our cultures.

Professor Lázaro Gonzales Dominguez, Mexico

Five Loaves and Two Fishes, He Qi, China

(Taken from an Indian Liturgy for Celebrating the Eucharist)

Smarana—Samarpana (Recalling and Offering)

(Theological comment: The entry from the world into the presence of God and the sending back into that world do not imply two unrelated realities. Being "awakened" to the presence of God in worship is intended to awaken us also to the presence of God in the world. Thus, throughout the liturgy there is interaction between God's life and the world's life. They are in "inseparable relationship" to use a long-held Indian ontological concept. The Bread-prayer, therefore, coming at the climax of our "Sharing" in God's life, is linked explicitly with the needs of the hungry, and the Redemption-prayer is linked explicitly with the deliverance of the oppressed poor in our land.)

Prayers for Church and World

(Various types of litany may be used here. Or this offering of intercessions may come after the Bread-Prayer later. When possible, lay people may lead and specific concerns of the time may be mentioned before the litany.)

Offering

Leader: Brothers and sisters, God's great love for us leads us to offer ourselves as a living sacrifice to him; for we hope to share in the perfect life-offering of Christ.

Congregation: This is the true worship we are to offer God.

Leader: Let us now bring our offerings to God as signs of our self-giving, praying for God's spirit to transform us and our gifts.

(As an offering lyric is sung, the worship leaders process to the place of offering and sharing. This may be a low table placed further behind the lamp. The leaders, having first sat behind the lamp, now sit behind the low table, preferably sitting on the floor or on a slightly raised platform. They may first process around the table. An offering of a tray of flowers, with other signs of God's goodness in creation, is brought forward with offering of money, and bread and wine for the Eucharist. During the following prayers, flowers are sprinkled on the place of offering; the response is sung if possible.)

Leader: Glory to God, Source of all bounty and beauty, whose fullness and fragrance transforms us.

Congregation: Creator God, we lift our hearts to you in thanks.

Leader: Glory to God, who has made covenant with all his creatures, and has promised never to forsake the creation he loves.

Congregation: Creator God, we lift our hearts to you in thanks.

Leader: Glory to God, who made us all in his image, and entrusted earth and her life to our care.

Congregation: Creator God, we lift our hearts to you in thanks.

(When the gifts of money and in kind are offered, the following prayers are made.)

Leader: Lord of the universe, these gifts are tokens of our labour in your world. We offer the work we do among and with our fellow-humans, asking you to lead us into your ways of justice and peace. As we care for this world you have given us, may we be filled with your compassion for all creatures, that we may live as fitting first-fruits of your new creation.

Congregation: Glory to God our Sustainer, who loves and cares for all.

(As the bread and wine are offered, the following prayers are made.)

Leader: O God, Redeemer of all things, with grateful thanks we offer this bread and wine, fruits of your earth and of our labour, and signs of your redemptive purpose for our lives and for all creation. By this bread and cup you assure us, in Christ, of a share in your being, your bliss, your purpose.

Congregation: Glory to God, our Redeemer, who saves us by his grace.

Saranam* in the Triune God

Leader: Our Creator God is with us to bless us;

Congregation: Saranam, saranam, saranam.

Leader: The Risen Lord is with us to bless us;

Congregation: Saranam, saranam, saranam.

Leader: The transforming Spirit is with us to bless us;

Congregation: Saranam, saranam, saranam.

(The offering bearers return; an alternative would be for all the helpers to sit on each side of the table of offering. A blessing may be given here for any who leave before the Sharing.)

*Refuge

Nama-smarana

(A recital of names of God that serve to recall the dramatic sets of divine redemption. This may be in the form of seven titles or groups of titles. A number of sets of such names my be prepared, each emphasizing themes to be brought out in that particular time of the church year. During the singing of the Namasmarana, the table is prepared for the Eucharistic meal.)

The Redemption Prayer

Leader: O God, Redeemer of the oppressed, at the last meal that your Son, Jesus Christ, shared with his disciples before his death, He took bread in his hands of compassion, gave you praise and thanks, and broke the bread. Then he said, "Take this bread, all of you, and eat it. This is my body. Do this to remember me."

Congregation: We celebrate through this bread the self-offering of our Saviour Christ.

Leader: Then after the meal he took the cup, offered praise and thanks to you, gave the cup to his disciples and said, "Take this, all of you, and drink from it; This is the cup of the new covenant of my blood, shed for you and for all, that sins may be forgiven. Do this to remember me.

Congregation: We celebrate through this cup the new covenant of our Saviour Christ.

The Bread Prayer

Leader: As this bread is broken and this wine poured out, O Seeker and Saviour of the lost, we remember again the poor and oppressed of the earth. We recall that your body was broken that the hungry might be nourished, the oppressed set free, replenished with the bread of new hope and new life.

Congregation: Christ has died, Christ has risen, Christ will come in glory.

Leader: As this bread was once scattered seed, O Bread of life, sown in the earth to die and rise to new life, so gather all peoples together in the one humanity of your coming new age. Restore the broken life of your creation; heal the disfigured body of your world; draw all creatures into yourself through the cross and in the power of your risen life. And grant to all the faithful departed a share in your bliss, that with them we too at the end may be welcomed into your kingdom through your inexhaustible grace, and guided by your indwelling Spirit.

Prasada (The Sharing)

(As the bread is lifted up prior to the congregation coming forward to share together in it, the following sentences are said.)

Leader: When we break bread, do we not share in the body of Christ?

Congregation: We seek to share your life, gracious God.

(As the cup is lifted up:)

Leader: When we take the cup, do we not share in the life-blood of Christ?

Congregation: We seek to share your life, gracious God.

Prayer for Darsana

Leader: Risen Lord;

Congregation: Be present, be present, even though we are unworthy for you to come to us. Only your peaceful presence can nourish us in faith, bind us together in love, and fill us with hope, so that we might share in your service. Amen.

Partaking

(As the bread and wine are distributed, suitable words are said.)

Exulting in God's New Age

(Prayer for the kingdom. The following may be in sung form.)

Leader: Having now shared in the feast that is God's sign of his coming kingdom, let us pray with confidence and hope;

Congregation: Our Father in heaven, holy be your name, your kingdom come, your will be done, on earth as in heaven. Give us today our daily bread. Forgive us our sins, as we forgive those who sin against us. Do not bring us to the test, but deliver us from evil.

Leader: Merciful God of all creation, Holy Parent of all peoples, through our Lord Jesus Christ, who united all things in his fullness, we join your whole creation in exultant praise of your bountiful goodness. You have now touched us with new life and filled us with new hope that your kingdom will come, that the hungry will be fed, that the oppressed will be set free from evil, that your reconciling work will be done, and the earth filled with your glory.

Congregation: For the kingdom, sovereign power, and supreme glory are yours alone, great Saviour of the world.

Preshana (Blessing and Commission)

(There may be a lyric or hymn sung as the worship-leaders move to the entrance, where the following is said.)

Leader: The God of peace will be with you and will grant you his peace at all times, his peace beyond our understanding, that purifies heart, mind, and body, until his kingdom comes. Amen.

Having shared this feast of God's love, go into the world to share his love in your life.

Congregation: In the name of Christ. Amen.

United Theological College, Bangalore, India

Preface

You are blessed, God, Father and Mother for us.
You have desired to be the God of our Hope!
You are blessed for Jesus of Nazareth
who opens for us the way to your kingdom
of truth, of life, of holiness and grace,
of justice, of love, and of peace!
You are blessed for your Spirit
who urges us to sing.

Invitation

*Let us remember in a moment of silence that we are invited to this table
not by any one church, or any one minister, but by the Lord Jesus Christ,
who calls us each one to join him.*

Commission

Leader: Go, with the promise that you will meet Christ when you meet one of the
least of your brothers and sisters.

Congregation: Yes. Amen.

United Congregational Church of South Africa

Table Blessing

Lord we give you thanks
because around this table
our strength revives
in the struggle against poverty.
Make of our gluttony,
our thirst for abundance
a new feeling
of justice and of hope.

Lord, may our meals
on an earth divided
one day be shared
in an earth reunited.
forgive us, now,
at this unjust meal,
until the whole earth
is nourished by your bread.

Jaci C. Maraschin, Brazil

I Am More than Flesh and Bone

"I am more than flesh and bone"
Says Christ
"I am body,
I am me.
Take this broken bread and be as me,
All of you
And I shall set you free."
"I am love and liveliness"
Says Christ
"I am blood,
I am me.
Take this outpoured wine and live my life,
Each of you
And I shall set you free."
We are body and the blood
Of Christ
Broken, shared,
Wine and bread—
Dreaming, praying, working, joyfully
For that day
When everyone is free!

Bill Wallace, Aotearoa/New Zealand

The Peace

All: Redeemer Christ, we are one body in you. We see our community gathered
together. We know others are gathered in your name at this time in other
places.
We cherish our unity in this diversity.
We look to you for guidance, we listen for your word, we hope for tomorrow.
We feel welcomed in and through Christ.

Leader: Let us now, in this new moment, come together and share the peace
which Jesus made possible: the peace of Christ.
Peace be with you.

Congregation: And also with you.

(Greet one another with gestures appropriate to the gathering.)

World Student Christian Federation

Closing Prayer

Leader: Having shared this tortilla together, having heard the words of Jesus Christ calling us to love of neighbor, having heard the words of contemporary prophets telling us who our neighbor is in this world, let us now join together by going out into our communities to love our neighbor!

Congregation: Loving God, make us good neighbors to all the suffering and wounded of our world. Even more, help us to see them as neighbors to us, bearers of our hope and salvation, calling us to conversion. Give us the courage to address the sources and structures of injustice, even if these are very close to home, and become prophets and workers in the process of transformation of this world—until it is a world that becomes what you created it to be, an image of you. And may all of us say together: Amen.

Janet Ross-Heiner, U.S.A./Nicaragua

Martha and Mary, He Qi, China

In these days of political strife in Zaire, the economy and nearly every sector of human existence is in a shambles. The Church of Jesus Christ in its human form, regardless of denomination (or "community" as is the term used here) is one of the only institutions in this present society that is "functioning" well. Thus the masses and even those who represent tumbling governmental structures are focusing more and more on the church to breathe renewed "life" into the country. So quite often in these times one hears expressions like: "The fact that we Zaireans are breathing today is a miracle!" "It is by the power of God that I have life today!" "Only the spilled blood of Jesus is holding back the flow of violent bloodshed of the Zairean people!" "God is miraculously feeding us in the daily miracle of fou-fou" (the staple food in the diet).

Suzette Goss-Geffrard, Zaire

Regarding prayer requests, a good long-standing one is for the safety and security of the Aytas. They have been exploited for decades, and their situation has continued to disintegrate.

Also, please solicit prayer for the translation teams involved in helping the people put the Scriptures into their own language. There are at least four major related language groups now working on translation. One New Testament is nearing completion after thirty years of tremendous adversity and difficulties. The people are suffering great and varied afflictions, particularly the translator who is past retirement age and in poor health.

Betsy H. Wrisley, Philippines

Roofs for the Roofless

"A roof is more than thatch and bamboo"—it is our symbol of new life in the village.

I am the Director of an Integrated Rural Development Organisation which my husband began, hoping to bring a better life to the poor. The organisation is a secular one, but its basic values are Christian. We feel that the Christian church is challenged today to be a creative community, and a new way of life and hope for the oppressed and needy has to be evolved through various ways.

Savithri Devanesen, India

Arogyalayam Trust

The name "Arogyalayam" has been chosen for our trust because it is a Tamil word meaning "place of healing." Arogyalayam Trust has as its primary objective the uplift of destitute and handicapped children.

As the smallest, youngest, poorest, least educated, most vulnerable part of our society, they are usually the first to be hurt, ignored, and taken advantage of.

Bonni-Belle Pickard, Kodaikanal, Tamil Nadu, India

For Greenville, Liberia, and for the Klao Bible translation project.

Nancy Lightfoot, Liberia

Greetings on behalf of the staff off the Common Ministry in Latin America and the Caribbean. The topmost needs in Latin America and the Caribbean are:

Haiti: the immediate return to democracy and the possibility of living in peace with justice.

Cuba: the immediate lifting of the economic embargo.

Guatemala: the safe return of the indigenous peoples living as refugees in the southern part of Mexico, to their lands; that the peace agreement be signed and kept by all parties. The possibility of peace with justice and respect of human rights, especially of the indigenous people.

El Salvador: the reconstruction process after twelve years of war.

Mexico: Peace with justice for the indigenous peoples of Chiapas. NAFTA with the needs and rights of the Mexicans, U.S. people, and Canadians in mind and heart.

Raquel Rodriguez, U.S.A.

This prayer is also by Birkha Khadka but is a request to the American churches for them to pray for the Nepali Church. This is a need, we feel, although it is not what you were asking for. Keith (Fleshman) helped him with the translation.

"We as Christians should pray for one another all around the world. If we are praying for each other we will get victory and blessing from God. Therefore, we are sending this request for prayer for the Nepali Christians. The past forty years the Nepali Church has been growing, but for thirty-eight years it was very difficult to preach and evangelize. By prayer the church was able to grow. Since the revolution we can preach and evangelize more freely.

Last year in Nepal a vision of Jesus was seen in Tansen over the mountain. After that vision more people are coming to Church. Many people are excited about it. Some people are also confused.

Now that more freedom has come to Nepal, should we stop praying? No! More prayer is needed. Please pray for the village fellowships in Nepal. Many people in these fellowships are young people and unbaptized new believers. These days many new fellowships in the village have begun.

These young people have to live in Hindu families. Every year they have many Hindu festivals in the homes, especially Desain and Tihar. At this time their Christian witness is seen—but they really need prayers because their parents and siblings can give them real pain. Is it possible that they will give their witness without the victory of God? Yes, God's victory is possible if we pray for them. In the village these immature believers are meeting. We Christians are few, but we pray.

We also know that your needs are the same and so we also pray for you."

June Fleshman, Nepal

This week our little church group also sent a refugee back to his home country of Syria. Seventy-five years old, a salesman who brings cars from France to Cyprus, Elazar, a Muslim, found himself without money or friends. Having nine thousand dollars in cash after a sale, he was staying in Turkey, but forgot to lock his door. When he came back to his room, he suddenly found his passport and money gone. It was the second time he had lost a passport. From what I have learned, some countries like his own treat such cases badly; the person may end up in confinement or worse. However, after extended efforts to get him an arrangement with the consulate and a temporary place to stay, he got on his way again. Trying to help one old man seems like a drop in the bucket, as Turkey is becoming more and more a country of many refugees—Kurdish, Bulgarian, Yugoslavian, Iraki, etc.

Lots of poor Kurdish people are around Istanbul now. I see them standing at the boat selling boat tokens—their clothes dirty, indicating that they have been sleeping on the street. They are fleeing terrible conditions in South-Eastern Turkey and Northern Irak, where thousands have been killed by the bombing of villages and crossfire between Turkey and Irak. The Kurds who have taken up arms against their native Irak call themselves the PKK.

Doug Wallace, Turkey

Since 1979, churches in China are reopening or being newly built at a rate of three every two days, making it perhaps the fastest growing church in the world.

Diane Allen, General Board of Global Ministries, United Methodist Church, U.S.A.

Front Page: Rwanda

It is not, you see,
that they are very far away—
the weeping children
of Haiti wash against
our very shores.
and it is not
that they
are black and naked,
pulitzer-proficient
photojournalists,
crazy with love,
have angled their lenses
on the fairest of blond
Bosnian orphans and
amputees with their
blown-to-bits
sleds.
it is rather, you see,
that we do not
care
that in Goma bloody bodies
lie bagged on
the street,
massacre, starvation,
cholera.
Wisely, it has been said that one
should not believe everything
one reads in the
papers—
that, irrefutably,
is true.
Rwandans do not die because
there are insufficient tankers in Zaire
to carry clean water
to refugee camps.
they die because
in Boston we wash newsprint
so easily off our
hands.

Maren C. Tirabassi, U.S.A., July 28, 1994

Robert Eddy, U.S.A.

PART V

Resources to Quicken the Heart: Poetry and Graphics for Worship

This book's agenda has been to broaden global understanding rather than to focus on the importance of artistic expression in worship. Nevertheless artistic material has appeared—as geographically diverse and thematically similar as the danced offertory from Ghana and the danced sermon from Bali—because for all people the celebration of the arts undergirds an appreciation of the whole person as worship participant.

Music, dance, sculpture, architecture are all profoundly expressive of the human spirit, but the two art forms that were contributed significantly to this book were poetry and black and white graphic art. We have shared these throughout the text. The last two chapters contain wonderful resources that did not fit with any other particular section but which are "gifts" for our communities.

And so this is the final part—which perhaps should be the first—for how can people of faith lift voice, join hands, walk the seasons of the earth, or become together the Body of Christ without truly quickened hearts?

Rini Templeton, U.S.A./Mexico

Poetry from the global community can be shared in many different ways by local congregations. Printed in newsletters and on bulletin covers, it gives opportunity for personal reflection or meditation during the prelude to worship. As oral reading in a service, poems can be recited by a single voice, by two or more readers in an antiphonal pattern, or by the congregation in unison. A danced interpretation of a poem can be a meaningful focus for worship. In either Christian Education classes or youth groups, poetry can stimulate discussion or a poetic or artistic response by young people which can then be shared with the congregation.

The poetry in this section is organized by author. We are grateful to the United Methodist hymnal for the privilege to reprint the first stanza of "Amazing Grace" in six Native American languages. Throughout this book, we have occasionally used multiple languages. Hearing many tongues in worship is as powerful and traditional as the Day of Pentecost itself.

The Body

You gave us this body that is your
    temple.
We don't want to destroy it
It is good to feel it free, like this
without bonds or wounds.
You gave us this body as an example
of harmony and of beauty;
don't let us turn it into
a reason for sadness
but let us express with joy
your spirit and the gift of life.
You gave us this body that perceives
the caresses of tenderness,
that knows how to speak with gestures
expressing its desires

You gave us this body that unites
reason with feelings;
don't let us make
it a prisoner of a mistake
but in everything glorify
and consecrate the Creator.
You gave us this body for life
We don't want it for death
but hunger and malnutrition
reduce it to misery.
You gave us this body for glory
and perfect plenitude
Don't let it become a negation of
    humanity
but in Christ restored, reveals us
    your image.

Simei Monteiro, Brazil

Amazing Grace in Six Native American Languages

Amazing Grace, how sweet the
   sound
that saved a wretch like me.
I once was lost, but now am found,
was blind but now I see.

     John Newton, England

Ooh nay thla nah, hee oo way gee
e gah gwoo yah hey ee
Naw gwoo joe sah, we you low say,
e gah gwoo yah ho nah.

     Cherokee

Nizhónígo joobá ditts' á
yisdáshíítínígíí,
Lah yóóííyá k'ad shénáhoosdzin,
doo eesh'íí da n't'éé

     Albert Tsosie, Navajo

Daw k'ee da ha dawtsahy he
   tsow'haw
daw k'ee da ha dawtsahy hee.
Bay dawtsahy taw, gaw aym
   owthaht'aw,
daw k'ee da ha dawtsahyh'ee.

     Kiowa

Po ya fek cha he thlat ah tet
ah non ah cha pa kas
Cha fee kee o funnan la kus
um e ha ta la yus.

     Creek

Shilombish holitopa ma!
ishmminti pulla cha
Hatak ilbusha pia ha
is pi yukpalashke.

     Choctaw

God

God is
a cloud forming,
an eagle soaring,
a voice from the wilderness
echoing through your ear.
Whispering, encouraging—
keep going, seek My glory,
don't worry, I'll keep
your fears.

     Juanita Helphrey, Hidatsa, U.S.A.

The Sigh

When it is necessary to drink so
much pain,
when a river of anguish
drowns us,
when we have wept many tears
and they flow like rivers
from our sad eyes,
only then
does the deep hidden sigh of our
neighbor
become our own.

     Julia Esquivel, Guatemala

Suspiro
Cuando se tiene que beber tanto
dolor
Cuando un río de angustia
ahoga nuestra respiración,
Cuando se ha llorado mucho
y las lágrimas brotan como ríos
de nuestros ojos tristes,
sólo entonces
el suspiro recóndito del prójimo
es nuestro propio suspiro!

     Julia Esquivel, Guatemala

For the People

(This song was written by a twenty-two-year-old student at Mahidol University who sang it at the demonstration against the return of Field Marshal Thanom. When police attacked the demonstrators, Nid was shot and killed.)

If I were a bird
and able to fly afar,
I would like to be a white dove
to guide the people to freedom.
If I were the cloud in the sky,
I would shelter and bring rains
to the rice field.
If I were a grain of sand
I would throw myself down
to make a path for the people.
I will sacrifice my life
for the suffering people.
I would sacrifice myself
no matter how many times
I would have to die.

    Nid, Thailand

The Way Home

Our "Home" is the realm of God.
It is where love and justice prevail,
and we are called by God
to make wherever we are
as much like home as possible.
We dare not feel "at home" in a
    world like this;
where one-third of the people live
    abundantly,
and two-thirds live in scarcity—
Two ghettos: one rich, the other
    poor.
In such a world we are refugees
dwelling on either side of a divid-
    ing wall
afraid to cross the boundary.
Christ breaks down the dividing
    wall.
"Home" happens when the walls
    come down,
and the ghettos are no more,
and we are all brothers and sisters.
The beginning of the way home
is the way of sharing!
Our footsteps down this aisle
to share with others
are the first short steps
of the long journey "home."

    Richard Wilcox, Spain

In Your Path

I love all your paths
that lead me to your House, Lord,
simple roads
dusty
neglected
bordered by simple houses.
Undeveloped roads
marked by the footprints
of working people:
builders of broad highways,
fancy houses,
gardens
and parks.
I love those paths
open to the rain
and to the good will
of their discounted residents.
Paths that lead me to the illiterate
    woman,
to the child who has no school,
to the old man who sells ice cream
from his worn-out wooden cart.
I love those paths
unimpressive
unattractive
that lead me to your brothers and
    sisters,
because You, poor with them,
speak to me from their indigence
and violently shake loose
all my assurances
binding me inescapably
into the secret tenderness
of your unknown suffering.
And so I know I am your friend,
because you reveal your secrets to
    me,
the secrets of a love without
    measure!

    Julia Esquivel, Guatemala

Deep in the Human Heart

Deep in the human heart
the fire of justice burns;
a vision of a world renewed
through radical concern.
As Christians we are called to set
the captives free,
to overthrow the evil pow'rs
and end hypocrisy.
This is our task today
to build a world of peace;
a world of justice, freedom, truth,
where kindness will increase;
a world from hunger free;
a world where people share,
where ev'ry person is of worth
and no one lives in fear.
We take the step of faith,
and leave the past behind
and move into the future's world
with open heart and mind.
By grace we work with Christ,
as one community,
to bring new hope and fuller life
to all humanity.

> Bill Wallace, Aotearoa/New
> Zealand

Unobserved

While
the preacher
assiduously laboured
to catch
both God
and congregation
in his word cage
Christ crept
into the aisle
as a small child
making a cross
with kneelers.

> Bill Wallace, Aotearoa/New
> Zealand

The Beach

Wedged between
the gentle inevitability
of the slap, slap, slapping tide
caressing the thighs
of the beach
and a wall
of bawdy
going nowhere
bar-room songs
spilling out
from the pub,
a new-dawn couple
resolutely advanced
into the enveloping
darkness
and
a child wandered,
moulding new patterns
on the top of the
waveless
waters of the bay.

God as I stand
on the beach
of my twilight days
help me painfully
to liberate all the
children and young lovers
imprisoned within me
and together
embrace
your multicoloured
fiesta of life.

> Bill Wallace, Aotearoa/New
> Zealand

Aotearoa (New Zealand)

Aotearoa,
Spirits' glorious home,
Mountain, lake and forest
Form our spirits' womb.
Bring to Tāne's garden[a]
Awe and tenderness;
Feel within your mauri[b]
Earth's divine caress.
Contemplate the koru[c]—
Live its spiral sign
As God's life unfolds within,
Like the Bread and Wine.
May this land of long white
clouds,
Bush and mountains tall
Be, within the pulsing seas,
Tapu[d] for us all.

Notes:

[a]Tāne—the mythical God of the forest; Tāne's
garden—the indigenous forest
[b]mauri—our life-force
[c]koru—the unfolding fern frond
[d]tapu—holy, sacred

> Bill Wallace, Aotearoa/New
> Zealand

Grandfather

Grandfather sings, I dance.
Grandfather speaks, I listen.
Now I sing, who will dance?
I speak, who will listen?
Grandfather hunts, I learn.
Grandfather fishes, I clean.
Now I hunt, who will learn?
I fish, who will clean?
Grandfather dies, I weep.
Grandfather buried, I am left
    alone.
When I am dead, who will cry?
When I am buried, who will be
    alone?

> Shirley Crawford, Native
> American, U.S.A.

Women Are Coming

Women are coming in
through the doors and windows
avenues and alleys.
They are coming in.
Coming with a strong wind,
coming with life and direction,
coming to question,
and coming to change.
Coming always with sweetness,
coming with great skill,
coming to bring delight,
and with many joys.
Coming to bring peace and
    healing,
coming to join their forces,
coming to work and to build,
and coming to go forward.
Coming to question,
coming to change,
coming to bring delight,
and coming to bring light.

> Valdomiro de Oliveira, Brazil

The Seed

Like an unwanted seed,
We were tossed aside,
Buried in the soil of greed,
Pushed down by tongues that lied.
Unnoticed we began to grow.
First our roots, then our stem.
Our branches began to show,
There are many of them.
Once again we will be strong,
A mighty Red Pine no one can
    bend.
Those that try will be wrong,
They will fail, there will be no
    end.
Our branches will spread across
    the land,
the unity of the branches will be
    our power,
Power by which to make our
    stand.
Once again our tree will tower.
—O shah wa shik a bee kwe

> Shelly Turner, Native American,
> U.S.A.

The Song of Netzahualcoyotl

I love the song of the "cenzontle"
bird of four hundred voices.
I love the color of green jade
and the perfume of the fragrant
    flowers,
but I love more my brother,
the human being.

Tlacuicac Netzahualcoyotl

(in Nahuatl)

In tlazohtla itlacuicac tzentzontli
totol in tzontli llacuicac.
In tlazohtla in xoxohuic in jade
iva i ahuialesh in xochime,
iva ocachi in tlazohtla nocni
tlacatl iva cihuatl.

> Translator: Sara Larson Wiegner,
> Mexico

Are You a Stranger to My Country, Lord?

Are you a stranger to my country, Lord?
My land of black roots and thick jungles
where the wild boar sharpens his tusks,
where the monkeys chatter in the trees,
and the peacock's shrill note
echoes through the mist-clad hills;
my land of brown, caked river mud
where the elephant and the leopard come to drink,
and the shambling bear with his dreamy eyes
sees the porcupine shedding his quills;
my land with its friezes of palmyra palms
etched sharply against the blue mountains;
my land of low-lying plains
with its miles of murmuring paddy fields
that stretch in undulating waves of green
to the distant horizon;
my land of sapphire skies and flaming sunsets,
my land of leaden grey skies piled high
with banks of monsoon clouds;
my land of stinging rain, of burning heat,
of dark nights, of enchanting moons
that dance behind the coconut fronds;
my land of tanks and pools
where the lazy buffalo wallows
and the red lotuses lie asleep?
No, you are no stranger, Lord,
for the wind whispers of you
and the waters chant your name.
The whole land is hushed in trembling expectancy,
awaiting your touch of creative love.

Chandran Devanesen, India

Floating Things

Dust particles
Scintillating
In the morning sun;
Coloured leaves
Swirling
Down to the ground;
Rainbowed bubbles
Drifting
With the breeze
Are floating things.
Floating things are
Graceful
Because they have
Submitted themselves
Totally
To a power
Greater than their own.
Take me Lord.
Make me
A floating thing.

Dayalan Devanesen, Australia/India

What is Old?

Old?
Who told you
That I
Am old?
I am scared
of myself
because I feel
so young and vital.
But I
am more scared
of you
When you look at me
as if
I have no right
to live!
What is youth?
What is age?
The body changes
even as the Seasons change,
With Spring
giving way to Summer
and Summer
giving way to Autumn
and Autumn
to Winter.
But life is as passionate
in Winter
as it was in spring,
a vital spark
that can leap
into flame
in any Season!
I thank you,
God,
that you shield
the flame
of life in me
with loving hands
that know when
to put it out
When the time comes
to enter
into another adventure,
another life
through the gateway
of death.

Chandran Devanesen, India

My World

This is my world
People,
Starving people. Working people.
Rich. Poor. Dying.
Cancer
Nuclear war—
I want to get away
from it all.
I've got myself
to worry about
to make secure.
Sometimes
I don't feel so sure.
Anyway,
there is still money
and myself.
I've got to cut myself out
from all that causes pain.
Still don't feel so good.
Something tells me
I'm out of place,
Out of step.
That preacher
said something
about
God
calling each one of us
to serve
the hungry, the sick,
the people
Rich. Poor. Young. Old.
What about me?
Can't I live for myself?
Must I answer?
I can't win.
I wonder why.
You know
This world
Maybe it is
God's.

Dayalan Devanesen, Australia/India

19 *Graphics*

Rini Templeton, U.S.A./Mexico

The black-and-white graphic art found throughout this book is the gift of several artists in the hope that congregations might share visual resources as well as the words, words, words so prevalent in much worship. These graphics may be reproduced in bulletins, newsletters, and for any other appropriate congregational use. When reproducing these pieces, please use the complete acknowledgment at the end of this book.

Rini Templeton

Our discovery of Rini Templeton was accidental and roundabout, but as we tracked down a flyer that came into our hands, we found a trail of people who spoke with great love about her artistic gifts and passion for justice.

Here are her words: "Other people call my work 'people's art,' I just call it my 'monitos' (little monkeys, a term used in Mexico for cartoons and comic strips). I'm not a theoretician. I'm a craft person. I make images. . . . People's art, perhaps I do not aspire to that because people's art would be art that comes from the people and returns to them. Art that is nourished by the traditions, the daily life, the struggles of the people, and returns to become theirs."*

Rini Templeton died suddenly in 1986, but her commitment to justice, peace, and an end to all exploitation lives on. *The Art of Rini Templeton* contains permission for activists to freely use the images in leaflets, picket signs, and newsletters. This one-time use is continued for the work we reproduce here. The Rini Templeton archives are being developed at the University of California at Santa Barbara, and it would be deeply appreciated if one copy of any piece that uses her artwork could be included in the archives by sending it to:

Ms. Elizabeth Martinez
c/o ISES
P.O. Box 2089
Oakland, CA 94609

*Elizabeth Martinez, ed., *The Art of Rini Templeton: Where There Is Life and Struggle* (Seattle: Real Comet Press, 1989), 9.

Rini Templeton, U.S.A./Mexico

Rini Templeton, U.S.A./Mexico

Rini Templeton, U.S.A., Mexico

Kimiyoshi Endo

Kimiyoshi Endo of Japan is a printmaker who has a life-long calling for art as well as being a minister with heavy pastoral responsibilities. He writes, "As a young man I was struggling, something like Van Gogh. Death, the pain of life, sadness, suffering, anxieties, and love were unsolved problems for me. I could not love myself, or others, or God. However, God showed love through the prayers of my family. Also Armin Kroehler, a missionary, encouraged me to live."*

It was Armin Kroehler who drew our attention to Kimiyoshi Endo's woodblock prints on Bible stories and we are delighted to be able to share them in this book.

*Judith Newton, *Haiku, Origami and More* (New York: Friendship Press, 1991), 70.

King of Kings, Kimiyoshi Endo, Japan

Calling the Wayward Sheep, Kimiyoshi Endo, Japan

Adam and Eve, He Qi, China

He Qi

An art instructor from Nanjing Union Theological Seminary, He Qi combines Asian images with Biblical themes. He states his belief this way: "Each country and each people should have its own artistic style and distinctive features. The more indigenous art is, the more international it will be. . . . A solitary flower is not spring; spring is spring because there is a riot of flowers."*

Paper cutting is an art form which began fifteen hundred years ago as a festive celebration of well wishes and good fortune during the lunar new year. Originally papercuts were in red and they were displayed on windows and doors to express joy. The art form has been expanded and used in many ways in contemporary Chinese culture. The Chinese church has recently begun using this traditional art form to make contemporary statements about the Christian faith.

He Qi believes that the indigenization of Christian art is an important mode of communication. The many papercuts that he has shared enrich our understanding of the nature of God and the people of China.

*Lois Cole, "The Shaping of a New Frontier: Christian Art in China," *China Talk: Newsletter of the United Methodist Church/China Program* 7, no. 1/2 (March 1992).

Wise and Foolish Virgins, He Qi, China

Ode to Joy, He Qi, China

Nativity Scene, He Qi, China

Good Samaritan, He Qi, China

Sister Helen David Brancato

Sister Helen David Brancato contributed designs she created for a curriculum on Central America for the Maryknoll Missioners in Ossining, New York. The curriculum was under the direction of Sister Jane Keegan.

Cross of the Americas, Sister Helen David Brancato, U.S.A.

Wise as Serpents, Midori Shibata, Japan

Midori Shibata

Midori Shibata is a stencil maker as well as a musician who organizes community concerts and teaches organ. She works with her husband at a "preaching point" in Otaru, Hokkaido.[*] Her beautiful designs for cards, bulletins, and programs show the influence of biblical themes and calligraphy.

[*]Judith Newton, *Haiku, Origami and More* (New York: Friendship Press, 1991), 70.

I am the vine, you are the branches.

(JOHN 15.5)

I Am the Vine, Midori Shibata, Japan

Midori Shibata, Japan

This print elaborates on the Kanji for love, which is "ai" in Japanese

Love, Midori Shibata, Japan

Untitled, Midori Shibata, Japan

Zhang Guijie

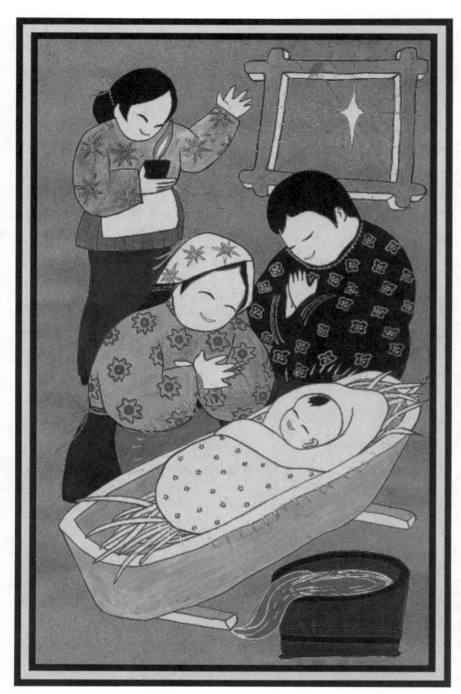

Born in a family of artists, Zhang Guijie was raised by her mother, a devout Christian, while her father was "re-educated" during the cultural revolution. A life-changing experience occurred when she was in the hospital as a child. Diane Allen tells the story in the "Mission News" of the Global Ministries Board of the United Methodist Church, "An unkempt raggedly clothed man—an artist with wounded hands—approached her bed. Suddenly he pulled from his spoiled coat a picture that was so lovely and captivating that she has never forgotten it. Featured in the picture was a dark forest against a dark mountain. Behind them, the bright red sun rose in joyous defiance."*

Zhang Guijie teaches at Nanjing Union Theological Seminary. The work we include in this book illustrates scripture texts. Women and their activities in the home and church are central. Diane Allen quotes her as suggesting, "perhaps women naturally see God more easily than men."*

*Diane Allen, "Zhang Guijie: Chinese Christian Artist," *Mission News, General Board of Global Ministries of the United Methodist Church* July–August 1993, 18C, 18D.

Nativity, Zhang Guijie, China

Rekindle the Gift of God, Zhang Guijie, China

Resurrection, Zhang Guijie, China

Resources to Quicken the Heart

Widow's Mite, Zhang Guijie, China

Other Artists

There are a variety of other graphic contributions throughout this book. The Middle East Council of Churches and the Protestant Christian Church in Bali are allowing their letterhead art to accompany written resources, and we are also including the Silver Jubilee Celebration symbol for the United Congregational Church of Southern Africa, as well as several designs from the Conference of European Churches. The Presbyterian Church (U.S.A.) has designated 1994–1995 "The Year with Africa," and has shared with us the graphics from their planning calendar.

Fumiko Takenaka, Japan

Family Values, Presbyterian Church, U.S.A.

The Spoken Word, Presbyterian Church, U.S.A.

Hospitality, Presbyterian Church, U.S.A.

Human Relationships, Presbyterian Church, U.S.A.

The photographs that reflect on each of our part themes are the gift of artist and photographer Robert Eddy, Kathy's husband. Fumiko and Masao Takenaka, Kathy's friends from Yale Divinity School, sent their personal book for friends, *Messages from Time to Time*, from which her art and his words were drawn.

Finally, Bill Wallace, pastor, author, and speaker on the contextualization of liturgy in Aotearoa/New Zealand, has been represented throughout these pages by prayers, hymn lyrics, and poetry. His photograph of Christ crucified in the Lenten section is a detail from a stained glass window he designed. It is with his poem that we close this chapter, because it lifts up the ultimate grace-filled hope that shapes all of the "images" of *Gifts of Many Cultures*.

The Image

Jailing
or liberating
the image
bears
and
unmasks
the power
and plight
of oppressed
and oppressor
in provokingly
unpacking
layered reality
of God-like
mystery-filled
life-evoking
pictures
of unlined
unframed
existing.*

*W. L. Wallace, *Singing the Circle*, Book 3: *Broken Bread, Broken Chains*, Christchurch, New Zealand, 1990. Used by permission.

Bank of candles in Chartres Cathedral, Robert Eddy

Source Notes

Permission to copy any of these worship resources—both words and pictures—is freely granted for use in church bulletins, newsletters, special programs, and educational events provided that the copyright notes and acknowledgments are included in the reproduction. Such free use does not extend to events (such as workshops and seminars) when admission is charged or registration fees collected or to reprints in books and other publications. These require the additional permission of the following copyright owners or United Church Press, 700 Prospect Avenue East, Cleveland, Ohio 44115-1100.

We wish to thank all those who have granted permission for the use of prayers and liturgical materials in this book. We have made every effort to trace and identify them correctly and to secure the necessary permissions for those which have been reprinted. If we have erred in any way in the source notes or have unwittingly infringed any copyright, we apologize sincerely. We would be glad to make the necessary corrections in subsequent editions of this book.

Part I: Resources to Lift Up Our Voices

Chapter 1: Gathering Words and Invocations

Page 4 "Lord, oil the hinges . . . ," reprinted from *With All God's People: The New Ecumenical Prayer Cycle: Orders of Service,* compiled by John Carden (Geneva: WCC Publications, 1989), 13. Copyright 1989, WCC Publications, World Council of Churches, Geneva, Switzerland.

Page 4 "God of Life . . . ," reprinted from *Poems, Prayers and Songs. Copyright 1993,* EGGYS Working Group on Liturgy and Bible Studies, Rio de Janeiro, Brazil, 18.

Page 4 "The light of the Great Spirit . . . ," reprinted from *Worship Resources,* compiled by Juanita J. Helphrey. Copyright 1991, Council for American Indian Ministries, United Church of Christ, Minneapolis, Minn., 9.

Page 4 "Like the sun . . . ," from 1987 *United Methodist Clergywomen's Consultation Resource Book,* 61. Reprinted by permission from *The United Methodist Book of Worship* (Nashville: United Methodist Publishing House, 1992), 472. Copyright 1992 The United Methodist Publishing House.

Page 5   "In the beginning, when it was very dark . . . ," reprinted from *Gloria Deo Worship Book, 10th Assembly, Prague CSFR.* Copyright 1992 Conference of European Churches, Geneva, Switz., 8.

Page 5   "Blessed is our God always . . . ," reprinted from "Morning Prayers for the Five Days of V General Assembly," Middle East Council of Churches, The Bible Society in Lebanon, Jan. 24, 1990.

Page 6   "Preparation and Approach to God," reprinted from *The Iona Community Worship Book,* by John L. Bell. Copyright 1988, Wild Goose Resource Group, Iona Community, Glasgow, Scot., 16.

Page 7   "Opening Responses," reprinted from "Universal Day of Prayer for Students," World Student Christian Federation, Feb. 14, 1993, 5.

Page 8   "Everything as it moves . . . ," reprinted from *Worship Resources,* compiled by Juanita J. Helphrey. Copyright 1991, Council for American Indian Ministries, United Church of Christ, Minneapolis, Minn., 28.

Page 8   "Father, Son and Holy Spirit . . . ," reprinted from *Gloria Deo Worship Book, 10th Assembly, Prague CSFR.* Copyright 1992 Conference of European Churches, Geneva, Switz., 11–12.

Page 9   "Longing for the God of Peace," reprinted from *Worship in an Indian Context,* edited by Eric J. Lott. Copyright 1986, The United Theological College, Bangalore, India, 88–90.

Page 10   "A people marked by life . . . ," reprinted from "Universal Day of Prayer for Students," World Student Christian Federation, Feb. 1992, unpaginated.

Page 10   "Come to be our hope . . . ," reprinted with changes by permission of the author, Jaci Maraschin, from *New Gestures New Gazes, Guide for Reading and Celebrating the Gospel of Luke,* edited by Nancy Pereira and Ernesto Cardoso. Copyright 1993, Institute for Religious Studies, Rio de Janeiro, Brazil, 33.

Page 11   "Invocation," reprinted from *Worship in an Indian Context,* edited by Eric J. Lott. Copyright 1986, The United Theological College, Bangalore, India, 99.

Page 11   "O God, we thank you . . . ," reprinted from *Worship Resources,* compiled by Juanita J. Helphrey. Copyright 1991, Council for American Indian Ministries, United Church of Christ, Minneapolis, Minn., 7.

Chapter 2: Prayers of Confession

Page 12   "Lord, thanks to you . . . ," reprinted from *With All God's People: The New Ecumenical Prayer Cycle,* compiled by John Carden (Geneva: WCC Publications, 1989) 155–56. Copyright 1989, WCC Publications, World Council of Churches, Geneva, Switzerland.

Page 12   "Grandfather, Grandmother . . . ," reprinted from *Worship Resources,* compiled by Juanita J. Helphrey. Copyright 1991, Council for American Indian Ministries, United Church of Christ, Minneapolis, Minn., 9.

Page 12   "Mercifully hear this prayer . . . ," reprinted from *Gloria Deo, Worship Book for CEC Assembly IX, Stirling, Scotland.* Copyright 1986, Conference of European Churches, Geneva, Switz., 89.

Page 12   "Forgiveness and Affirmation," reprinted from *Singing the Circle, Book 3: Broken Bread, Broken Chains*. Copyright 1990, W. L. Wallace, Christchurch, N.Z., 63.

Page 14   "Eternal God, we confess . . . ," reprinted from *Your Will Be Done*. Copyright 1986, CCA Youth, Christian Conference of Asia, Shatin, Hong Kong, 121.

Page 14   "Prayer of Confession," reprinted by permission of the author. All rights reserved. Copyright 1993, Kate Compston, 44 Western Way, Alverstoke, Gosport, PO 12 2NQ, Eng., unpaginated.

Page 15   "Earthmaker our Father . . . ," reprinted from *Worship Resources*, compiled by Juanita J. Helphrey. Copyright 1991, Council for American Indian Ministries, United Church of Christ, Minneapolis, Minn., 4.

Page 15   "Our Hawaiian sisters and brothers . . . ," reprinted by permission of the author from "Pono (to make right)," *New Conversations*, Spring 1993, published by United Church Board for Homeland Ministries.

Page 16   "Revelation," reprinted from *The Certainty of Spring: Poems by a Guatemalan in Exile*, by Julia Esquivel. Copyright 1993, Ecumenical Program on Central America and the Caribbean (EPICA), Washington, D.C., unpaginated.

Page 16   "Lord God, we have given . . . ," reprinted from *Gloria Deo, Worship Book for CEC Assembly IX, Stirling, Scotland*. Copyright 1986, Conference of European Churches, Geneva, Switz., 70.

Page 17   "Penitence," reprinted by permission of the author, Barbara de Souza, from a women's health group graduation service.

Page 18   "The Liturgy of 1997, Hong Kong," reprinted from *Your Will Be Done*. Copyright 1986, CCA Youth, Christian Conference of Asia, Shatin, Hong Kong, 87–88.

Page 19   "Prayer of Confession," reprinted from the Twenty- fourth Assembly Closing Service of the United Congregational Church of Southern Africa, Oct. 2, 1990, 2–3.

Chapter 3: Prayers of Praise and Thanksgiving

Page 20   "We thank you, God . . . ," reprinted from *Singing the Circle, Book 1: Sacred Earth, Holy Darkness*. Copyright 1990, W. L. Wallace, Christchurch, N.Z., 47.

Page 20   "Thank you, Creator . . . ," reprinted by permission of the author, Sue Ellen Herne, from *The United Methodist Book of Worship* (Nashville: United Methodist Publishing House, 1992), 558. Copyright 1992 The United Methodist Publishing House.

Page 21   "Ho, Grandfather, Grandmother . . . ," reprinted from *Worship Resources*, compiled by Juanita J. Helphrey. Copyright 1991, Council for American Indian Ministries, United Church of Christ, Minneapolis, Minn., 9.

Page 22   "For the earth and all . . . " reprinted from *With All God's People: The New Ecumenical Prayer Cycle: Orders of Service*, compiled by John Carden (Geneva: WCC Publications, 1989), 63. Copyright 1989, WCC Publications, World Council of Churches, Geneva, Switzerland.

Page 23   "You found out what we were doing . . . ," reprinted from *The Iona Community Worship Book,* by John L. Bell. Copyright 1988, Wild Goose Resource Group, Iona Community, Glasgow, Scot., 52.

Page 23   "Blessed Is My God—A Prayer," reprinted by permission of the translator, Barbara de Souza, "Mulheres—Vida Nova Liturgia," Cadern no. 2, Centro de Esterdos Cristiano—8, 1989.

Page 23   "O Lord, Our God . . . ," reprinted from *Your Will Be Done.* Copyright 1986, CCA Youth, Christian Conference of Asia, Shatin, Hong Kong, 123.

Page 24   "Lord of lords, Creator . . . ," reprinted from *With All God's People: The New Ecumenical Prayer Cycle: Orders of Service,* compiled by John Carden (Geneva: WCC Publications, 1989), 68. Copyright 1989, WCC Publications, World Council of Churches, Geneva, Switzerland.

Page 26   "The Directions," reprinted from *Worship Resources,* compiled by Juanita J. Helphrey. Copyright 1991, Council for American Indian Ministries, United Church of Christ, Minneapolis, Minn., 32.

Page 27   "Rejoice in the Lord," reprinted from *With All God's People: The New Ecumenical Prayer Cycle: Orders of Service,* compiled by John Carden (Geneva: WCC Publications, 1989), 64. Copyright 1989, WCC Publications, World Council of Churches, Geneva, Switzerland.

Page 28   "Thanksgiving for the Sun," reprinted by permission of the author, Edith Wolfe, from *Na Himeni Haipule Hawaii,* unpaginated.

Chapter 4: Prayers of Petition and Intercession

Page 29   "O God, that we may receive . . . ," reprinted with changes from *Die Schoensten Gebete der Erde.* Copyright 1964, Suedwest Verlag, Munich, Ger.

Page 29   "Lord Hear Us," reprinted from the Third General Assembly, Nicosia–Cyprus, Nov. 28–Dec. 4, 1980, Middle East Council of Churches, The Bible Society in Lebanon, unpaginated.

Page 30   "O God: Enlarge my heart . . . ," reprinted from *With All God's People: The New Ecumenical Prayer Cycle,* compiled by John Carden (Geneva: WCC Publications, 1989), 279. Copyright 1989, WCC Publications, World Council of Churches, Geneva, Switzerland.

Page 30   "Lord, make us realize . . . ," reprinted from *Your Will Be Done.* Copyright 1986, CCA Youth, Christian Conference of Asia, Shatin, Hong Kong, 145.

Page 30   "Be mindful, O Lord, of us . . . ," reprinted from *Gloria Deo Worship Book,* 10th Assembly, Prague CSFR. Copyright 1992 Conference of European Churches, Geneva, Switz., 35–36.

Page 31   "Lord, Hear Us," reprinted from the Third General Assembly, Nicosia–Cyprus, Nov. 28–Dec. 4, 1980, Middle East Council of Churches, The Bible Society in Lebanon.

Page 31   "Grandfather, Great Spirit . . . ," a Dakota prayer, reprinted by permission from E. Russell Carter, *The Gift Is Rich* (New York : Friendship Press, 1968), 59. Copyright 1955 and 1968, Friendship Press, Inc.

Page 31   "Let us pray for all religious communities . . . ," reprinted from *With All God's People: The New Ecumenical Prayer Cycle: Orders of Service*, compiled by John Carden (Geneva: WCC Publications, 1989), 98. Copyright 1989, WCC Publications, World Council of Churches, Geneva, Switzerland.

Page 33   "Look Graciously, O Lord . . . ," attributed to "Morning and Evening Prayer," Church of Pakistan, reprinted by permission from *The United Methodist Book of Worship* (Nashville: United Methodist Publishing House, 1992), 515. Copyright 1992 The United Methodist Publishing House.

Page 33   "God Our Creator . . . ," reprinted from *With All God's People: The New Ecumenical Prayer Cycle*, compiled by John Carden (Geneva: WCC Publications, 1989), 73–74. Copyright 1989, WCC Publications, World Council of Churches, Geneva, Switzerland.

Page 33   "Lord most giving and resourceful . . . ," reprinted from *Worship Resources*, compiled by Juanita J. Helphrey. Copyright 1991, Council for American Indian Ministries, United Church of Christ, Minneapolis, Minn., 6.

Page 34   "Lord, in your mercy . . . ," reprinted by permission of the author, Jabez Bryce, from *With All God's People: The New Ecumenical Prayer Cycle*, compiled by John Carden (Geneva: WCC Publications, 1989), 227–28. Copyright 1989, WCC Publications, World Council of Churches, Geneva, Switzerland.

Page 34   "Prayers of Intercession from Europe," reprinted from "Universal Day of Prayer for Students," World Student Christian Federation, Feb., 1993, 10.

Page 35   "Let us pray . . . ," reprinted from *With All God's People: The New Ecumenical Prayer Cycle*, compiled by John Carden (Geneva: WCC Publications, 1989), 179. Copyright 1989, WCC Publications, World Council of Churches, Geneva, Switzerland.

Page 35   "Prayer for Peace," reprinted from *With All God's People: The New Ecumenical Prayer Cycle*, compiled by John Carden (Geneva: WCC Publications, 1989), 213–14. Copyright 1989, WCC Publications, World Council of Churches, Geneva, Switzerland.

Page 35   "Lord, hear us . . . ," reprinted from the Third General Assembly, Nicosia–Cyprus, Nov. 28–Dec. 4, 1980, Middle East Council of Churches, The Bible Society in Lebanon.

Page 36   "Song and Prayer," reprinted from International Women's Day by World Student Christian Federation, March 8, 1992.

Page 37   "O Great Spirit . . . ," reprinted from *Worship Resources*, compiled by Juanita J. Helphrey. Copyright 1991, Council for American Indian Ministries, United Church of Christ, Minneapolis, Minn., 5.

Page 37   "Pray for us, brothers and sisters . . . ," reprinted from *With All God's People: The New Ecumenical Prayer Cycle*, compiled by John Carden (Geneva: WCC Publications, 1989), 41. Copyright 1989, WCC Publications, World Council of Churches, Geneva, Switzerland.

Page 37   "Grant us prudence in proportion . . . ," reprinted from *Gloria Deo, Worship Book for CEC Assembly IX, Stirling, Scotland.* Copyright 1986, Conference of European Churches, Geneva, Switz., 90.

Page 38   "Lord, make me an instrument of your peace . . . ," reprinted from *Gloria Deo Worship Book, 10th Assembly, Prague CSFR.* Copyright 1992 Conference of European Churches, Geneva, Switz., 48–49.

Chapter 5: Resources Relating to Scripture

Page 40　"Matthew 11: 28–30," reprinted from *With All God's People: The New Ecumenical Prayer Cycle*, compiled by John Carden (Geneva: WCC Publications, 1989), 312–13. Copyright 1989, WCC Publications, World Council of Churches, Geneva, Switzerland.

Page 40　"Revelation 3:20," reprinted from *The Iona Community Worship Book*, by John L. Bell. Copyright 1988, Wild Goose Resource Group, Iona Community, Glasgow, Scot., 49.

Page 41　"Matthew 20:1–16," reprinted from *Gloria Deo Worship Book*, *10th Assembly, Prague CSFR*. Copyright 1992 Conference of European Churches, Geneva, Switz., 29–30.

Page 41　"Genesis 28:17," reprinted from *Singing the Circle, Book 3: Broken Bread, Broken Chains*. Copyright 1990, W. L. Wallace. Christchurch, N.Z., 59.

Page 42　"Psalm 137 (Psalm from Ceara)," reprinted from *Net: Information Bulletin of the Latin American Liturgy Network* 3, no. 4 (Feb. 1994): 8.

Page 43　"Daniel 3/You are a Lord of Fire . . . " reprinted from *With All God's People: The New Ecumenical Prayer Cycle: Orders of Service*, compiled by John Carden (Geneva: WCC Publications, 1989), 77. Copyright 1989, WCC Publications, World Council of Churches, Geneva, Switzerland.

Page 43　"Psalm 107:1–9 (Come, let us do service . . .)," reprinted from *Worship Resources*, compiled by Juanita J. Helphrey. Copyright 1991, Council for American Indian Ministries, United Church of Christ, Minneapolis, Minn., 30.

Pages 44–46　"Mark 5:25–34 (A Procession for Liberation Done by Women)," reprinted by permission of the translator, Barbara de Souza, from a group work, Projeto Mulher, Methodist Seminary, 1992 Conference, Sao Paulo, Brazil.

Page 47　"Luke 10:30–37 (Aboriginal Traveller)," reprinted from *Your Will Be Done*. Copyright 1986, CCA Youth, Christian Conference of Asia, Shatin, Hong Kong, 77.

Page 48　"Our Father who art in heaven . . . ," reprinted from *Worship Resources*, compiled by Juanita J. Helphrey. Copyright 1991, Council for American Indian Ministries, United Church of Christ, Minneapolis, Minn., 27.

Page 48　"O Great Spirit . . . ," reprinted from *Worship Resources*, compiled by Juanita J. Helphrey. Copyright 1991, Council for American Indian Ministries, United Church of Christ, Minneapolis, Minn., 14.

Page 49　"Our Father who are in this our land . . . ," reprinted from *With All God's People: The New Ecumenical Prayer Cycle*, compiled by John Carden (Geneva: WCC Publications, 1989), 256. Copyright 1989, WCC Publications, World Council of Churches, Geneva, Switzerland.

Page 49　"Our father who is in heaven . . . ," reprinted from *New Gestures, New Gazes: Guide for Reading and Celebrating the Gospel of Luke*, edited by Nancy Pereira and Ernesto Cardoso. Copyright 1993, Institute for Religious Studies, Rio de Janeiro, Brazil, 55.

Page 49　"O most compassionate Life-Giver . . . ," reprinted from *Singing the Circle, Book 3: Broken Bread, Broken Chains*. Copyright 1990, W. L. Wallace, Christchurch, N.Z., 64.

Page 52   "Life's Source and Sustainer . . . ," reprinted from *Worship in an Indian Context*, edited by Eric J. Lott. Copyright 1986, The United Theological College, Bangalore, India, 25–26.

Chapter 6: Offering Resources

Page 53   "All Things of Earth are holy . . . ," reprinted from *Singing the Circle, Book 3: Broken Bread, Broken Chains.* Copyright 1990, W. L. Wallace, Christchurch, N.Z., 57.

Page 53   "O God, to those who have hunger . . . ," reprinted from *With All God's People: The New Ecumenical Prayer Cycle,* compiled by John Carden (Geneva: WCC Publications, 1989), 125. Copyright 1989, WCC Publications, World Council of Churches, Geneva, Switzerland.

Page 53   "For fish and poi . . . ," reprinted by permission of the author, Edith Wolfe, from *Na Himeni Haipule Hawaii,* unpaginated.

Page 54   "Offering," reprinted from *Worship in an Indian Context,* edited by Eric J. Lott. Copyright 1986, The United Theological College, Bangalore, India, 16.

Page 54   "Offertory," reprinted from the Twenty-fifth Assembly Opening Service of the United Congregational Church of Southern Africa, Oct. 2, 1991, 6.

Chapter 7: Benedictions

Page 56   "May it be blessed . . . ," reprinted from *Worship Resources,* compiled by Juanita J. Helphrey. Copyright 1991, Council for American Indian Ministries, United Church of Christ, Minneapolis, Minn., 6.

Page 56   "May our senses be awakened . . . ," reprinted from *Singing the Circle, Book 1: Sacred Earth, Holy Darkness.* Copyright 1990, W. L. Wallace, Christchurch, New Zealand, 49.

Page 56   "Go into the world . . . ," reprinted from *Haiku, Origami and More,* by Judith Newton. Copyright 1991, Friendship Press, 81.

Page 56   "Closing Responses," by George Macleod. Reprinted from *The Iona Community Worship Book,* by John L. Bell. Copyright 1988, Wild Goose Resource Group, Iona Community, Glasgow, Scot., 16.

Page 56   "Hands that join . . . ," reprinted from *New Gestures, New Gazes: Guide for Reading and Celebrating the Gospel of Luke,* edited by Nancy Pereira and Ernesto Cardoso. Copyright 1993, Institute for Religious Studies, Rio de Janeiro, Brazil, 39.

Page 57   "Sisters and brothers . . . ," reprinted by permission of the author. All rights reserved. Copyright Kate Compston, 44 Western Way, Alverstoke, Gosport, PO 12 2NQ, Eng., 1993, unpaginated.

Page 57   "May the God of justice and creativity . . . " reprinted from *Singing the Circle, Book 1: Sacred Earth, Holy Darkness.* Copyright 1990, W. L. Wallace, Christchurch, N.Z., 49.

Page 57   "A Blessing," reprinted by permission of the translator, Barbara de Souza, "Mulheres—Vida Nova Liturgia," Cadern no. 2, Centro de Esterdos Cristiano—8, 1989.

Page 57   "O you people, be healed . . . " reprinted from *Worship Resources*, compiled by Juanita J. Helphrey. Copyright 1991, Council for American Indian Ministries, United Church of Christ, Minneapolis, Minn., 4.

Page 58   "May the blessing of God who risked everything . . . ," reprinted from *With All God's People: The New Ecumenical Prayer Cycle: Orders of Service*, compiled by John Carden (Geneva: WCC Publications, 1989), 13. Copyright 1989, WCC Publications, World Council of Churches, Geneva, Switzerland.

Page 58   "Through the days to come . . . ," reprinted from *Haiku, Origami and More*, by Judith Newton. Copyright 1991, Friendship Press, 81.

Page 59   "Blessing and Sending Out on the Closing Worship," reprinted from *Net: Information Bulletin of the Latin American Liturgy Network* 2, no. 3 (Apr. 1993): 22.

Page 59   "We must close the meeting . . . ," reprinted from the Twenty-fourth Assembly Service of the United Congregational Church of Southern Africa, Oct. 2, 1990, 7–8.

Page 59   "May the warm winds of heaven . . . ," reprinted by permission from *The United Methodist Book of Worship* (Nashville: United Methodist Publishing House, 1992), 456. Copyright 1992 The United Methodist Publishing House.

Part II: Resources to Join Hands Together

Chapter 8: Words, Proverbs, and Sayings

Page 63   "Bhajan . . . ," reprinted from *Worship in an Indian Context*, edited by Eric J. Lott. Copyright 1986, The United Theological College, Bangalore, India, 13.

Page 63   "A candle-light . . . ," reprinted from *Your Will Be Done*. Copyright 1986, CCA Youth, Christian Conference of Asia, Shatin, Hong Kong, 15.

Page 64   "Pono," reprinted by permission of the author, Paul Sherry, from "Pono (to make right)," *New Conversations*, Spring 1993. Published by United Church Board for Homeland Ministries.

Page 65   "Benediction: Psalm 19:14," reprinted by permission of the author, Edith Wolfe, from *Na Himeni Haipule Hawaii*, unpaginated.

Page 65   "The prison cell . . . ," reprinted from *Your Will Be Done*. Copyright 1986, CCA Youth, Christian Conference of Asia, Shatin, Hong Kong, 1.

Page 66   "Het che tu aloh," reprinted from Worship Resources, compiled by Juanita J. Helphrey. Copyright 1991, Council for American Indian Ministries, United Church of Christ, Minneapolis, Minn., 7.

Chapter 9: Descriptions of Worship from the Global Community

Page 68   "In our church in Zimbabwe . . . ," from a letter from Allen Myrick, Zimbabwe, May 12, 1993.

Page 68   "As I explained to you . . . ," from a letter from John Huegel, Mexico, Feb. 24, 1993.

Page 68   "One of the things . . . ," from a letter from Phyl Asher, Nepal, May 9, 1994.

Page 70   " . . . then I will return hopefully . . . ," from a letter from Barbara de Souza, Brazil, Apr. 1, 1993.

Page 70   "The spontaneity of Zairean worship . . . ," from a letter from Suzette Goss-Geffrard, Zaire, June 8, 1993.

Page 70   "It is the rare occasion . . . ," from a letter from Alison Buttrick, Chile, Feb. 1993.

Page 70   "I believe that viewing the gospel . . . ," reprinted from *Singing the Circle, Book 1: Sacred Earth, Holy Darkness*. Copyright 1990, W. L. Wallace, Christchurch, N.Z., 6.

Page 71   "For a Quinceañera," reprinted by permission from *The United Methodist Book of Worship* (Nashville: United Methodist Publishing House, 1992), 531–31. Copyright 1992 The United Methodist Publishing House.

Page 71   "About prayer . . . ," reprinted from *With All God's People: The New Ecumenical Prayer Cycle*, compiled by John Carden (Geneva: WCC Publications, 1989), 309. Copyright 1989, WCC Publications, World Council of Churches, Geneva, Switzerland.

Page 71   "*Tonsung Kido* (Pray Aloud)," reprinted by permission from *The United Methodist Book of Worship* (Nashville: United Methodist Publishing House, 1992), 445. Copyright 1992 The United Methodist Publishing House.

Page 74   "Breathing" ("In a short period . . . "), reprinted from *Worship in an Indian Context*, edited by Eric J. Lott. Copyright 1986, The United Theological College, Bangalore, India, 13.

Pages 76–77   "New Life in Liturgy," reprinted from *New Gestures, New Gazes: Guide for Reading and Celebrating the Gospel of Luke*, edited by Nancy Pereira and Ernesto Cardoso. Copyright 1993, Institute for Religious Studies, Rio de Janeiro, Brazil, 29, 305.

Pages 77–78   "Remembering in Hawaii," reprinted by permission of the author, Edith Wolfe, from *Na Himeni Haipule Hawaii*, unpaginated.

Pages 78–80   "Multifaceted Indian Worship," reprinted from *Worship in an Indian Context*, edited by Eric J. Lott. Copyright 1986, The United Theological College, Bangalore, India, 2–4.

Chapter 10: Worship Services and Baptism, Wedding and Funeral Resources

Pages 84–85   "Ohana—Devotions for the Family," reprinted by permission of the author, Edith Wolfe, from *Na Himeni Haipule Hawaii*, unpaginated.

Pages 89–94   "India (Sharing Earth's Life)," reprinted from *Worship in an Indian Context*, edited by Eric J. Lott. Copyright 1986, The United Theological College, Bangalore, India, 17–26.

Pages 95–97   "Brazil (Worship Services . . .)," reprinted from *Whole Life, Holy Life*, by Ernesto Barros Cardoso. Copyright 1993, Rio de Janeiro, Brazil, 65–72.

Page 98   "Resources for Infant Baptism," reprinted from *Singing the Circle, Book 3: Broken Bread, Broken Chains*. Copyright 1990. W. L. Wallace, Christchurch, N.Z., 67.

Page 100   "Continuing Christian, Buddhist Dialogue," reprinted from *Occasional Bulletin*, Taiwan Church Press, Sept. 1992 15.

Pages 101–2   "Funeral Resources," reprinted from *Singing the Circle, Book 3: Broken Bread, Broken Chains*. Copyright 1990, W. L. Wallace, Christchurch, N.Z. 68–70.

Page 102   "Through the Rivers of Our Tears," reprinted from *Singing the Circle, Book 2: Darkness and Light*. Copyright 1990, W. L. Wallace, Christchurch, N.Z., 42.

Chapter 11: Youth Offerings

Page 104   "Praise Given by Students," reprinted from "Universal Day of Prayer for Students," World Student Christian Federation, Feb. 9, 1992, 4.

Page 109   "Keep the ocean clean . . . ," reprinted from *1985 Prayer Calendar*, General Board of Global Ministries, The United Methodist Church, 104.

Page 110   "Exactly at this time . . . ," reprinted from *New Gestures, New Gazes: Guide for Reading and Celebrating the Gospel of Luke*, edited by Nancy Pereira and Ernesto Cardoso. Copyright 1993, Institute for Religious Studies, Rio de Janiero, Brazil, 55.

Pages 110–11   "Sonia's Baptism," reprinted from *El Salvador: A Spring Whose Waters Never Run Dry*, edited by Scott Wright et al. Copyright 1990, Ecumenical Program on Central America and the Caribbean (EPICA), 52–53.

Pages 111–13   "Universal Day of Prayer for Students," reprinted from "Universal Day of Prayer for Students," World Student Christian Federation, Feb. 1994, 3, 5, 12–13.

Chapter 12: Affirmations and Statements of Faith; Prayers of Commitment and Dedication

Pages 114–15   "Earth Credo," reprinted by permission of the author, Elizabeth Tapia, from *A Time to Speak*. Copyright 1993, published through the efforts of the General Board of Global Ministries of the United Methodist Church and Youth and Young Adult Ministries, in coordination with the United Methodist Youth Fellowship in the Philippines and the Methodist Youth Fellowship in Korea. Manila, Philippines, 18.

Page 115   "We believe in you, O God . . . ," reprinted by permission from *The United Methodist Book of Worship* (Nashville: United Methodist Publishing House, 1992), 811. Copyright 1992 The United Methodist Publishing House.

Page 115   "Affirmation of Peace and Justice," reprinted from *With All God's People: The New Ecumenical Prayer Cycle,* compiled by John Carden (Geneva: WCC Publications, 1989), 80. Copyright 1989, WCC Publications, World Council of Churches, Geneva, Switzerland.

Pages 116–17   "Affirmation," reprinted by permission of the author. All rights reserved. Copyright Kate Compston, 44 Western Way, Alverstoke, Gosport, PO 12 2NQ, Eng., 1993, unpaginated.

Page 116–117   "The Creation Covenant," reprinted from *Singing the Circle, Book 1: Sacred Earth, Holy Darkness.* Copyright 1990, W. L. Wallace, Christchurch, N.Z., 48.

Page 117   "I Am a Woman," reprinted from *Your Will Be Done.* Copyright 1986, CCA Youth, Christian Conference of Asia, Shatin, Hong Kong, 49.

Page 118   "Renewal of the Covenant," reprinted from Silver Jubilee Covenant Service of the United Congregational Church of Southern Africa, 1992, 14.

Page 119   "We believe in God . . . ," "Profession of Faith of the Christian Base Communities," reprinted from *El Salvador: A Spring Whose Waters Never Run Dry,* edited by Scott Wright et al. Copyright 1990, Ecumenical Program on Central America and the Caribbean (EPICA), 48–49.

Page 120   "I believe our responsibility . . . ," reprinted from *Your Will Be Done.* Copyright 1986, CCA Youth, Christian Conference of Asia, Shatin, Hong Kong, 129.

Page 120   "Asian Methodist Youth Seminar Statement," reprinted from *A Time to Speak.* Copyright 1993, published through the efforts of the General Board of Global Ministries of the United Methodist Church and Youth and Young Adult Ministries, in coordination with the United Methodist Youth Fellowship in the Philippines and the Methodist Youth Fellowship in Korea, Manila, Philippines, 88–89.

Pages 120–21   "The Social Creed of Methodist Youths in Asia," reprinted from *A Time to Speak.* Copyright 1993, published through the efforts of the General Board of Global Ministries of the United Methodist Church and Youth and Young Adult Ministries, in coordination with the United Methodist Youth Fellowship in the Philippines and the Methodist Youth Fellowship in Korea, Manila, Philippines, 90.

Page 121   "Affirmation of Our Discipleship," reprinted from *A Time to Speak.* Copyright 1993, published through the efforts of the General Board of Global Ministries of the United Methodist Church and Youth and Young Adult Ministries, in coordination with the United Methodist Youth Fellowship in the Philippines and the Methodist Youth Fellowship in Korea, Manila, Philippines, 10.

Page 121   "An Indian Prayer," reprinted from *Worship Resources,* compiled by Juanita J. Helphrey. Copyright 1991, Council for American Indian Ministries, United Church of Christ, Minneapolis, Minn., 12.

Page 122   "The Star Light of Commitment," reprinted from *Your Will Be Done.* Copyright 1986, CCA Youth, Christian Conference of Asia, Shatin, Hong Kong, 12–13.

Page 123   "New Responsibility," reprinted by permission of the author. All rights reserved. Copyright Kate Compston, 44 Western Way, Alverstoke, Gosport, PO 12 2NQ, Eng., 1988, unpaginated.

Page 124   "Our Prayer," reprinted from *Your Will Be Done*. Copyright 1986, CCA Youth, Christian Conference of Asia, Shatin, Hong Kong, 95.

Page 124   "God of all Tenderness . . . ," reprinted from *Singing the Circle, Book 3: Broken Bread, Broken Chains*. Copyright 1990 W. L. Wallace, Christchurch, New Zealand, 59.

Page 125   "Call to Commitment," reprinted from *A Time to Speak*. Copyright 1993, published through the efforts of the General Board of Global Ministries of the United Methodist Church and Youth and Young Adult Ministries, in coordination with the United Methodist Youth Fellowship in the Philippines and the Methodist Youth Fellowship in Korea, Manila, Philippines, 22–23.

Pages 126–28   "Offering of our Life and Labours to God in Gratitude and Praise," reprinted from Silver Jubilee Covenant Service of the United Congregational Church of Southern Africa, 1992, 11–12.

Page 129   "Prayer for Dedication of a Bible," printed by permission of the author, Kathy Wonson Eddy. All rights reserved.

Part III: Resources to Walk the Sacred Seasons and Holy Days

Chapter 13: Advent, Christmas, and Epiphany

Page 132   "Waiting," reprinted from *The Certainty of Spring: Poems by a Guatemalan in Exile* by Julia Esquivel. Copyright 1993 Ecumenical Program on Central America and the Caribbean (EPICA), Washington D.C., unpaginated.

Pages 132–33   "Advent Wreath Liturgy," printed by permission of the author, Thomas McNair. All rights reserved.

Page 133   "Remember not the former things . . . ," reprinted from *Gloria Deo Worship Book, 10th Assembly, Prague CSFR*. Copyright 1992 Conference of European Churches Geneva, Switz., 9–10.

Page 134   "Stranger at the Door," printed by permission of the author, Maren C. Tirabassi. All rights reserved.

Page 134   "A Celtic Rune of Hospitality," reprinted from *Gloria Deo, Worship Book for CEC Assembly IX, Stirling, Scotland*. Copyright 1986, Conference of European Churches, Geneva, Switz., 118.

Pages 136–38   "Las Posadas," reprinted by permission from *The United Methodist Book of Worship* (Nashville: United Methodist Publishing House, 1992), 266–68. Translation and adaptation copyright 1992 The United Methodist Publishing House.

Page 140   "God of Gods . . . ," reprinted by permission from *The Cross Is Lifted*, by Chandran Devanesen. Copyright 1954, Friendship Press.

Page 140   "If Mary and Joseph . . . ," reprinted from *1985 Prayer Calendar*, General Board of Global Ministries, The United Methodist Church, 18.

Page 144   "Living Water," reprinted from *Messages from Time to Time: A Book Celebrating the Fortieth Wedding Anniversary of Masao and Fumiko Takenaka*.

Page 145   "Epiphany," reprinted from *With All God's People: The New Ecumenical Prayer Cycle: Orders of Service*, compiled by John Carden (Geneva: WCC Publications, 1989), 23. Copyright 1989, WCC Publications, World Council of Churches, Geneva, Switzerland.

Page 146   "We offer you, O Ruler . . . " from the Assembly of the International Missionary Society, Ghana. Reprinted from *With All God's People: The New Ecumenical Prayer Cycle: Orders of Service*, compiled by John Carden (Geneva: WCC Publications, 1989), 27. Copyright 1989, WCC Publications, World Council of Churches, Geneva, Switzerland.

Page 146   "From the East," reprinted from *Lilies of the Field*, by Wang Weifan. Copyright by The Upper Room, Nashville, Tenn., 9.

Chapter 14: Lent and Easter

Page 147   "O Christ, as the spear . . . ," reprinted from *With All God's People: The New Ecumenical Prayer Cycle*, compiled by John Carden (Geneva: WCC Publications, 1989), 259. Copyright 1989, WCC Publications, World Council of Churches, Geneva, Switzerland.

Page 147   "Lent, 1991," printed by permission of the author, Maren C. Tirabassi. All rights reserved.

Page 147   "Yisu ke pichhe . . . ," reprinted from *With All God's People: The New Ecumenical Prayer Cycle*, compiled by John Carden (Geneva: WCC Publications, 1989), 317. Copyright 1989, WCC Publications, World Council of Churches, Geneva, Switzerland.

Page 148   "Benediction," reprinted from *With All God's People: The New Ecumenical Prayer Cycle*, compiled by John Carden (Geneva: WCC Publications, 1989), 35. Copyright 1989, WCC Publications, World Council of Churches, Geneva, Switzerland.

Page 148   "As the needle turns . . . ," reprinted from *With All God's People: The New Ecumenical Prayer Cycle*, compiled by John Carden (Geneva: WCC Publications, 1989), 37. Copyright 1989, WCC Publications, World Council of Churches, Geneva, Switzerland.

Page 149   "Arising from the Ashes," reprinted from *El Salvador: A Spring Whose Waters Never Run Dry*, edited by Scott Wright et al. Copyright 1990, Ecumenical Program on Central America and the Caribbean (EPICA), 60–61.

Pages 150–51   "Nama-Kirtana," reprinted from *Worship in an Indian Context*, edited by Eric J. Lott. Copyright 1986, The United Theological College, Bangalore, India, 57–59.

Pages 152–56   "Ideas to Celebrate the Passion and Resurrection," reprinted from *Net: Information Bulletin of the Latin American Liturgy Network* 2, no. 3 (Apr. 1993): 13–16.

Page 156   "O Majesty, O Magnificence . . . ," reprinted from *Sabbaths, Sacraments and Seasons: A Collection of Meditations, Prayers and Canticles*, by Arnold Kenseth. Copyright 1982, Windhover Press, Amherst, Mass., 151.

Page 158   "The Cross," reprinted from *The Iona Community Worship Book*, by John L. Bell. Copyright 1988, Wild Goose Resource Group, Iona Community, Glasgow, Scot., 90.

Page 158   "Crosses," reprinted from *Singing the Circle, Book 1: Sacred Earth, Holy Darkness*. Copyright 1990, W. L. Wallace, Christchurch, N.Z., 46.

Page 160   "In the Fields Where Rice Is Planted," reprinted from *Singing the Circle, Book 2: Darkness and Light*. Copyright 1990, W. L. Wallace, Christchurch, N.Z., 35.

Page 163   "Resurrection," reprinted from *The Certainty of Spring: Poems by a Guatemalan in Exile* by Julia Esquivel. Copyright 1993. Ecumenical Program on Central America and the Caribbean (EPICA), Washington, D.C., unpaginated.

Page 164   "In Thy Hand," reprinted from *Messages from Time to Time: A Book Celebrating the Fortieth Wedding Anniversary of Masao and Fumiko Takenaka*.

Page 164   "Collect," reprinted from *With All God's People: The New Ecumenical Prayer Cycle*, compiled by John Carden (Geneva: WCC Publications, 1989), 43. Copyright 1989, WCC Publications, World Council of Churches, Geneva, Switzerland.

Page 164   "Sharing through Interceding," reprinted from *Worship in an Indian Context*, edited by Eric J. Lott. Copyright 1986, The United Theological College, Bangalore, India, 85–86.

Page 165   "Let us pray for the whole world . . . ,' reprinted from *With All God's People: The New Ecumenical Prayer Cycle*, compiled by John Carden (Geneva: WCC Publications, 1989), 42–43. Copyright 1989, WCC Publications, World Council of Churches, Geneva, Switzerland.

Page 166   "Strong and gentle Christ . . . ," reprinted from *Singing the Circle, Book 3: Broken Bread, Broken Chains*. Copyright 1990, W. L. Wallace, Christchurch, N.Z., 55.

Page 166   "Messenger of Marvels," reprinted by permission of the author. All rights reserved. Copyright Kate Compston, 44 Western Way, Alverstoke, Gosport, PO 12 2NQ, Eng., 1993, unpaginated.

Page 167   "And the Waters Will Flow from Your Altar, Lord," reprinted by permission of the author, Simei Monteiro, from *Whole Life, Holy Life*, by Ernesto Barros Cardoso. Copyright 1993, Rio de Janeiro, Brazil, 43.

Chapter 15: Pentecost, Saints, and the Marking of Seasons and Days

Page 169   "The Hope of the Coming of Christ," reprinted by permission of the author, Jaci C. Maraschin, from *Whole Life, Holy Life*, by Ernesto Barros Cardoso. Copyright 1993, Rio de Janeiro, Brazil, 49.

Page 169   "Pieces, Pieces, a world in pieces . . . ," reprinted from *Poems, Prayers and Songs*. Copyright 1993, EGGYS Working Group on Liturgy and Bible Studies, Rio de Janeiro, Brazil, #20.

Page 170   "Lord, Holy Spirit . . . ," reprinted from *On the Occasion of the Dedication of the New Centre in Hong Kong*. Copyright 1993, Christian Conference of Asia, 16.

Page 170   "Open Your Hearts," reprinted from *Lilies of the Field*, by Wang Weifan. Copyright by The Upper Room, Nashville, Tenn., 51.

Page 171   "The God of Columba," reprinted from *The Iona Community Worship Book*, by John L. Bell. Copyright 1988, Wild Goose Resource Group, Iona Community, Glasgow, Scot., 89.

Page 172   "Sanctuary Prayer," reprinted from *With All God's People: The New Ecumenical Prayer Cycle*, compiled by John Carden (Geneva: WCC Publications, 1989), 60. Copyright 1989, WCC Publications, World Council of Churches, Geneva, Switzerland.

Page 173   "Some Acts of Commemoration of Contemporary Witnesses," reprinted from *With All God's People: The New Ecumenical Prayer Cycle*, compiled by John Carden (Geneva: WCC Publications, 1989), 59. Copyright 1989, WCC Publications, World Council of Churches, Geneva, Switzerland.

Page 173   "#16670," reprinted from *With All God's People: The New Ecumenical Prayer Cycle*, compiled by John Carden (Geneva: WCC Publications, 1989), 143. Copyright 1989, WCC Publications, World Council of Churches, Geneva, Switzerland.

Page 174   "Remembering Archbishop Oscar Romero," reprinted from *El Salvador: A Spring Whose Waters Never Run Dry*, edited by Scott Wright et al. Copyright 1990, Ecumenical Program on Central America and the Caribbean (EPICA), 46–47.

Page 176   "Remembrances," reprinted from *Net: Information Bulletin of the Latin American Liturgy Network* 2, no. 3 (Apr. 1993): 22.

Page 177   "Remembrance," reprinted by permission of the author. All rights reserved. Copyright Kate Compston, 44 Western Way, Alverstoke, Gosport, PO 12 2NQ, Eng., 1993, unpaginated.

Page 178   "Canticles," reprinted from *Sabbaths, Sacraments and Seasons: A Collection of Meditations, Prayers and Canticles*. Copyright 1982 by Arnold Kenseth, Windhover Press, Amherst, Mass.: Winter, 135; Spring, 141; Summer, 152; Autumn, 157.

Page 179   "A God for All Seasons," reprinted by permission of the author. All rights reserved. Copyright Kate Compston, 44 Western Way, Alverstoke, Gosport, PO 12 2NQ, Eng., 1993, unpaginated.

Pages 179–80   "Mid-Winter," reprinted from *Singing the Circle, Book 1: Sacred Earth, Holy Darkness*. Copyright 1990, W. L. Wallace, Christchurch, N.Z., 54, 80.

Pages 180–81   "Body Moments for the Other-Festivals," printed by permission of the author, Maren C. Tirabassi. All rights reserved.

Part IV: Resources for Communion in the Body of Christ

Chapter 16: Sacramental Prayers, Practices, and Services

Page 184   "Eucharist," reprinted from *The Certainty of Spring: Poems by a Guatemalan in Exile*, by Julia Esquivel. Copyright 1993, Ecumenical Program on Central America and the Caribbean (EPICA), Washington D.C., unpaginated.

Page 184   "Communion," reprinted from *With All God's People: The New Ecumenical Prayer Cycle*, compiled by John Carden (Geneva: WCC Publications, 1989), 231. Copyright 1989, WCC Publications, World Council of Churches, Geneva, Switzerland.

Page 184   "The Breaking of Bread" reprinted from *A Time to Speak*. Copyright 1993, published through the efforts of the General Board of Global Ministries of the United Methodist Church and Youth and Young Adult Ministries, in coordination with the United Methodist Youth Fellowship in the Philippines and the Methodist Youth Fellowship in Korea, Manila, Philippines, 23.

Page 186   "God Is Rice," reprinted from *Messages from Time to Time: A Book Celebrating the Fortieth Wedding Anniversary of Masao and Fumiko Takenaka*.

Page 189   "Communion Prayer," reprinted from "Universal Day of Prayer for Students," World Student Christian Federation, Feb. 1994, 18.

Pages 193–96   "Taken from an Indian Liturgy for Celebrating the Eucharist," reprinted from *Worship in an Indian Context*, edited by Eric J. Lott. Copyright 1986, The United Theological College, Bangalore, India, 68–77.

Page 197   "Preface" ("You are blessed, God, Father and Mother for us . . ."), reprinted from the Twenty-fourth Assembly Opening Service of the United Congregational Church of Southern Africa, Sept. 26, 1990, 4–6.

Page 197   "Table Blessing," reprinted by permission of the author, Jaci C. Maraschin, from *New Gestures, New Gazes: Guide for Reading and Celebrating the Gospel of Luke*, edited by Nancy Pereira and Ernesto Cardoso. Copyright 1993, Institute for Religious Studies, Rio de Janeiro, Brazil, 53.

Page 198   "I Am More than Flesh and Blood," reprinted from *Singing the Circle, Book 3: Broken Bread, Broken Chains*. Copyright 1990, W. L. Wallace, Christchurch, N.Z., 16.

Page 198   "The Peace," reprinted from "Universal Day of Prayer for Students," World Student Christian Federation, Feb. 1994, 17.

Chapter 17: Prayers for Those Gathered into This Book

Page 200   "In these days of political strife . . . ," from a letter from Suzette Goss-Geffrard, Zaire June 8, 1993.

Page 200   "Regarding prayer requests . . . ," from a letter from Betsy H. Wrisley, Philippines, May 13, 1993.

Page 200   "Roofs for the Roofless," from a letter from Savithri Devanesen, India, June 16, 1993.

Page 201   "Arogyalayam Trust," from a letter from Bonni-Belle Pickard, India, Apr. 17, 1993.

Page 201   "For Greenville, Liberia and for . . . ," from a letter from Nancy Lightfoot, Liberia, Apr. 20, 1993.

Page 201   "Greetings on behalf of staff . . . ," from a letter from Raquel Rodriguez, Common Ministry in Latin America and the Caribbean, United Church Board of World Ministries and Christian Church (Disciples of Christ) Division of Overseas Ministries, July 22, 1994.

Pages 201–2   "This prayer is also by Birkha Khadka, but is a request . . . ," from a letter from June Fleshman, Nepal, Sept. 23, 1993.

Page 202   "This week our church group also sent a refugee . . . ," from a letter from Doug Wallace, Turkey, Feb. 18, 1993.

Page 203   "Front Page: Rwanda," printed by permission of the author, Maren C. Tirabassi. All rights reserved.

Page 203   "Since 1979, churches in China are reopening . . . ," from a letter from Diane Allen, General Board of Global Ministries, United Methodist Church, undated.

Part V: Resources to Quicken the Heart

Chapter 18: Poetry

Page 206   "The Body," reprinted by permission of the author, Simei Monteiro, from *Whole Life, Holy Life*, by Ernesto Barros Cardoso. Copyright 1993, Rio de Janeiro, Brazil, 24.

Page 207   "God," reprinted from *Worship Resources*, compiled by Juanita J. Helphrey. Copyright 1991, Council for American Indian Ministries, United Church of Christ, Minneapolis, Minn., 17.

Page 207   "Amazing Grace," words: John Newton, 1779 (st. 6 anon.); phonetic transcription in Cherokee, Kiowa, Creek, Choctaw as sung in Oklahoma Indiana Missionary Conference; Navajo phonetic transcription by Albert Tsosie L(1 Chr 17:16–17). Reprinted from *The United Methodist Hymnal*.

Page 207   "The Sigh," reprinted from *The Certainty of Spring: Poems by a Guatemalan in Exile*, by Julia Esquivel. Copyright 1993, Ecumenical Program on Central America and the Caribbean (EPICA), Washington, D.C., unpaginated.

Page 208   "For the People," reprinted from *Your Will Be Done*. Copyright 1986, CCA Youth, Christian Conference of Asia, Shatin, Hong Kong, 42.

Illustration Notes

Part I: Resources to Lift Up Our Voices

Page 2   *Mexican Father and Son*, by Robert Eddy. Used by permission.

Page 4   Untitled (Central American Church), by Rini Templeton.* Reprinted by permission from *The Art of Rini Templeton: Where There Is Life and Struggle*, ed. Elizabeth Martinez (Seattle: The Real Comet Press, 1989), 131. Copyright 1989, The Capp Street Foundation/Rini Templeton Memorial Fund. The Real Comet Press, Seattle.

Page 5   Middle East Council of Churches letterhead symbol, used by permission of Souha Khoury.

Page 12   *Prodigal Son*, by He Qi. Used by permission.

Page 15   Untitled (Cemetery Scene), by Rini Templeton.* Reprinted by permission from *The Art of Rini Templeton: Where There Is Life and Struggle*, ed. Elizabeth Martinez (Seattle: The Real Comet Press, 1989), 26. Copyright 1989, The Capp Street Foundation/Rini Templeton Memorial Fund. The Real Comet Press, Seattle.

Page 20   Untitled (Harvest Scene), by Rini Templeton.* Reprinted by permission from *The Art of Rini Templeton: Where There Is Life and Struggle*, ed. Elizabeth Martinez (Seattle: The Real Comet Press, 1989), 162. Copyright 1989, The Capp Street Foundation/Rini Templeton Memorial Fund. The Real Comet Press, Seattle.

Page 29   *Woman at the Well*, by He Qi. Used by permission.

Page 39   *Four Kinds of Soil*, by Kimiyoshi Endo. Used by permission.

Page 40   Untitled (Man from Nepal with Burden). Reprinted from *With All God's People: The New Ecumenical Prayer Cycle*, compiled by John Carden (Geneva: WCC Publications, 1989), 313. Copyright 1989, WCC Publications, World Council of Churches, Geneva.

Page 46   *Good Samaritan*, by He Qi. Used by permission.

Page 50   *Lord's Prayer in Arabic*. Reprinted from *Your Will Be Done* (Hong Kong, 1986), 142. Copyright 1986, CCA Youth, Christian Conference of Asia, Shatin, Hong Kong.

Page 53   *Benefactor*, by Zhang Guijie. Mission and Promotion of the Presbyterian Church, U.S.A. Reproduced by permission from *1993–94 Presbyterian Planning Calendar*.

Page 54   *Sharing* (Africa-based art), by J. Foster. Mission and Promotion of the Presbyterian Church, U.S.A. Reproduced by permission from *1994–95 Presbyterian Planning Calendar*, relating to the theme "Walking with Africans—A Healing Journey," from the designation of 1994–95 as the "Year with Africa."

Page 56   Untitled (Bicycle Riders), by Rini Templeton.* Reprinted by permission from *The Art of Rini Templeton: Where There Is Life and Struggle*, ed.

Elizabeth Martinez (Seattle: The Real Comet Press, 1989), 162. Copyright 1989, The Capp Street Foundation/Rini Templeton Memorial Fund. The Real Comet Press, Seattle.

Part II: Resources to Join Hands Together

Page 60   *Hands*, by Robert Eddy. Used by permission.

Page 62   *El Salvador Cross*, by Sister Helen David Brancato. Used by permission.

Page 64   *Words for Peace*. Source unknown.

Page 66   *P'ing-an*, calligraphy. Courtesy of Virginia Thelin.

Page 67   *Hsing-t'u*, calligraphy. Courtesy of Virginia Thelin.

Page 67   *K'eiwa*, calligraphy. Courtesy of John Moss.

Page 69   *Vine and Branches*, by Kimiyoshi Endo. Used by permission.

Page 72   Reprinted from Conference of European Churches, *Prayers, Hymns*, copyright April 1989. Used by permission of Isabel Best. Artist unknown.

Page 81   *Water into Wine*, by He Qi. Used by permission.

Page 83   Protestant Christian Church in Bali, letterhead symbol. Used by permission of Bishop I. Wayan Mastra.

Page 85   Reprinted from Conference of European Churches, *Prayers, Hymns*, copyright April 1989. Used by permission of Isabel Best. Artist unknown.

Page 99   Reprinted from Conference of European Churches, *Prayers, Hymns*, copyright April 1989. Used by permission of Isabel Best. Artist unknown.

Page 104   Untitled (Children Playing Basketball), by Rini Templeton.* Reprinted by permission from *The Art of Rini Templeton: Where There Is Life and Struggle*, ed. Elizabeth Martinez (Seattle: The Real Comet Press, 1989), 24. Copyright 1989, The Capp Street Foundation/Rini Templeton Memorial Fund. The Real Comet Press, Seattle.

Page 111   Reprinted from Conference of European Churches, *Prayers, Hymns*, copyright April 1989. Used by permission of Isabel Best. Artist unknown.

Page 114   *Resurrection*, by He Qi. Used by permission.

Page 117   Reprinted from Conference of European Churches, *Prayers, Hymns*, copyright April 1989. Used by permission of Isabel Best. Artist unknown.

Page 118   Reprinted from Conference of European Churches, *Prayers, Hymns*, copyright April 1989. Used by permission of Isabel Best. Artist unknown.

Page 122   *Star Light of Commitment*. Reprinted from *Your Will Be Done* (Hong Kong, 1986), 13. Copyright 1986, CCA, Youth Christian Conference of Asia, Shatin, Hong Kong.

Page 123   Reprinted from Conference of European Churches, *Prayers, Hymns*, copyright April 1989. Used by permission of Isabel Best. Artist unknown.

Page 125   Reprinted from Conference of European Churches, *Prayers, Hymns*, copyright April 1989. Used by permission of Isabel Best. Artist unknown.

Page 128   United Congregational Church of Southern Africa Silver Jubilee Symbol. Used by permission of Samuel Arends.

Part III: Resources to Walk the Sacred Seasons and Watch the Holy Days

Page 130   *Walking in the Woods*, by Robert Eddy. Used by permission.

Page 132   *Annunciation*, by He Qi. Used by permission.

Page 135   *Feliz Navidad y Una Vida Digna*, by Rini Templeton.* Reprinted by permission from *The Art of Rini Templeton: Where There Is Life and Struggle*, ed. Elizabeth Martinez (Seattle: The Real Comet Press, 1989), 114. Copyright 1989, The Capp Street Foundation/Rini Templeton Memorial Fund. The Real Comet Press, Seattle.

Page 139   *Nativity*, by Midori Shibata. Used by permission.

Page 144   *Living Water*, by Fumiko Takenaka. Used by permission.

Page 145   Reprinted from Conference of European Churches, *Prayers, Hymns*, copyright April 1989. Used by permission of Isabel Best. Artist unknown.

Page 146   *Flight into Egypt*, by He Qi. Used by permission.

Page 147   *Carrying the Cross*, by He Qi. Used by permission.

Page 151   *Palm Sunday*, by He Qi. Used by permission.

Page 157   Untitled (Christ Crucified), by Bill Wallace. Used by permission.

Page 159   Untitled (Women of Prophecy), by Rini Templeton.* Reprinted by permission from *The Art of Rini Templeton: Where There Is Life and Struggle*, ed. Elizabeth Martinez (Seattle: The Real Comet Press, 1989), 189. Copyright 1989, The Capp Street Foundation/Rini Templeton Memorial Fund. The Real Comet Press, Seattle.

Page 161   Untitled (Empty Tomb), by Midori Shibata. Used by permission.

Page 167   Reprinted from Conference of European Churches, *Prayers, Hymns*, copyright April 1989. Used by permission of Isabel Best. Artist unknown.

Page 168   *Pentecost*, by Zhang Guijie. Mission and Promotion of the Presbyterian Church, U.S.A. Reproduced by permission from *1993–94 Presbyterian Planning Calendar*.

Page 169   *Alpha and Omega*, by Midori Shibata. Used by permission.

Page 174   *Our Ancestors* (Africa-based art), by J. Foster. Mission and Promotion of the Presbyterian Church, U.S.A. Reproduced from *1994–95 Presbyterian Planning Calendar*, relating to the theme, "Walking with Africans—A Healing Journey," from the designation of 1994–95 as the "Year with Africa."

Page 177   Reprinted from Conference of European Churches, *Prayers, Hymns*, copyright April 1989. Used by permission of Isabel Best. Artist unknown.

Part IV: Resources for Communion in the Body of Christ

Page 182   *Jamaican Farmworker and Child*, by Robert Eddy. Used by permission.

Page 184   *Last Supper*, by He Qi. Used by permission.

Page 186   Untitled (God Is Rice), by Fumiko Takenaka. Used by permission.

Page 192   *Five Loaves and Two Fishes*, by He Qi. Used by permission.

Page 200   *Martha and Mary*, by He Qi. Used by permission.

Part V: Resources to Quicken the Heart

Page 204   *Boys Dancing in Art Gallery*, by Robert Eddy. Used by permission.

Page 206   Untitled (Coffeeworkers), by Rini Templeton.* Reprinted by permission from *The Art of Rini Templeton: Where There Is Life and Struggle*, ed. Elizabeth Martinez (Seattle: The Real Comet Press, 1989), 162. Copyright 1989, The Capp Street Foundation/Rini Templeton Memorial Fund. The Real Comet Press, Seattle.

Page 213   Untitled (City Workers), by Rini Templeton.* Reprinted by permission from *The Art of Rini Templeton: Where There Is Life and Struggle*, ed. Elizabeth Martinez (Seattle: The Real Comet Press, 1989), 169. Copyright 1989, The Capp Street Foundation/Rini Templeton Memorial Fund. The Real Comet Press, Seattle.

Page 214   Untitled (City on Fire), by Rini Templeton.* Reprinted by permission from *The Art of Rini Templeton: Where There Is Life and Struggle*, ed. Elizabeth Martinez (Seattle: The Real Comet Press, 1989), 170. Copyright 1989, The Capp Street Foundation/Rini Templeton Memorial Fund. The Real Comet Press, Seattle.

Page 214   Untitled (Village at Peace), by Rini Templeton.* Reprinted by permission from *The Art of Rini Templeton: Where There Is Life and Struggle*, ed. Elizabeth Martinez (Seattle: The Real Comet Press, 1989), 25. Copyright 1989, The Capp Street Foundation/Rini Templeton Memorial Fund. The Real Comet Press, Seattle.

Page 215   Untitled (Lights on Mountain), by Rini Templeton.* Reprinted by permission from *The Art of Rini Templeton: Where There Is Life and Struggle*, ed. Elizabeth Martinez (Seattle: The Real Comet Press, 1989), introduction. Copyright 1989, The Capp Street Foundation/Rini Templeton Memorial Fund. The Real Comet Press, Seattle.

Page 216   *King of Kings*, by Kimiyoshi Endo. Used by permission.

Page 217   *Calling the Wayward Sheep*, by Kimiyoshi Endo. Used by permission.

Page 218   *Adam and Eve*, by He Qi. Used by permission.

Page 219   *Wise and Foolish Virgins*, by He Qi. Used by permission.

Page 220   *Ode to Joy*, by He Qi. Used by permission.

Page 221   *Nativity Scene*, by He Qi. Used by permission.

Page 222   *Good Samaritan*, by He Qi. Used by permission.

Page 223   Untitled (Cross of the Americas), by Sister Helen David Brancato. Used by permission.

Page 224   *Wise as Serpents*, by Midori Shibata. Used by permission.

Page 225   *I Am the Vine*, by Midori Shibata. Used by permission.

Page 225   Untitled (Shepherds and Stars), by Midori Shibata. Used by permission.

Page 226   *Love*, calligraphy by Midori Shibata. Used by permission.

Page 227   Untitled (Jesus on the Star of David), by Midori Shibata. Used by permission.

Page 228   *Nativity*, by Zhang Guijie. Mission and Promotion of the Presbyterian Church, U.S.A. Reproduced by permission from 1993–94 *Presbyterian Planning Calendar*.

Page 229   *Rekindle the Gift of God*, by Zhang Guijie. Mission and Promotion of the Presbyterian Church, U.S.A. Reproduced by permission from *1993–94 Presbyterian Planning Calendar*.

Page 230   *Resurrection*, by Zhang Guijie. Mission and Promotion of the Presbyterian Church, U.S.A. Reproduced by permission from *1993–94 Presbyterian Planning Calendar*.

Page 231   *Widow's Mite*, by Zhang Guijie. Mission and Promotion of the Presbyterian Church, U.S.A. Reproduced by permission from *1993–94 Presbyterian Planning Calendar*.

Page 232   Untitled (Cranes), by Fumiko Takenaka. Used by permission.

Page 233   *Human Relationships* (Africa-based art), by J. Foster. Mission and Promotion of the Presbyterian Church, U.S.A. Reproduced from *1994–95 Presbyterian Planning Calendar*, relating to the theme, "Walking with Africans—A Healing Journey," from the designation of 1994–95 as the "Year with Africa."

Page 233   *Family Values* (Africa-based art), by J. Foster. Mission and Promotion of the Presbyterian Church, U.S.A.. Reproduced from *1994–95 Presbyterian Planning Calendar*, relating to the theme, "Walking with Africans—A Healing Journey," from the designation of 1994–95 as the "Year with Africa."

Page 233   *Hospitality* (Africa-based art), by J. Foster. Mission and Promotion of the Presbyterian Church, U.S.A.. Reproduced from *1994–95 Presbyterian Planning Calendar*, relating to the theme, "Walking with Africans—A Healing Journey," from the designation of 1994–95 as the "Year with Africa."

Page 233   *The Spoken Word* (Africa-based art), by J. Foster. Mission and Promotion of the Presbyterian Church, U.S.A. Reproduced from *1994–95 Presbyterian Planning Calendar*, relating to the theme, "Walking with Africans—A Healing Journey," from the designation of 1994–95 as the "Year with Africa."

Page 235   *Bank of Candles in Chartres Cathedral, May 1993*, by Robert Eddy. Used by permission.

*The Rini Templeton archives are being developed at the University of California at Santa Barbara, and it would be deeply appreciated if one copy of any piece which uses her artwork could be included in them by sending the piece to:

Ms. Elizabeth Martinez
c/o ISES
P.O. Box 2089
Oakland, CA 94609

Index of Origins

Material in this index is arranged by country of origin or cultural background of author. Many pieces will be found in two places. For example, materials cited by the name of an American Indian nation or tribe of origin will also be listed both under American Indian and Native American. However, the designation of continents—Africa, Latin America, and so on—appears *only* for those items for which we had no more specific source reference.